W9-BBH-016

THE MODERN STUDENT'S LIBRARY

ENGLISH POETS
OF THE
EIGHTEENTH CENTURY

THE MODERN STUDENT'S LIBRARY

EACH VOLUME EDITED BY A LEADING AMERICAN AUTHORITY

This series is composed of such works as are conspicuous in the province of literature for their enduring influence. Every volume is recognized as essential to a liberal education and will tend to infuse a love for true literature and an appreciation of the qualities which cause it to endure.

A descriptive list of the volumes published in this series appears in the last pages of this volume

CHARLES SCRIBNER'S SONS

ENGLISH POETS
OF THE
EIGHTEENTH CENTURY

SELECTED AND EDITED WITH AN INTRODUCTION

BY

ERNEST BERNBAUM
PROFESSOR OF ENGLISH AT THE UNIVERSITY OF ILLINOIS

CHARLES SCRIBNER'S SONS
NEW YORK CHICAGO BOSTON

Printed in the United States of America
E

TO

CHESTER NOYES GREENOUGH

LOVER AND MASTER OF EIGHTEENTH-CENTURY LITERATURE

PREFACE

The text of this collection of poetry is authentic and not bowdlerized. The general reader will, I hope, be gratified to find that its pages display no pedantic or scholastic traits. His pleasure in the poetry itself will not be distracted by a marginal numbering of the lines; by index-figures and footnotes; or by antiquated peculiarities of spelling, capitalization, and elision. Except where literal conventions are essential to the poet's purpose,—as in *The Castle of Indolence*, *The Schoolmistress*, or Chatterton's poems,—I have followed modern usage. Dialect words are explained in the glossary; and the student who may wish to consult the context of any passage will find the necessary references in the unusually full table of contents. Whenever the title of a poem gives too vague a notion of its substance, or whenever its substance is miscellaneous, I have supplied [bracketed] captions for the extracts; except for these, there is nothing on the pages of the text besides the poets' own words.

Originality is not the proper characteristic of an anthologist, and in the choice of extracts I have rarely indulged my personal likings when they conflicted with time-honored preferences; yet this anthology,—the first published in a projected series of four or five volumes comprising the English poets from Elizabethan to Victorian times,—has certain minor features that may be deemed objectionably novel. Much the greater portion of the volume has of course, as usual, been given to those poems (by Pope, Thomson, Collins, Gray, Goldsmith, Crabbe, Cowper, and Burns) which have been loved or admired from their day to our own. But I have ventured to admit also a few which, though forgotten to-day, either were popular in the eighteenth century or possess marked historical significance. In other words, I present not solely what the twentieth century considers enduringly great in the poetry of the eighteenth, but also a little—proportionately very little—of what the eighteenth century itself (perhaps mistakenly) considered interesting. This secondary purpose accounts for my inclusion of passages from such neglected authors as Mandeville, Brooke, Day, and Darwin. The passages of this sort are too infrequent to annoy him who reads for æsthetic pleasure only; and to the student they will illustrate movements in the spirit of the age which would otherwise be unrepresented, and which, as the historical introduction points out, are an integral part of its thought and feeling. The inclusion of passages from "Ossian," though almost unprecedented, requires, I think, no defense against the literal-minded protest that they are written in "prose."

Students of poetical history will find it illuminating to read the passages in chronological order (irrespective of authorship); and in order to facilitate this method I have given in the table of contents the date of each poem.

E. B.

CONTENTS

INTRODUCTION

I. ORTHODOXY AND CLASSICISM QUIESCENT

(1700–1725)

The clearest portrayal of the prominent features of an age may sometimes be seen in poems which reveal what men desire to be rather than what they are; and which express sentiments typical, even commonplace, rather than individual. John Pomfret's *Choice* (1700) is commonplace indeed; it was never deemed great, but it was remarkably popular. "No composition in our language," opined Dr. Johnson, "has been oftener perused,"—an opinion quite incredible until one perceives how intimately the poem harmonizes with the prevalent mood of its contemporary readers. It was written by a clergyman (a circumstance not insignificant); its form is the heroic couplet; its content is a wish for a peaceful and civilized mode of existence. And what is believed to satisfy that longing? A life of leisure; the necessaries of comfort plentifully provided, but used temperately; a country-house upon a hillside, not too distant from the city; a little garden bordered by a rivulet; a quiet study furnished with the classical Roman poets; the society of a few friends, men who know the world as well as books, who are loyal to their nation and their church, and whose conversation is intellectually vigorous but always polite; the occasional companionship of a woman of virtue, wit, and poise of manner; and, above all, the avoidance of public or private contentions. Culture and peace—and the greater of these is peace! The sentiment characterizes the first quarter of the eighteenth century.

The poets of that period had received an abundant heritage from the Elizabethans, the Cavaliers, Dryden, and Milton. It was a poetry of passionate love, chivalric honor, indignant satire, and sublime faith. Much of it they admired, but their admiration was tempered with fear. They heard therein the tones of violent generations,—of men whose intensity, though yielding extraordinary beauty and grandeur, yielded also obscurity and extravagance; men whom the love of women too often impelled to utter fantastic hyperbole, and the love of honor to glorify preposterous adventures; quarrelsome men, who assailed their opponents with rancorous personalities; doctrinaires, who employed their fiery energy of mind in the creation of rigid systems of religion and government; uncompromising men, who devoted to the support of those systems their fortunes and lives, drenched the land in the blood of a civil war, executed a king, presently restored his dynasty, and finally exiled it again, thus maintaining during half a century a general insecurity of life and property which checked the finer growths of civilization. Their successors trusted that the compromise of 1688 had reduced political and sectarian affairs to a state of calm equilibrium; and they desired to cultivate the fruits of serenity by fostering in all things the spirit of moderation. In poetry, as in life, they tended more and more to discountenance manifestations of vehemence. Even the poetry of Dryden, with its reflections of the stormy days through which he had struggled, seemed to them, though gloriously leading the way toward perfection, to fall short of equability of temper and smoothness of form. To work like Defoe's *True-Born Englishman* (1701) and *Hymn to the Pillory* (1703), combative in spirit and free in style, they gave only guarded and temporary approval.

Inevitably the change of mood entailed losses. Sir Henry Wotton's *Character of a Happy Life* (c. 1614) treats the same theme as Pomfret's *Choice*; but Pomfret's contemporaries were rarely if ever visited by such gleams as shine in Wotton's lines describing the happy man as one

who never understood
How deepest wounds are given by praise,

and as one

Who God doth late and early pray
More of his grace than gifts to lend.

Such touches of penetrative wisdom and piety, like many other precious qualities, are of an age that had passed. In the poetry of 1700–1725, religion forgoes mysticism and exaltation; the intellectual life, daring and subtlety; the imagination, exuberance and splendor. Enthusiasm for moral ideals declines into steadfast approval of ethical principles. Yet these were changes in tone and manner rather than in fundamental views. The poets of the period were conservatives. They were shocked by the radicalism of Mandeville, the Nietzsche of his day, who derided the generally accepted moralities as shallow delusions, and who by means of a clever fable supported a materialistic theory which implied that in the struggle for existence nothing but egotism could succeed:

> Fools only strive
> To make a great and honest hive.

Obloquy buried him; he was a sensational exception to the rule. As a body, the poets of his time retained the orthodox traditions concerning God, Man, and Nature.

Their theology is evidenced by Addison, Watts, and Parnell. It is a Christianity that has not ceased to be stern and majestic. In Addison's *Divine Ode*, the planets of the firmament proclaim a Creator whose power knows no bounds. In the hymns of Isaac Watts, God is as of old a jealous God, obedience to whose eternal will may require the painful sacrifice of temporal earthly affections, even the sacrifice of our love for our fellow-creatures; a just God, who by the law of his own nature cannot save unrepentant sin from eternal retribution; yet an adored God, whose providence protects the faithful amid stormy vicissitudes,—

> Under the shadow of whose throne
> The saints have dwelt secure.

Spirits as gentle and kindly as Parnell insist that the only approach to happiness lies through a religious discipline of the feelings, and protest that death is not to be feared but welcomed—as the passage from a troublous existence to everlasting peace. In most of the poetry of the time, religion, if at all noticeable, is a mere undercurrent; but whenever it rises to the surface, it reflects the ancient creed.

Traditional too is the general conception of human character. Man is still thought of as a complex of lofty and mean qualities, widely variable in their proportion yet in no instance quite dissevered. To interpret—not God or Nature—but this self-contradictory being, in both his higher and his lower manifestations and possibilities, remains the chief vocation of the poets. They have not ceased the endeavor to lend dignity to life by portraying its nobler features. Addison, in *The Campaign*, glorifies the national hero whose brilliant victories thwarted the great monarch of France on his seemingly invincible career toward the hegemony of Europe, the warrior Marlborough, serene of soul amid the horror and confusion of battle. Tickell, in his noble elegy on Addison, not only, while voicing his own grief, illustrates the beauty of devoted friendship, but also, when eulogizing his subject, holds up to admiration, as a type to be revered, the wise moralist, cultured and versatile man of letters, and adept in the art of virtuous life. Pope, in the most ambitious literary effort of the day, his translation of the *Iliad*, labors to enrich the treasury of English poetry with an epic that sheds radiance upon the ideals and manners of an heroic age. In such attempts to exalt the grander phases of human existence, the poets were, however, owing to their fear of enthusiasm, never quite successful. It is significant that though most critics consider Pope's Homer no better than a mediocre performance, none denies that his *Rape of the Lock* is, in its kind, perfection.

Here, as in the *vers de société* of Matthew Prior and Ambrose Philips, the age was illuminating with the graces of poetry something it really understood and delighted in,—the life of leisure and fashion; and here, accordingly, is its most original and masterly work. *The Rape of the Lock* is the product of a society which had the good sense and good breeding to try to laugh away incipient quarrels, and which greeted with airy banter the indiscreet act of an enamoured young gallant,—the kind of act which vulgarity meets with angry lampoons or rude violence. The poem is an idyll quite as much as a satire. The follies of fashionable life are treated with nothing severer than light raillery; and its actually distasteful features,—its lapses into stupidity, its vacuous restlessness, its ennui,—are cunningly suppressed. But all that made it seem the height of human felicity is preserved, and enhanced in charm. "Launched on the bosom of the silver Thames," one glides to Hampton Court amid youth and gayety and melting music; and for the nonce this realm of "airs, flounces, and furbelows," of merry chit-chat, and of pleasurable excitement, seems as important as it is to those exquisite creatures of fancy that hover about the heroine, assiduous guardians of her "graceful ease and sweetness void of pride." Of that admired world likewise are the lovers that Matthew Prior creates, who woo neither with stormy passion nor with mawkish whining, but in a courtly manner; lovers who deem an epigram a finer tribute than a sigh. So the tender fondness of a middle-aged man for an infant is elevated above the commonplace by assuming the tone of playful gallantry.

The ignobler aspects of life,—nutriment of the comic sense,—were not ignored. The new school of poets, however deficient in the higher vision, were keen observers of actuality; and among them the satiric spirit, though not militant as in the days of Dryden, was still active. The value which they attached to social culture is again shown in the persistence of the sentiment that as man grew in civility he became less ridiculous. The peccadilloes of the upper classes they treated with comparatively gentle humor, and aimed their strokes of satire chiefly against the lower. Rarely did they idealize humble folk: Gay's *Sweet William's Farewell to Black-Eyed Susan* is in this respect exceptional. Their typical attitude is seen in his *Shepherd's Week*, with its ludicrous picture of rustic superstition and naive amorousness; and in Allan Ramsay's *Gentle Shepherd*, where the pastoral, once remote from life, assumes the manners and dialect of the countryside in order to arouse laughter.

The obvious fact that these poets centered their attention upon Man, particularly in his social life, and that their most memorable productions are upon that theme, led posterity to complain that they wholly lacked interest in Nature, were incapable of delineating it, and did not feel its sacred influence. The last point in the indictment,—and the last only,—is quite true. No one who understood and believed, as they did, the doctrines of orthodoxy could consistently ascribe divinity to Nature. To them Nature exhibited the power of God, but not his will; and the soul of Man gained its clearest moral light directly from a *super*natural source. This did not, however, imply that Nature was negligible. The celebrated essays of Addison on the pleasures of the imagination (*Spectator*, Nos. 411–414) base those pleasures upon the grandeur of Nature; upon its variety and freshness, as of "groves, fields, and meadows in the opening of the Spring"; and upon its beauty of form and color. The works of Nature, declares Addison, surpass those of art, and accordingly "we always find the poet in love with a country life." Such was the theory; the practice was not out of accord therewith. Passages appreciative of the lovelier aspects of Nature, and not, despite the current preference for general rather than specific terms, inaccurate as descriptions, were written between 1700 and 1726 by Addison himself, Pope, Lady Winchilsea, Gay, Parnell, Dyer, and many others. Nature worshippers they were not. Nature lovers they can be justly styled,—if such love may discriminate between the beautiful and the ugly aspects of the natural. It is characteristic that Berkeley, in his *Prospect of Planting Arts and Learning in America*, does not indulge the fancy that the wilderness is of itself uplifting; it requires, he assumes, the aid of human culture and wisdom,—"the rise of empire and of arts,"—to develop its potentialities.

A generation which placidly adhered to the orthodox sentiments of its predecessors was of course not moved to revolutionize poetical theories or forms. Its theories are authoritatively stated in Pope's *Essay on Criticism*; they embrace principles of good sense and mature taste which are easier to condemn than to confute or supersede. In poetical diction the age cultivated clearness, propriety, and dignity: it rejected words so minutely particular as to suggest pedantry or specialization; and it refused to sacrifice simple appropriateness to inaccurate vigor of utterance or meaningless beauty of sound. Its favorite measure, the decasyllabic couplet, moulded by Jonson, Sandys, Waller, Denham, and Dryden, it accepted reverently, as an heirloom not to be essentially altered but to be polished until it shone more brightly than ever. Pope perfected this form, making it at once more artistic and more natural. He discountenanced on the one hand run-on lines, alexandrines, hiatus, and sequence of monosyllables; on the other, the resort to expletives and the mechanical placing of cæsura. If his verse does not move with the "long resounding pace" of Dryden at his best, it has a movement better suited to the drawing-room: it is what Oliver Wendell Holmes terms

> The straight-backed measure with the stately stride.

Thus in form as in substance the poetry of the period voiced the mood, not of carefree youth, nor yet of vehement early manhood, but of still vigorous middle age,—a phase of existence perhaps less ingratiating than others, but one which has its rightful hour in the life of the race as of the individual. The sincere and artistic expression of its feelings will be denied poetical validity only by those whose capacity for appreciating the varieties of poetry is limited by their lack of experience or by narrowness of sympathetic imagination.

II. ORTHODOXY AND CLASSICISM ASSAILED (1726–1750)

During the second quarter of the century, Pope and his group remained dominant in the realm of poetry; but their mood was no longer pacific. Their work showed a growing seriousness and acerbity. Partly the change was owing to disappointment: life had not become so highly cultured, literature had not prospered so much, nor displayed so broad a diffusion of intelligence and taste, as had been expected. Pope's *Dunciad*, *Epistle to Dr. Arbuthnot*, and ironic satire on the state of literature under "Augustus" (George II, the "snuffy old drone from the German hive"), brilliantly express this indignation with the intellectual and literary shortcomings of the times.

A cause of the change of mood which was to be of more lasting consequence than the failure of the age to put the traditional ideal more generally into practice, was the appearance of a distinctly new ideal,—one which undermined the very foundations of the old. This new spirit may be termed sentimentalism. In prose literature it had already been stirring for about twenty-five years, changing the tone of comedy, entering into some of the periodical essays, and assuming a philosophic character in the works of Lord Shaftesbury. Its chief doctrines, rhapsodically promulgated by this amiable and original enthusiast, were that the universe and all its creatures constitute a perfect harmony; and that Man, owing to his innate moral and æsthetic sense, needs no supernatural revelation of religious or ethical truth, because if he will discard the prejudices of tradition, he will instinctively, when face to face with Nature, recognize the Spirit which dwells therein,—and, correspondingly, when in the presence of a good deed he will recognize its morality. In other words, God and Nature are one; and Man is instinctively good, his cardinal virtue being the love of humanity, his true religion the love of Nature. Be therefore of good cheer: evil merely appears to exist, sin is a figment of false psychology; lead mankind to return to the natural, and they will find happiness.

The poetical possibilities of sentimentalism were not grasped by any noteworthy poet before Thomson. *The Seasons* was an innovation, and its novelty lay not so much in the choice of the subject as in the interpretation. Didactic as well as descriptive, it was designed not merely to present realistic pictures but to arouse certain explicitly stated thoughts and feelings. Thomson had absorbed some of Shaftesbury's ideas. Such sketches as that of the hardships which country folk suffer in winter, contrasted with the thoughtless gayety of city revelers, and inculcating the lesson of sympathy, are precisely in the vein that sentimentalism encouraged. So, too, the tendency of Shaftesbury to deify Nature appears in several ardent passages. The choice of blank verse as the medium of this liberal and expansive train of thought was appropriate. It should not be supposed, however, that Thomson accepted sentimentalism in its entirety or fully understood its ultimate bearings. The author of *Rule, Britannia* praised many things,—like commerce and industry and imperial power,—that are not favored by the thorough sentimentalist. Often he was inconsistent: his *Hymn to Nature* is in part a pantheistic rhapsody, in part a monotheistic Hebrew psalm. Essentially an indolent though receptive mind, he made no effort to trace the new ideas to their consequences; he vaguely considered them not irreconcilable with the old.

A keener mind fell into the same error. Pope, in the *Essay on Man*, tried to harmonize the orthodox conception of human character with sentimental optimism. As a collection of those memorable half-truths called aphorisms, the poem is admirable; as an attempt to unite new half-truths with old into a consistent scheme of life, it is fallacious. No creature composed of such warring elements as Pope describes in the superb antitheses that open Epistle II, can ever become in this world as good and at the same time as happy as Epistle IV vainly asserts. Pope, charged with heresy, did not repeat this endeavor to console mankind; he returned to his proper element, satire. But his effort to unite the new philosophy with the old psychology is striking evidence of the attractiveness and growing vogue of Shaftesbury's theories.

It was minor poets who first expressed sentimental ideas without inconsistency. As early as 1732, anonymous lines in the *Gentleman's Magazine* advanced what must have seemed the outrageously paradoxical thought that the savage in the wilderness was happier than civilized man. Two years later Soame Jenyns openly assailed in verse the orthodox doctrines of sin and retribution. These had long been assailed in prose; and under the influence of the attacks, within the pale of the Church itself, some ministers had suppressed or modified the sterner aspects of the creed,—a movement which Young's satires had ridiculed in the person of a lady of fashion who gladly entertained the notion that the Deity was too well-bred to call a lady to account for her offenses. Jenyns versified this effeminization of Christianity, charged orthodoxy with attributing cruelty to God, and asserted that faith in divine and human kindness would banish all wrong and discord from the world. In 1735 a far more important poet of sentimentalism arose in Henry Brooke, an undeservedly neglected pioneer, who, likewise drawing his inspiration from Shaftesbury, developed its theories with unusual consistency and fullness. His *Universal Beauty* voiced his sense of the divine immanence in every part of the cosmos, and emphasized the doctrine that animals, because they unhesitatingly follow the promptings of Nature, are more lovely, happy, and moral than Man, who should learn from them the individual and social virtues, abandon artificial civilization, and follow instinct. Brooke, in the prologue of his *Gustavus Vasa*, shows that he foresaw the political bearings of this theory; it is, in his opinion, peculiarly a people "guiltless of courts, untainted, and unread" that, illumined by Nature, understands and upholds freedom: but this was a thought too advanced to be general at this time even among Brooke's fellow-sentimentalists.

Though sentimental literature bore the seeds of revolution, its earliest effect upon its devotees was to create, through flattery of human character, a feeling of good-natured complacency. Against this optimism the traditional school reacted in two ways,—derisive and hortatory. Pope, Young, and Swift satirized with masterful skill the inherent weaknesses and follies of mankind, the vigor of their strokes drawing from the sentimentalist Whitehead the feeble but significant protest, *On Ridicule*, deprecating satire as discouraging to benevolence. On the other hand, Wesley's hymns fervently summoned to repentance and piety; while Young's *Night Thoughts*, yielding to the new influence only in its form (blank verse), reasserted the hollowness of earthly existence, the justice of God's stern will, and the need of faith in heavenly immortality as the only adequate satisfaction of the spiritual elements in Man.

The literary powers of Pope, Swift, and Young were far superior to those of the opposed school, which might have been overborne had not a second generation of sentimentalists arisen to voice its claims in a more poetical manner.

These newcomers,—Akenside, J. G. Cooper, the Wartons, and Collins,—all of them very young, appeared between 1744 and 1747; and each rendered distinct service to their common cause. The least original of the group, John Gilbert Cooper, versified in *The Power of Harmony* Shaftesbury's cosmogony. More independently, Mark Akenside developed out of the same doctrine of universal harmony the theory of æsthetics that was to guide the school,—the theory that the true poet is created not by culture and discipline at all, but owes to the impress of Nature—that beauty which is goodness—his imagination, his taste, and his moral vision. Though comparatively ardent and free in manner, Akenside pursued the customary, didactic method. Less abstract, more nearly an utterance of personal feeling, was Joseph Warton's *Enthusiast, or the Lover of Nature*, historically a remarkable poem, which, through its expression of the author's tastes and preferences, indicated briefly some of the most important touchstones of the sentimentalism (*videlicet*, "romanticism") of the future. Warton found odious such things as artificial gardens, commerical interests, social and legal conventions, and a formal Addisonian style; he yearned for mountainous wilds, unspoiled savages, solitudes where the voice of Wisdom was heard above the storms, and poetry that was "wildly warbled." His younger brother Thomas, who wrote *The Pleasures of Melancholy*, and sonnets showing an interest in non-classical antiquities, likewise felt the need of new literary gods to sanction the practices of their school: Pope and Dryden were accordingly dethroned; Spenser, Shakespeare, and the young Milton, all of whom were believed to warble wildly, were invoked.

William Collins was the most gifted of this band of enthusiasts. His general views were theirs: poetry is in his mind associated with wonder and ecstacy; and it finds its true themes, as the *Ode on Popular Superstitions* shows, in the weird legends, the pathetic mischances, and the blameless manners of a simple-minded folk remote from cities. Unlike his fellows, Collins had moments of great lyric power, and gave posterity a few treasured poems. His further distinction is that he desired really to create that poetical world about which Akenside theorized and for which the Wartons yearned. Unhappily, however, he too often peopled it with allegorical figures who move in a hazy atmosphere; and his melody is then more apparent than his meaning.

The hopeful spirit of these enthusiasts found little encouragement in the poems with which the period closed,—Gray's *Ode on Eton* and *Hymn to Adversity*, and Johnson's *Vanity of Human Wishes*.

> Some bold adventurers disdain
> The limits of their little reign,

wrote Gray, adding with the wisdom of disillusion,

> Gay hopes are theirs, by fancy fed,
> Less pleasing when possessed.

He was speaking of schoolboys whose ignorance is bliss; but the general tenor of his mind allows us to surmise that he also smiled pityingly upon some of the aspirations of the youthful sentimentalists. Dr. Johnson's hostility to them was, of course, outspoken. He laughed uproariously at their ecstatic manner, and ridiculed the cant of sensibility; and in solemn mood he struck in *The Vanity of Human Wishes* another blow at the heresy of optimism. In style the contrast between these poems and those of the Wartons and Collins is marked. Heirs of the Augustans, Johnson and Gray have perfect control over their respective diction and metres: here are no obscurities or false notes; Johnson sustains with superb dignity the tone of moral grandeur; Gray is ever felicitous. Up to the mid-century then, despite assailants, the classical school held its supremacy; for its literary art was incomparably more skillful than that of its enemies.

III. THE PROGRESS OF SENTIMENTALISM (1751–1775)

During the 1750's sentimental poetry did not fulfill the expectations which the outburst of 1744 had seemed to promise. It sank to lower levels, and its productions are noteworthy only as signs of the times and presages of the future. Richard Jago wrote some bald verses intended to foster opposition to hunting, and love for the lower animals,—according to the sentimental view really the "little brothers" of Man. John Dalton's crude *Descriptive Poem* apostrophized what was regarded as the "savage grandeur" of the Lake country; it is interesting only because it mentions Keswick, Borrowdale, Lodore, and Skiddaw, half a century later to become sacred ground. The practical dilemma of the sentimentalist,—drawn toward solitude by his worship of Nature, and toward society by his love for Man,—was described by Whitehead in *The Enthusiast*, the humanitarian impulse being finally given the preference. Though the last of these pieces is not contemptible in style, none of these writers had sufficient ardor to compel attention; and if sentimentalism had not been steadily disseminated through other literary forms, especially the novel, it might well have been regarded as a lost cause.

The great poet of this decade was Gray, whose *Elegy Written in a Country Churchyard*, by many held the noblest English lyric, appeared in 1751. His classical ideal of style, according to which poetry should have, in his words, "extreme conciseness of expression," yet be "pure, perspicuous, and musical," was realized both in the *Elegy* and in the otherwise very different *Pindaric Odes.* The ethical and religious implications of the *Elegy*, its piety, its sense of the frailties as well as the merits of mankind, are conservative. Nor is there in the *Pindaric Odes* any violation of classical principles. Gray never deviates into a pantheistic faith, a belief in human perfection, a conception of poetry as instinctive imagination unrestrained, or any other essential tenet of sentimentalism. Yet the influence of the new spirit upon him may be discerned. It modified his choice of subjects, and slightly colored their interpretation, without causing him to abandon the classical attitude. The *Elegy* treats with reverence what the Augustans had neglected,—the tragic dignity of obscure lives; *The Progress of Poesy* emphasizes qualities (emotion and sublimity) which the *Essay on Criticism* had not stressed; and *The Bard* presents a wildly picturesque figure of ancient days. Gray felt that classicism might quicken its spirit and widen its interests without surrendering its principles, that a classical poem might be a popular poem; and the admiration of posterity supports his belief.

An astounding and epochal event was the publication (1760 ff.) of the poems attributed to Ossian. Their "editor and translator," James Macpherson, author of a forgotten sentimental epic, alleged that Ossian was a Gaelic poet of the third century A. D., who sang the loves and wars of the heroes of his people, brave warriors fighting the imperial legions of Rome; and that his poems had been orally transmitted until now, fifteen centuries later, they had been taken down from the lips of Scotch peasants. It was a fabrication as ingenious as brazen. As a matter of fact, Macpherson had found only an insignificant portion of his extensive work in popular ballads; and what little he had found he had expanded and changed out of all semblance to genuine ancient legend. Both the guiding motive of his prose-poem (it is his as truly as *King Lear* is Shakespeare's), and the furore of welcome which greeted it, may be understood by recalling the position of the sentimental school on the eve of its appearance. The sentimentalists were maintaining that civilization had corrupted tastes, morals, and poetry, that it had perverted Man from his instinctive goodness, and that only by a return to communion with Nature could humanity and poetry be redeemed. But all this was based merely on philosophic theory, and could find no confirmation in history or literature: history knew of no innocent savages; and even as unsophisticated literature as Homer was then supposed to be, disclosed no heroes perfect in the sentimental virtues.

Ossian appeared; and the truth of sentimentalism seemed historically established. For here was poetry of the loftiest tone, composed in the unlearned Dark Ages, and answering the highest expectations concerning poetry inspired by Nature only. (Was not a distinguished Professor of Rhetoric saying, "Ossian's poetry, more perhaps than that of any other writer, deserves to be styled the poetry of the heart"?) And here was the record of a nature-people whose conduct stood revealed as flawless. "Fingal," Macpherson himself accommodatingly pointed out, "exercised every manly virtue in Caledonia while Heliogabalus disgraced human nature in Rome." More than fifty years afterwards Byron compared Homer's Hector, greatly to his disadvantage, with Ossian's Fingal: the latter's conduct was, in his admirer's words, "uniformly illustrious and great, without one mean or inhuman action to tarnish the splendor of his fame." The benevolent magnanimity of the heroes, the sweet sensibility of the heroines, their harmony with Nature's moods (traits which Macpherson had supplied from his own imagination), were the very traits that won the enthusiasm of the public. The poem in its turn stimulated the sentimentalism which had produced it; and henceforth the new school contended on even terms with the old.

One of the effects of the progress of sentimentalism was the decline of satire. Peculiarly the weapon of the classical school, it had fallen into unskillful hands: Churchill, though keen and bold, lacked the grace of Pope and the power of Johnson. Goldsmith might have proved a worthier successor; but though his genius for style was large, his capacity for sustained indignation was limited. Even his *Retaliation* is humorous in spirit rather than satiric. He was a being of conflicting impulses; and in his case at least, the style is not precisely the man. His temperament was emotional and affectionate; by nature he was a sentimentalist. But his inclinations were restrained, partly by the personal influence of Dr. Johnson, partly by his own admiration for the artistic traditions of the classicists. He despised looseness of style, considered blank verse unfinished, and cultivated what seemed to him the more polished elegance of the heroic couplet. The vacillation of his views appears in the difference between the sentiments of *The Traveller* and those of *The Deserted Village.* The former is a survey of the nations of Europe, the object being to discover a people wholly admirable. Merit is found in Italians, Swiss, French, Dutch, and English,—but never perfection; even the free and happy Swiss are disgusting in the vulgar sensuality of their pleasures; happiness is nowhere. One is not surprised to learn that Dr. Johnson contributed at least a few lines to a poem with so orthodox a message.

In *The Deserted Village,* on the other hand, Goldsmith employed the classical graces to point a moral which from the classical point of view was false. His sympathetic feelings had now been captivated by the notion of rural innocence. The traits of character which he attributed to the village inhabitants,—notably to the immortal preacher who, entertaining the vagrants,

> Quite forgot their vices in their woe,—

are those exalted in the literature of sentimentalism, as, for example, in his contemporary, Langhorne's *Country Justice. The Deserted Village* was in point of fact an imaginative idyll,—the supreme idyll of English poetry; but Goldsmith insisted that it was a realistic record of actual conditions. Yet he could never have observed such an English village, either in its depopulated and decayed state (as Macaulay has remarked), or in its rosy prosperity and unsullied virtue; his economic history and theory were misleading. Like Macpherson, but through self-delusion rather than intent, he was engaged in an effort to deceive by giving sentimental doctrines a basis of apparent actuality. But the world has forgotten or forgiven his pious fraud in its gratitude for the loveliness of his art.

IV. THE TRIUMPH OF SENTIMENTALISM

(1776–1800)

Goldsmith's application of sentimental ideas to contemporary affairs foreshadowed what was to be one of the marked tendencies of the movement in the last quarter of the century. Thus in 1777 Thomas Day interpreted the American Revolution as a conflict between the pitiless tyranny of a corrupt civilization and the appealing virtues of a people who had found in sequestered forests and prairies the abiding place of Freedom and the only remaining opportunity "to save the ruins of the human name." At the same time the justification of sentimentalism on historical grounds was strengthened by the young antiquarian and poet, Thomas Chatterton. Like Macpherson, he answers to Pope's description of archaizing authors,—

> Ancients in words, mere moderns in their sense.

He fabricated, in what he thought to be Middle English, a body of songs and interludes, which he attributed to a monk named Thomas Rowleie, and which showed that, in the supposedly unsophisticated simplicity of medieval times, charity to Man and love for Nature had flourished as beautifully as lyric utterance. Even more lamentable than Chatterton's early death is the fact that his fanciful and musical genius was shrouded in so grotesque a style.

In 1781 appeared a new poet of real distinction, George Crabbe, now the hope of the conservatives. Edmund Burke, who early in his great career had assailed the radicals in his ironic *Vindication of Natural Society*, and who to the end of his life contended against them in the arena of politics, on reading some of Crabbe's manuscripts, rescued this cultured and ingenuous man from obscurity and distress; and Dr. Johnson presently aided him in his literary labors. In *The Library* Crabbe expressed the reverence of a scholarly soul for the garnered wisdom of the past, and satirized some of the popular writings of the day, including sentimental fiction. He would not have denied the world those consolations which flow from the literature that mirrors our hopes and dreams; but his honest spirit revolted when such literature professed to be true to life. His acquaintance with actual conditions in humble circles, and with hardships, was as personal as Goldsmith's; but he was not the kind of poet who soothes the miseries of mankind by ignoring them. In *The Village* he arose with all the vigor and intensity of insulted common sense to refute the dreamers who offered a rose-colored picture of country life as a genuine portrayal of truth and nature. So evident was his mastery of his subject, his clearness of perception, and his earnestness of feeling, that he attracted immediate attention; and he might well have led a new advance under the ancient standards. But silence fell upon Crabbe for many years; and this proved to be the last occasion in the poetical history of the century that a powerful voice was raised in behalf of the old cause.

The poet who became the favorite of moderate sentimentalists, in what were called "genteel" circles, was William Cowper. He presented little or nothing that could affright the gentle emotions, and much that pleasurably stimulated them. He enriched the poetry of the domestic affections, and had a vein of sadness which occasionally, as in *To Mary*, deepened into the most touching pathos. In *The Task*, a discursive familiar essay in smooth-flowing blank verse, he dwelt fondly upon those satisfactions which his life of uneventful retirement offered; intimated that truth and wisdom were less surely found by poring upon books than by meditating among beloved rural scenes; and, turning his sad gaze toward the distant world of action, deplored that mankind strained "the natural bond of brotherhood" by tolerating cruel imprisonments, slavery, and warfare. Such humanitarian views, when they seek the aid of religious ethics, ought normally to find support in that sentimentalized Christianity which professes the entire goodness of the human heart; but the discordant element in Cowper's mind was his inclination towards Calvinism, which goes to the opposite extreme by insisting on total depravity. Personally he believed that he had committed the unpardonable sin (against the Holy Spirit),—a dreadful thought which underlies his tragic poem, *The Castaway;* and probably unwholesome, though well-intentioned, was the influence upon him of his spiritual adviser, John Newton, whose gloomy theology may be seen in the hymn, *The Vision of Life in Death.* Cowper's sense of the reality of evil not only distracted his mind to madness, but also prevented him from carrying his sentimental principles to their logical goal. What the hour demanded were poets who, discountenancing any mistrust of the natural emotions, should give them free rein. They were found at last in Burns and in Blake.

The sentimentalists had long yearned for the advent of the ideal poet. Macpherson had presented him,—but as of an era far remote; latterly Beattie, in *The Minstrel,* had set forth his growth under the inspiration of Nature,—but in a purely imaginary tale. Suddenly Burns appeared: and the ideal seemed incarnated in the living present. The Scottish bard was introduced to the world by his first admirers as "a heaven-taught ploughman, of humble unlettered station," whose "simple strains, artless and unadorned, seem to flow without effort from the native feelings of the heart"; and as "a signal instance of true and uncultivated genius." The real Burns, though indeed a genius of song, was far better read than the expectant world wished to believe, particularly in those whom he called his "bosom favorites," the sentimentalists Mackenzie and Sterne; and his sense of rhythm and melody had been trained by his emulation of earlier Scotch lyricists, whose lilting cadences flow towards him as highland rills to the gathering torrent. Sung to the notes of his native tunes, and infused with the local color of Scotch life, the sentimental themes assumed the freshness of novelty. Giving a new ardor to revolutionary tendencies, Burns revolted against the orthodoxy of the "Auld Lichts," depicting its representatives as ludicrously hypocritical. He protested against distinctions founded on birth or rank, as in *A Man's a Man for A' That;* and, on the other hand, he idealized the homely feelings and manners of the "virtuous populace" in his immortal *Cotter's Saturday Night.* He scorned academic learning, and protested that true inspiration was rather to be found in "ae spark o' Nature's fire,"—or at the nearest tavern:

> Leese me on drink! it gies us mair
> Than either school or college.

Like Sterne, who boasted that his pen governed him, Burns praised and affected the impromptu:

> But how the subject theme may gang,
> Let time or chance determine;
> Perhaps it may turn out a sang,
> Perhaps turn out a sermon.

His Muse was to be the mood of the moment. Herein he brought to fulfillment the sentimental desire for the liberation of the emotions; but his work, taken as a whole, can scarcely be said to vindicate the faith that the emotions, once freed, would manifest instinctive purity. At his almost unrivalled best, he can sing in the sweetest strains the raptures or pathos of innocent youthful love, as in *Sweet Afton* or *To Mary in Heaven;* but straightway sinking from that elevation of feeling to the depths of vulgarity or grossness, he will chant with equal zest and skill the indulgence of the animal appetites.* He hails the joys of life, but without discriminating between the higher and the lower. Yet these exuberant animal spirits which, unrestrained by conscience or taste, drove him too often into scurrility, gave his work that passion—warm, throbbing, and personal—which had been painfully wanting in earlier poets of sensibility. It was his emotional intensity as well as his lyric genius that made him the most popular poet of his time.

In Burns, sentimentalism was largely temperamental, unreflective, and concrete. In William Blake, the singularity of whose work long retarded its due appreciation, sentimentalism was likewise temperamental; but, unconfined to actuality, became far broader in scope, more spiritual, and more consistently philosophic. Indeed, Blake was the ultimate sentimentalist of the century. A visionary and

*** In this edition, the poems of Burns, unlike those of the other poets, are printed not in the order of their publication but as nearly as ascertainable in that of their composition.**

symbolist, he passed beyond Shaftesbury in his thought, and beyond any poet of the school in his endeavor to create a new and appropriate style. His contemporary, Erasmus Darwin, author of *The Botanic Garden*, was trying to give sentimentalism a novel interpretation by describing the life of plants in terms of human life; but, Darwin being destitute of artistic sense, the result was grotesque. Blake, by training and vocation an engraver, was primarily an artist; but, partly under Swedenborgian influences, he had grasped the innermost character of sentimentalism, perceived all its implications, and carried them fearlessly to their utmost bounds. To him every atom of the cosmos was literally spiritual and holy; the divine and the human, the soul and the flesh, were absolutely one; God and Man were only two aspects of pervasive "mercy, pity, peace, and love." Nothing else had genuine reality. The child, its vision being as yet unclouded by false teachings, saw the universe thus truly; and Blake, therefore, in *Songs of Innocence*, gave glimpses of the world as the child sees it,—a guileless existence amid the peace that passes all understanding. He hymned the sanctity of animal life: even the tiger, conventionally an incarnation of cruelty, was a glorious creature of divine mould; to slay or cage a beast was, the *Auguries of Innocence* protested, to incur anathema. *The Book of Thel* allegorically showed the mutual interdependence of all creation, and reprehended the maiden shyness that shrinks from merging its life in the sacrificial union which sustains the whole.

To Blake the great enemy of truth was the cold logical reason, a truncated part of Man's spirit, which was incapable of attaining wisdom, and which had fabricated those false notions that governed the practical world and constrained the natural feelings. Instances of the unhappiness caused by such constraint, he gave in *Songs of Experience*, where *The Garden of Love* describes the blighting curse which church law had laid upon free love. To overthrow intellectualism and discipline, Man must liberate his most precious faculty, the imagination, which alone can reveal the spiritual character of the universe and the beauty that life will wear when the feelings cease to be unnaturally confined. Temporarily Blake rejoiced when the French Revolution seemed to usher in the millennium of freedom and peace; and his interpretation of its earlier incidents in his poem on that theme* illustrates in style and spirit the highly original nature of his mind. More than any predecessor he understood how the peculiarly poetical possibilities of sentimentalism might be elicited, namely by emphasizing its mystical quality. Thus under his guidance mysticism, which in the early seventeenth century had sublimated the religious poetry of the orthodox, returned to sublimate the poetry of the radicals; and with that achievement the sentimental movement reached its climax.

Burns died in 1796; Blake, lost in a realm of symbolism, became unintelligible; and temporarily sentimentalism suffered a reaction. The French Revolution, with its Reign of Terror, and the rise of a military autocrat, though supported, even after Great Britain had taken up arms against Napoleon, by some "friends of humanity" who placed universal brotherhood above patriotism, seemed to the general public to demonstrate that the sentimental theories and hopes were untrue to life and led to results directly contrary to those predicted. Once again, in Canning's caustic satires of *The Anti-Jacobin*, conservatism raised its voice. But by this time sentimentalism was too fully developed and widely spread to be more than checked. Under the new leadership of Wordsworth, Coleridge, and Southey, the movement, chastened and modified by experience, resumed its progress; and the fame of its new leaders presently dimmed the memory of those pioneers who in the eighteenth century had undermined the foundations of orthodoxy, slowly upbuilt a new world of thought, gradually fashioned a poetic style more suited to their sentiments than the classical, and thus helped to plunge the modern world into that struggle which, in life and in literature, rages about us still.

ERNEST BERNBAUM

* *The French Revolution* was suppressed at the time, and has been recovered only in our own day by Dr. John Sampson, who first published it in the admirable Clarendon Press edition of Blake.

ENGLISH POETS OF THE EIGHTEENTH CENTURY

JOHN POMFRET

THE CHOICE

If Heaven the grateful liberty would give,
That I might choose my method how to live;
And all those hours propitious fate should lend,
In blissful ease and satisfaction spend.

I. The Gentleman's Retirement

Near some fair town I'd have a private seat,
Built uniform, not little, nor too great:
Better, if on a rising ground it stood;
Fields on this side, on that a neighbouring wood.
It should within no other things contain,
But what are useful, necessary, plain:
Methinks 'tis nauseous, and I'd ne'er endure,
The needless pomp of gaudy furniture.
A little garden, grateful to the eye;
And a cool rivulet run murmuring by,
On whose delicious banks a stately row
Of shady limes, or sycamores, should grow.
At th' end of which a silent study placed,
Should with the noblest authors there be graced:
Horace and Virgil, in whose mighty lines
Immortal wit, and solid learning, shines;
Sharp Juvenal and amorous Ovid too,
Who all the turns of love's soft passion knew:
He that with judgment reads the charming lines,
In which strong art with stronger nature joins,
Must grant his fancy does the best excel;
His thoughts so tender, and expressed so well:

With all those moderns, men of steady sense,
Esteemed for learning, and for eloquence.
In some of these, as fancy should advise,
I'd always take my morning exercise:
For sure no minutes bring us more content,
Than those in pleasing useful studies spent.

II. His Fortune and Charity

I'd have a clear and competent estate,
That I might live genteelly, but not great:
As much as I could moderately spend;
A little more, sometimes t' oblige a friend.
Nor should the sons of poverty repine
At fortune's frown, for they should taste of mine;
And all that objects of true pity were,
Should be relieved with what my wants could spare;
For what our Maker has too largely given,
Should be returned in gratitude to Heaven.
A frugal plenty should my table spread,
With healthy, not luxurious, dishes fed;
Enough to satisfy, and something more,
To feed the stranger, and the neighb'ring poor.
Strong meat indulges vice, and pampering food
Creates diseases, and inflames the blood.
But what's sufficient to make nature strong,
And the bright lamp of life continue long,
I'd freely take, and as I did possess,
The bounteous Author of my plenty bless.

III. His Hospitality and Temperance

I'd have a little cellar, cool and neat,
With humming ale and virgin wine replete.
Wine whets the wit, improves its native force,
And gives a pleasant flavour to discourse;
By making all our spirits debonair,
Throws off the lees and sediment of care.
But as the greatest blessing Heaven lends
May be debauched, and serve ignoble ends;
So, but too oft, the grape's refreshing juice
Does many mischievous effects produce.

My house should no such rude disorders know,
As from high drinking consequently flow;
Nor would I use what was so kindly given,
To the dishonour of indulgent Heaven.
If any neighbour came, he should be free,
Used with respect, and not uneasy be,
In my retreat, or to himself or me.
What freedom, prudence, and right reason give,
All men may, with impunity, receive:
But the least swerving from their rules too much,
And what's forbidden us, 'tis death to touch.

IV. His Company

That life may be more comfortable yet,
And all my joys refined, sincere, and great;
I'd choose two friends, whose company would be
A great advance to my felicity:
Well-born, of humours suited to my own,
Discreet, that men as well as books have known;
Brave, generous, witty, and exactly free
From loose behaviour or formality;
Airy and prudent, merry but not light;
Quick in discerning; and in judging, right;
They should be secret, faithful to their trust,
In reasoning cool, strong, temperate, and just;
Obliging, open, without huffing, brave;
Brisk in gay talking, and in sober, grave;
Close in dispute, but not tenacious; tried
By solemn reason, and let that decide;
Not prone to lust, revenge, or envious hate;
Nor busy meddlers with intrigues of state;
Strangers to slander, and sworn foes to spite,
Not quarrelsome, but stout enough to fight;
Loyal and pious, friends to Cæsar; true
As dying martyrs to their Makers too.
In their society I could not miss
A permanent, sincere, substantial bliss.

V. His Lady and Converse

Would bounteous Heaven once more indulge, I'd choose
(For who would so much satisfaction lose
As witty nymphs in conversation give?)
Near some obliging modest fair to live:
For there's that sweetness in a female mind,
Which in a man's we cannot [hope to] find;
That, by a secret but a powerful art,
Winds up the spring of life, and does impart
Fresh, vital heat to the transported heart.
  I'd have her reason all her passions sway;
Easy in company, in private gay;
Coy to a fop, to the deserving free;
Still constant to herself, and just to me.
She should a soul have for great actions fit;
Prudence and wisdom to direct her wit;
Courage to look bold danger in the face,
Not fear, but only to be proud or base;
Quick to advise, by an emergence pressed,
To give good counsel, or to take the best.
  I'd have th' expressions of her thoughts be such,
She might not seem reserved, nor talk too much:
That shows a want of judgment and of sense;
More than enough is but impertinence.
Her conduct regular, her mirth refined;
Civil to strangers, to her neighbours kind;
Averse to vanity, revenge, and pride;
In all the methods of deceit untried;
So faithful to her friend, and good to all,
No censure might upon her actions fall:
Then would e'en envy be compelled to say
She goes the least of womankind astray.
  To this fair creature I'd sometimes retire;
Her conversation would new joys inspire;
Give life an edge so keen, no surly care
Would venture to assault my soul, or dare
Near my retreat to hide one secret snare.
But so divine, so noble a repast
I'd seldom, and with moderation, taste:
For highest cordials all their virtue lose,
By a too frequent and too bold an use;

And what would cheer the spirits in distress
Ruins our health when taken to excess.

VI. His Peaceable Life

I'd be concerned in no litigious jar;
Beloved by all, not vainly popular.
Whate'er assistance I had power to bring
T' oblige my company, or to serve my king,
Whene'er they called, I'd readily afford,
My tongue, my pen, my counsel, or my sword.
Lawsuits I'd shun, with as much studious care,
As I would dens where hungry lions are;
And rather put up injuries, than be
A plague to him who'd be a plague to me.
I value quiet at a price too great
To give for my revenge so dear a rate:
For what do we by all our bustle gain,
But counterfeit delight for real pain?

VII. His Happy Death

If Heaven a date of many years would give,
Thus I'd in pleasure, ease, and plenty live.
And as I near approach[ed] the verge of life,
Some kind relation (for I'd have no wife)
Should take upon him all my worldly care
While I did for a better state prepare.
Then I'd not be with any trouble vexed,
Nor have the evening of my days perplexed;
But by a silent and a peaceful death,
Without a sigh, resign my aged breath.
And, when committed to the dust, I'd have
Few tears, but friendly, dropped into my grave;
Then would my exit so propitious be,
All men would wish to live and die like me.

DANIEL DEFOE

From THE TRUE-BORN ENGLISHMAN

The Romans first with Julius Cæsar came,
Including all the nations of that name,
Gauls, Greeks, and Lombards, and, by computation,
Auxiliaries or slaves of every nation.
With Hengist, Saxons; Danes with Sueno came;
In search of plunder, not in search of fame.
Scots, Picts, and Irish from th' Hibernian shore,
And conquering William brought the Normans o'er.
All these their barbarous offspring left behind,
The dregs of armies, they of all mankind;
Blended with Britons, who before were here,
Of whom the Welsh ha' blessed the character.
From this amphibious ill-born mob began
That vain, ill-natured thing, an Englishman.

. . . .

And lest by length of time it be pretended
The climate may this modern breed ha' mended,
Wise Providence, to keep us where we are,
Mixes us daily with exceeding care.
We have been Europe's sink, the jakes where she
Voids all her offal outcast progeny.
From our fifth Henry's time, the strolling bands
Of banished fugitives from neighbouring lands
Have here a certain sanctuary found:
Th' eternal refuge of the vagabond,
Where, in but half a common age of time,
Borrowing new blood and manners from the clime,
Proudly they learn all mankind to contemn;
And all their race are true-born Englishmen.
Dutch, Walloons, Flemings, Irishmen, and Scots,
Vaudois, and Valtelins, and Huguenots,
In good Queen Bess's charitable reign,
Supplied us with three hundred thousand men.
Religion—God, we thank thee!—sent them hither,
Priests, Protestants, the Devil and all together:

Of all professions and of every trade,
All that were persecuted or afraid;
Whether for debt or other crimes they fled,
David at Hachilah was still their head.
The offspring of this miscellaneous crowd,
Had not their new plantations long enjoyed,
But they grew Englishmen, and raised their votes
At foreign shoals for interloping Scots.
The royal branch from Pictland did succeed,
With troops of Scots and Scabs from North-by-Tweed.
The seven first years of his pacific reign
Made him and half his nation Englishmen.
Scots from the northern frozen banks of Tay,
With packs and plods came whigging all away;
Thick as the locusts which in Egypt swarmed,
With pride and hungry hopes completely armed;
With native truth, diseases, and no money,
Plundered our Canaan of the milk and honey.
Here they grew quickly lords and gentlemen,—
And all their race are true-born Englishmen.

. . . .

The wonder which remains is at our pride,
To value that which all wise men deride.
For Englishmen to boast of generation
Cancels their knowledge, and lampoons the nation.
A true-born Englishman's a contradiction,
In speech an irony, in fact a fiction;
A banter made to be a test of fools,
Which those that use it justly ridicules;
A metaphor invented to express
A man akin to all the universe.

From A HYMN TO THE PILLORY

Hail hieroglyphic state-machine,
Contrived to punish fancy in!
Men that are men in thee can feel no pain,
And all thy insignificants disdain.
Contempt, that false new word for shame,
Is, without crime, an empty name,

A shadow to amuse mankind,
But never frights the wise or well-fixed mind:
Virtue despises human scorn,
And scandals innocence adorn.

. . . .

Sometimes, the air of scandal to maintain,
Villains look from thy lofty loops in vain;
But who can judge of crimes by punishment
Where parties rule and L[ord]s subservient?
Justice with change of interest learns to bow,
And what was merit once is murder now:
Actions receive their tincture from the times,
And as they change, are virtues made or crimes.
Thou art the state-trap of the law,
But neither can keep knaves nor honest men in awe;
These are too hardened in offence,
And those upheld by innocence.

. . . .

Thou art no shame to truth and honesty,
Nor is the character of such defaced by thee
Who suffer by oppressive injury.
Shame, like the exhalations of the sun,
Falls back where first the motion was begun;
And he who for no crime shall on thy brows appear
Bears less reproach than they who placed him there.

But if contempt is on thy face entailed,
Disgrace itself shall be ashamed;
Scandal shall blush that it has not prevailed
To blast the man it has defamed.
Let all that merit equal punishment
Stand there with him, and we are all content.

. . . .

Thou bugbear of the law, stand up and speak,
Thy long misconstrued silence break;
Tell us who 'tis upon thy ridge stands there,
So full of fault and yet so void of fear;
And from the paper in his hat,
Let all mankind be told for what.
Tell them it was because he was too bold,
And told those truths which should not ha' been told,

Extol the justice of the land,
Who punish what they will not understand.
Tell them he stands exalted there
For speaking what we would not hear;
And yet he might have been secure
Had he said less or would he ha' said more.
Tell them that this is his reward
And worse is yet for him prepared,
Because his foolish virtue was so nice
As not to sell his friends, according to his friends' advice.

And thus he's an example made,
To make men of their honesty afraid,
That for the time to come they may
More willingly their friends betray;
Tell them the m[en] who placed him here
Are sc[anda]ls to the times;
But at a loss to find his guilt,
They can't commit his crimes.

JOSEPH ADDISON

From THE CAMPAIGN

Behold in awful march and dread array
The long-extended squadrons shape their way!
Death, in approaching terrible, imparts
An anxious horror to the bravest hearts;
Yet do their beating breasts demand the strife,
And thirst of glory quells the love of life.
No vulgar fears can British minds control:
Heat of revenge and noble pride of soul
O'er look the foe, advantaged by his post,
Lessen his numbers, and contract his host;
Though fens and floods possessed the middle space,
That unprovoked they would have feared to pass,
Nor fens nor floods can stop Britannia's bands
When her proud foe ranged on their borders stands.

But, O my Muse, what numbers wilt thou find
To sing the furious troops in battle joined!
Methinks I hear the drum's tumultuous sound
The victor's shouts and dying groans confound,
The dreadful burst of cannon rend the skies,
And all the thunder of the battle rise!
'Twas then great Marlborough's mighty soul was proved,
That, in the shock of charging hosts unmoved,
Amidst confusion, horror, and despair,
Examined all the dreadful scenes of war:
In peaceful thought the field of death surveyed,
To fainting squadrons sent the timely aid,
Inspired repulsed battalions to engage,
And taught the doubtful battle where to rage.
So when an angel by divine command
With rising tempests shakes a guilty land,
Such as of late o'er pale Britannia passed,
Calm and serene he drives the furious blast,
And, pleased th' Almighty's orders to perform,
Rides in the whirlwind, and directs the storm.

[DIVINE ODE]

I

The spacious firmament on high,
With all the blue ethereal sky,
And spangled heavens, a shining frame,
Their great Original proclaim.
Th' unwearied sun from day to day
Does his Creator's power display;
And publishes to every land
The work of an almighty hand.

II

Soon as the evening shades prevail,
The moon takes up the wondrous tale;
And nightly to the listening earth
Repeats the story of her birth:
Whilst all the stars that round her burn,
And all the planets in their turn,

Confirm the tidings as they roll,
And spread the truth from pole to pole.

III

What though in solemn silence all
Move round the dark terrestrial ball;
What though nor real voice nor sound
Amidst their radiant orbs be found?
In reason's ear they all rejoice,
And utter forth a glorious voice:
Forever singing as they shine,
'The hand that made us is divine.'

MATTHEW PRIOR

TO A CHILD OF QUALITY FIVE YEARS OLD

THE AUTHOR FORTY

Lords, knights, and squires, the numerous band
  That wear the fair Miss Mary's fetters,
Were summoned, by her high command,
  To show their passions by their letters.

My pen amongst the rest I took,
  Lest those bright eyes that cannot read
Should dart their kindling fires, and look
  The power they have to be obeyed.

Nor quality nor reputation
  Forbid me yet my flame to tell;
Dear five years old befriends my passion,
  And I may write till she can spell.

For while she makes her silk-worms beds
  With all the tender things I swear,
Whilst all the house my passion reads
  In papers round her baby's hair,

She may receive and own my flame;
  For though the strictest prudes should know it,
She'll pass for a most virtuous dame,
  And I for an unhappy poet.

Then, too, alas! when she shall tear
  The lines some younger rival sends,
She'll give me leave to write, I fear,
  And we shall still continue friends;

For, as our different ages move,
'Tis so ordained (would fate but mend it!)
That I shall be past making love
  When she begins to comprehend it.

TO A LADY

SHE REFUSING TO CONTINUE A DISPUTE WITH ME, AND LEAVING ME IN THE ARGUMENT

Spare, generous victor, spare the slave
  Who did unequal war pursue,
That more than triumph he might have
  In being overcome by you.

In the dispute whate'er I said,
  My heart was by my tongue belied,
And in my looks you might have read
  How much I argued on your side.

You, far from danger as from fear,
  Might have sustained an open fight:
For seldom your opinions err;
  Your eyes are always in the right.

Why, fair one, would you not rely
  On reason's force with beauty's joined?
Could I their prevalence deny,
  I must at once be deaf and blind.

Alas! not hoping to subdue,
  I only to the fight aspired;
To keep the beauteous foe in view
  Was all the glory I desired.

But she, howe'er of victory sure,
Contemns the wreath too long delayed,
And, armed with more immediate power,
Calls cruel silence to her aid.

Deeper to wound, she shuns the fight:
She drops her arms, to gain the field;
Secures her conquest by her flight,
And triumphs when she seems to yield.

So when the Parthian turned his steed
And from the hostile camp withdrew,
With cruel skill the backward reed
He sent, and as he fled he slew.

[THE DYING HADRIAN TO HIS SOUL]

Poor, little, pretty, fluttering thing,
Must we no longer live together?
And dost thou prune thy trembling wing
To take thy flight, thou know'st not whither?
Thy humorous vein, thy pleasing folly,
Lies all neglected, all forgot:
And pensive, wavering, melancholy,
Thou dread'st and hop'st, thou know'st not what.

A BETTER ANSWER

Dear Chloe, how blubbered is that pretty face!
Thy cheek all on fire, and thy hair all uncurled!
Prithee quit this caprice, and (as old Falstaff says)
Let us e'en talk a little like folks of this world.

How canst thou presume thou hast leave to destroy
The beauties which Venus but lent to thy keeping?
Those looks were designed to inspire love and joy;
More ordinary eyes may serve people for weeping.

To be vexed at a trifle or two that I writ,
Your judgment at once and my passion you wrong;
You take that for fact which will scarce be found wit:
Od's life! must one swear to the truth of a song?

What I speak, my fair Chloe, and what I write, shows
The difference there is betwixt nature and art:
I court others in verse, but I love thee in prose;
And they have my whimsies, but thou hast my heart.

The god of us verse-men (you know, child), the sun,
How after his journeys he sets up his rest;
If at morning o'er earth 'tis his fancy to run,
At night he reclines on his Thetis's breast.

So when I am wearied with wandering all day,
To thee, my delight, in the evening I come:
No matter what beauties I saw in my way;
They were but my visits, but thou art my home.

Then finish, dear Chloe, this pastoral war,
And let us like Horace and Lydia agree;
For thou art a girl as much brighter than her
As he was a poet sublimer than me.

BERNARD DE MANDEVILLE

From THE GRUMBLING HIVE; OR, KNAVES TURNED HONEST

A spacious hive, well stocked with bees,
That lived in luxury and ease;
And yet as famed for laws and arms,
As yielding large and early swarms;
Was counted the great nursery
Of sciences and industry.

. . . .

Vast numbers thronged the fruitful hive;
Yet those vast numbers made 'em thrive;
Millions endeavouring to supply
Each others lust and vanity,
While other millions were employed
To see their handiworks destroyed;

They furnished half the universe,
Yet had more work than labourers.
Some with vast stocks, and little pains,
Jumped into business of great gains;
And some were damned to scythes and spades,
And all those hard laborious trades
Where willing wretches daily sweat
And wear out strength and limbs, to eat;
While others followed mysteries
To which few folks bind prentices,
That want no stock but that of brass,
And may set up without a cross,—
As sharpers, parasites, pimps, players,
Pickpockets, coiners, quacks, soothsayers,
And all those that in enmity
With downright working, cunningly
Convert to their own use the labour
Of their good-natured heedless neighbour.
These were called knaves; but bar the name,
The grave industrious were the same:
All trades and places knew some cheat,
No calling was without deceit.

. . . .

Thus every part was full of vice,
Yet the whole mass a paradise:
Flattered in peace, and feared in wars,
They were th' esteem of foreigners,
And lavish of their wealth and lives,
The balance of all other hives.
Such were the blessings of that state;
Their crimes conspired to make them great.

. . . .

The root of evil, avarice,
That damned, ill-natured, baneful vice,
Was slave to prodigality,
That noble sin; whilst luxury
Employed a million of the poor,
And odious pride a million more;
Envy itself, and vanity,
Were ministers of industry;

Their darling folly—fickleness
In diet, furniture, and dress—
That strange, ridiculous vice, was made
The very wheel that turned the trade.
Their laws and clothes were equally
Objects of mutability;
For what was well done for a time,
In half a year became a crime.

. . . .

How vain is mortal happiness!
Had they but known the bounds of bliss,
And that perfection here below
Is more than gods can well bestow,
The grumbling brutes had been content
With ministers and government.
But they, at every ill success,
Like creatures lost without redress,
Cursed politicians, armies, fleets;
While every one cried, 'Damn the cheats!'
And would, though conscious of his own,
In others barbarously bear none.
One that had got a princely store
By cheating master, king, and poor,
Dared cry aloud, 'The land must sink
For all its fraud'; and whom d'ye think
The sermonizing rascal chid?
A glover that sold lamb for kid!
The least thing was not done amiss,
Or crossed the public business,
But all the rogues cried brazenly,
'Good Gods, had we but honesty!'
Mercury smiled at th' impudence,
And others called it want of sense,
Always to rail at what they loved:
But Jove, with indignation moved,
At last in anger swore he'd rid
The bawling hive of fraud; and did.
The very moment it departs,
And honesty fills all their hearts,
There shews 'em, like th' instructive tree,
Those crimes which they're ashamed to see,

Which now in silence they confess
By blushing at their ugliness;
Like children that would hide their faults
And by their colour own their thoughts,
Imagining when they're looked upon,
That others see what they have done.
But, O ye Gods! what consternation!
How vast and sudden was th' alternation!
In half an hour, the nation round,
Meat fell a penny in the pound.

. . . .

Now mind the glorious hive, and see
How honesty and trade agree.
The show is gone; it thins apace,
And looks with quite another face.
For 'twas not only that they went
By whom vast sums were yearly spent;
But multitudes that lived on them,
Were daily forced to do the same.
In vain to other trades they'd fly;
All were o'erstocked accordingly.

. . . .

As pride and luxury decrease,
So by degrees they leave the seas.
Not merchants now, but companies,
Remove whole manufactories.
All arts and crafts neglected lie:
Content, the bane of industry,
Makes 'em admire their homely store,
And neither seek nor covet more.
So few in the vast hive remain,
The hundredth part they can't maintain
Against th' insults of numerous foes,
Whom yet they valiantly oppose,
Till some well-fenced retreat is found,
And here they die or stand their ground.
No hireling in their army's known;
But bravely fighting for their own
Their courage and integrity
At last were crowned with victory.
They triumphed not without their cost,
For many thousand bees were lost.

Hardened with toil and exercise,
They counted ease itself a vice;
Which so improved their temperance
That, to avoid extravagance,
They flew into a hollow tree,
Blessed with content and honesty.

THE MORAL:

Then leave complaints: fools only strive
To make a great an honest hive.
T' enjoy the world's conveniences,
Be famed in war, yet live in ease,
Without great vices, is a vain
Utopia seated in the brain.

ISAAC WATTS

THE HAZARD OF LOVING THE CREATURES

Where'er my flattering passions rove,
  I find a lurking snare;
'Tis dangerous to let loose our love
  Beneath th' eternal fair.

Souls whom the tie of friendship binds,
  And things that share our blood,
Seize a large portion of our minds,
  And leave the less for God.

Nature has soft but powerful bands,
  And reason she controls;
While children with their little hands
  Hang closest to our souls.

Thoughtless they act th' old Serpent's part;
  What tempting things they be!
Lord, how they twine about our heart,
  And draw it off from Thee!

Our hasty wills rush blindly on
  Where rising passion rolls,
And thus we make our fetters strong
  To bind our slavish souls.

Dear Sovereign, break these fetters off,
  And set our spirits free;
God in Himself is bliss enough;
  For we have all in Thee.

THE DAY OF JUDGMENT

When the fierce north-wind with his airy forces
Rears up the Baltic to a foaming fury;
And the red lightning with a storm of hail comes
    Rushing amain down;

How the poor sailors stand amazed and tremble,
While the hoarse thunder, like a bloody trumpet,
Roars a loud onset to the gaping waters,
    Quick to devour them.

Such shall the noise be, and the wild disorder
(If things eternal may be like these earthly),
Such the dire terror when the great Archangel
    Shakes the creation;

Tears the strong pillars of the vault of heaven,
Breaks up old marble, the repose of princes.
See the graves open, and the bones arising,
    Flames all around them!

Hark, the shrill outcries of the guilty wretches!
Lively bright horror and amazing anguish
Stare through their eyelids, while the living worm lies
    Gnawing within them.

Thoughts like old vultures, prey upon their heart-strings,
And the smart twinges, when the eye beholds the
Lofty Judge frowning, and a flood of vengeance
    Rolling afore Him.

Hopeless immortals! how they scream and shiver,
While devils push them to the pit wide-yawning
Hideous and gloomy, to receive them headlong
Down to the centre!

Stop here, my fancy: (all away, ye horrid
Doleful ideas!) come, arise to Jesus,
How He sits God-like! and the saints around Him
Throned, yet adoring!

O may I sit there when He comes triumphant,
Dooming the nations! then arise to glory,
While our hosannas all along the passage
Shout the Redeemer.

O GOD, OUR HELP IN AGES PAST

O God, our help in ages past,
Our hope for years for to come,
Our shelter from the stormy blast,
And our eternal home:

Under the shadow of Thy throne,
Thy saints have dwelt secure;
Sufficient is Thine arm alone,
And our defense is sure.

Before the hills in order stood,
Or earth received her frame,
From everlasting Thou art God,
To endless years the same.

A thousand ages in Thy sight
Are like an evening gone;
Short as the watch that ends the night
Before the rising sun.

Time, like an ever-rolling stream,
Bears all its sons away;
They fly forgotten, as a dream
Dies at the opening day.

O God, our help in ages past;
Our hope for years to come;
Be thou our guard while troubles last,
And our eternal home!

A CRADLE HYMN

Hush! my dear, lie still and slumber,
Holy angels guard thy bed!
Heavenly blessings without number
Gently falling on thy head.

Sleep, my babe; thy food and raiment,
House and home, thy friends provide;
All without thy care or payment:
All thy wants are well supplied.

How much better thou'rt attended
Than the Son of God could be,
When from Heaven He descended
And became a child like thee!

Soft and easy is thy cradle:
Coarse and hard thy Saviour lay,
When His birthplace was a stable
And His softest bed was hay.

Blessèd babe! what glorious features—
Spotless fair, divinely bright!
Must He dwell with brutal creatures?
How could angels bear the sight?

Was there nothing but a manger
Cursèd sinners could afford
To receive the heavenly stranger?
Did they thus affront their Lord?

Soft, my child: I did not chide thee,
Though my song might sound too hard;
'Tis thy mother sits beside thee,
And her arms shall be thy guard.

Yet to read the shameful story
  How the Jews abused their King,
How they served the Lord of Glory,
  Makes me angry while I sing.

See the kinder shepherds round Him,
  Telling wonders from the sky!
Where they sought Him, there they found Him,
  With His virgin mother by.

See the lovely babe a-dressing;
  Lovely infant, how He smiled!
When He wept, the mother's blessing
  Soothed and hushed the holy child.

Lo, He slumbers in His manger,
  Where the hornèd oxen fed;
Peace, my darling; here's no danger,
  Here's no ox a-near thy bed.

'Twas to save thee, child, from dying,
  Save my dear from burning flame,
Bitter groans and endless crying,
  That thy blest Redeemer came.

May'st thou live to know and fear him,
  Trust and love Him all thy days;
Then go dwell forever near Him,
  See His face, and sing His praise!

ALEXANDER POPE

FROM AN ESSAY ON CRITICISM

'Tis hard to say, if greater want of skill
Appear in writing or in judging ill;
But, of the two, less dangerous is th' offense
To tire our patience, than mislead our sense.
Some few in that, but numbers err in this,
Ten censure wrong for one who writes amiss;
A fool might once himself alone expose,
Now one in verse makes many more in prose.
'Tis with our judgments as our watches, none
Go just alike, yet each believes his own.
In poets as true genius is but rare,
True taste as seldom is the critic's share;
Both must alike from heaven derive their light,
These born to judge, as well as those to write.
Let such teach others who themselves excel,
And censure freely who have written well.
Authors are partial to their wit, 'tis true,
But are not critics to their judgment too?

. . . .

But you who seek to give and merit fame
And justly bear a critic's noble name,
Be sure yourself and your own reach to know,
How far your genius, taste, and learning go;
Launch not beyond your depth, but be discreet,
And mark that point where sense and dulness meet.

. . . .

First follow Nature, and your judgment frame
By her just standard, which is still the same:
Unerring Nature, still divinely bright,
One clear, unchanged, and universal light,
Life, force, and beauty, must to all impart,
At once the source, and end, and test of art.
Art from that fund each just supply provides,
Works without show, and without pomp presides:

In some fair body thus th' informing soul
With spirit feeds, with vigour fills the whole.
Each motion guides, and every nerve sustains;
Itself unseen, but in th' effects, remains.
Some, to whom Heaven in wit has been profuse,
Want as much more, to turn it to its use;
For wit and judgment often are at strife,
Though meant each other's aid, like man and wife.
'Tis more to guide than spur the Muse's steed;
Restrain his fury, than provoke his speed;
The wingèd courser, like a generous horse,
Shows most true mettle when you check his course.
Those rules of old discovered, not devised,
Are Nature still, but Nature methodized;
Nature, like liberty, is but restrained
By the same laws which first herself ordained.
You, then, whose judgment the right course would steer,
Know well each ancient's proper character;
His fable, subject, scope in every page;
Religion, country, genius of his age:
Without all these at once before your eyes,
Cavil you may, but never criticise.
Be Homer's works your study and delight,
Read them by day, and meditate by night;
Thence form your judgment, thence your maxims bring,
And trace the Muses upward to their spring.
Still with itself compared, his text peruse;
And let your comment be the Mantuan Muse.
When first young Maro in his boundless mind
A work t' outlast immortal Rome designed,
Perhaps he seemed above the critic's law,
And but from nature's fountains scorned to draw:
But when t' examine every part he came,
Nature and Homer were, he found, the same.
Convinced, amazed, he checks the bold design;
And rules as strict his laboured work confine
As if the Stagirite o'erlooked each line.
Learn hence for ancient rules a just esteem;
To copy nature is to copy them.
Some beauties yet no precepts can declare,
For there's a happiness as well as care.

Music resembles poetry, in each
Are nameless graces which no methods teach,
And which a master-hand alone can reach.
If, where the rules not far enough extend,
(Since rules were made but to promote their end)
Some lucky license answer to the full
Th' intent proposed, that license is a rule.
Thus Pegasus, a nearer way to take,
May boldly deviate from the common track;
From vulgar bounds with brave disorder part,
And snatch a grace beyond the reach of art,
Which without passing through the judgment, gains
The heart, and all its end at once attains.
In prospects thus, some objects please our eyes,
Which out of nature's common order rise,
The shapeless rock, or hanging precipice.
Great wits sometimes may gloriously offend,
And rise to faults true critics dare not mend.
But tho' the ancients thus their rules invade,
(As kings dispense with laws themselves have made)
Moderns, beware! or if you must offend
Against the precept, ne'er transgress its end;
Let it be seldom and compelled by need;
And have, at least, their precedent to plead.
The critic else proceeds without remorse,
Seizes your fame, and puts his laws in force.
I know there are, to whose presumptuous thoughts
Those freer beauties, e'en in them, seem faults.
Some figures monstrous and misshaped appear,
Considered singly, or beheld too near,
Which, but proportioned to their light or place,
Due distance reconciles to form and grace.
A prudent chief not always must display
His powers in equal ranks, and fair array,
But with th' occasion and the place comply,
Conceal his force, nay, seem sometimes to fly.
Those oft are stratagems which errors seem,
Nor is it Homer nods, but we that dream.

. . . .

A little learning is a dangerous thing;
Drink deep, or taste not the Pierian spring:

There shallow draughts intoxicate the brain,
And drinking largely sobers us again.
Fired at first sight with what the Muse imparts,
In fearless youth we tempt the heights of arts,
While from the bounded level of our mind,
Short views we take, nor see the lengths behind;
But more advanced, behold with strange surprise
New distant scenes of endless science rise!
So pleased at first the towering Alps we try,
Mount o'er the vales, and seem to tread the sky,
Th' eternal snows appear already past,
And the first clouds and mountains seem the last;
But, those attained, we tremble to survey
The growing labours of the lengthened way,
Th' increasing prospects tire our wandering eyes,
Hills peep o'er hills, and Alps on Alps arise!
  A perfect judge will read each work of wit
With the same spirit that its author writ:
Survey the whole, nor seek slight faults to find
Where nature moves, and rapture warms the mind;
Nor lose, for that malignant dull delight,
The gen'rous pleasure to be charmed with wit.
But in such lays as neither ebb, nor flow,
Correctly cold, and regularly low,
That shunning faults, one quiet tenor keep;
We cannot blame indeed—but we may sleep.
In wit, as nature, what affects our hearts
Is not th' exactness of peculiar parts:
'Tis not a lip, or eye, we beauty call,
But the joint force and full result of all.
Thus when we view some well-proportioned dome,
(The world's just wonder, and e'en thine, O Rome!)
No single parts unequally surprise,
All comes united to th' admiring eyes;
No monstrous height, or breadth, or length appear;
The whole at once is bold, and regular.
  Whoever thinks a faultless piece to see,
Thinks what ne'er was, nor is, nor e'er shall be.
In every work regard the writer's end,
Since none can compass more than they intend;
And if the means be just, the conduct true,
Applause, in spite of trivial faults, is due;

As men of breeding, sometimes men of wit,
T' avoid great errors, must the less commit:
Neglect the rules each verbal critic lays,
For not to know some trifles, is a praise.
Most critics, fond of some subservient art,
Still make the whole depend upon a part:
They talk of principles, but notions prize,
And all to one loved folly sacrifice.
Once on a time, La Mancha's knight, they say,
A certain bard encountering on the way,
Discoursed in terms as just, with looks as sage,
As e'er could Dennis of the Grecian stage;
Concluding all were desperate sots and fools,
Who durst depart from Aristotle's rules.
Our author, happy in a judge so nice,
Produced his play, and begged the knight's advice;
Made him observe the subject, and the plot,
The manners, passions, unities, what not?
All which, exact to rule, were brought about,
Were but a combat in the lists left out.
'What! leave the combat out?' exclaims the knight;
Yes, or we must renounce the Stagirite.
'Not so, by Heaven' (he answers in a rage),
'Knights, squires, and steeds, must enter on the stage.'
So vast a throng the stage can ne'er contain.
'Then build a new, or act it in a plain.'
Thus critics, of less judgment than caprice,
Curious not knowing, not exact but nice,
Form short ideas; and offend in arts
(As most in manners) by a love to parts.
Some to conceit alone their taste confine,
And glitt'ring thoughts struck out at every line;
Pleased with a work where nothing's just or fit;
One glaring chaos and wild heap of wit.
Poets like painters, thus unskilled to trace
The naked nature and the living grace,
With gold and jewels cover every part,
And hide with ornaments their want of art.
True wit is nature to advantage dressed,
What oft was thought, but ne'er so well expressed;
Something, whose truth convinced at sight we find,
That gives us back the image of our mind.

As shades more sweetly recommend the light,
So modest plainness sets off sprightly wit.
For works may have more wit than does 'em good,
As bodies perish through excess of blood.
  Others for language all their care express,
And value books, as women, men, for dress:
Their praise is still,—the style is excellent;
The sense, they humbly take upon content.
Words are like leaves; and where they most abound,
Much fruit of sense beneath is rarely found.
False eloquence, like the prismatic glass,
Its gaudy colours spreads on every place;
The face of nature we no more survey,
All glares alike, without distinction gay:
But true expression, like th' unchanging sun,
Clears and improves whate'er it shines upon,
It gilds all objects, but it alters none.
Expression is the dress of thought, and still
Appears more decent, as more suitable;
A vile conceit in pompous words expressed,
Is like a clown in regal purple dressed:
For different styles with different subjects sort,
As several garbs with country, town, and court.
Some by old words to fame have made pretence,
Ancients in phrase, mere moderns in their sense;
Such laboured nothings, in so strange a style,
Amaze th' unlearn'd, and make the learnèd smile.
Unlucky, as Fungoso in the play,
These sparks with awkward vanity display
What the fine gentleman wore yesterday;
And but so mimic ancient wits at best,
As apes our grandsires, in their doublets dressed.
In words, as fashions, the same rule will hold;
Alike fantastic, if too new, or old:
Be not the first by whom the new are tried,
Nor yet the last to lay the old aside.
  But most by numbers judge a poet's song;
And smooth or rough, with them, is right or wrong:
In the bright Muse though thousand charms conspire,
Her voice is all these tuneful fools admire;
Who haunt Parnassus but to please their ear,

Not mend their minds; as some to church repair,
Not for the doctrine, but the music there.
These equal syllables alone require,
Though oft the ear the open vowels tire;
While expletives their feeble aid do join,
And ten low words oft creep in one dull line:
While they ring round the same unvaried chimes,
With sure returns of still expected rhymes;
Where'er you find 'the cooling western breeze,'
In the next line, it 'whispers through the trees;'
If crystal streams 'with pleasing murmurs creep,'
The reader's threatened (not in vain) with 'sleep':
Then, at the last and only couplet fraught
With some unmeaning thing they call a thought,
A needless Alexandrine ends the song,
That, like a wounded snake, drags its slow length along.
Leave such to tune their own dull rhymes, and know
What's roundly smooth or languishingly slow;
And praise the easy vigour of a line,
Where Denham's strength, and Waller's sweetness join.
True ease in writing comes from art, not chance,
As those move easiest who have learned to dance.
'Tis not enough no harshness gives offence,
The sound must seem an echo to the sense.
Soft is the strain when Zephyr gently blows,
And the smooth stream in smoother numbers flows;
But when loud surges lash the sounding shore,
The hoarse, rough verse should like the torrent roar.
When Ajax strives some rock's vast weight to throw,
The line too labours, and the words move slow;
Not so, when swift Camilla scours the plain,
Flies o'er th' unbending corn, and skims along the main.
Hear how Timotheus' varied lays surprise,
And bid alternate passions fall and rise!
While, at each change, the son of Libyan Jove
Now burns with glory, and then melts with love;
Now his fierce eyes with sparkling fury glow,
Now sighs steal out, and tears begin to flow:
Persians and Greeks like turns of nature found,
And the world's victor stood subdued by sound!
The power of music all our hearts allow,
And what Timotheus was, is Dryden now.

Avoid extremes; and shun the fault of such,
Who still are pleased too little or too much.
At every trifle scorn to take offence,
That always shows great pride, or little sense;
Those heads, as stomachs, are not sure the best,
Which nauseate all, and nothing can digest.
Yet let not each gay turn thy rapture move;
For fools admire, but men of sense approve:
As things seem large which we through mists descry,
Dulness is ever apt to magnify.
Some foreign writers, some our own despise;
The ancients only, or the moderns prize.
Thus wit, like faith, by each man is applied
To one small sect, and all are damned beside.
Meanly they seek the blessing to confine,
And force that sun but on a part to shine,
Which not alone the southern wit sublimes,
But ripens spirits in cold northern climes;
Which from the first has shone on ages past,
Enlights the present, and shall warm the last;
Though each may feel increases and decays,
And see now clearer and now darker days.
Regard not, then, if wit be old or new,
But blame the false, and value still the true.
Some ne'er advance a judgment of their own,
But catch the spreading notion of the town;
They reason and conclude by precedent,
And own stale nonsense which they ne'er invent.
Some judge of author's names, not works, and then
Nor praise nor blame the writings, but the men.
Of all this servile herd, the worst is he
That in proud dulness joins with Quality.
A constant critic at the great man's board,
To fetch and carry nonsense for my Lord.
What woful stuff this madrigal would be,
In some starved hackney sonneteer, or me?
But let a Lord once own the happy lines,
How the wit brightens! how the style refines!
Before his sacred name flies every fault,
And each exalted stanza teems with thought!

. . . .

Learn then what morals critics ought to show,
For 'tis but half a judge's task, to know.
'Tis not enough, taste, judgment, learning join;
In all you speak, let truth and candour shine:
That not alone what to your sense is due
All may allow; but seek your friendship too.
  Be silent always when you doubt your sense;
And speak, though sure, with seeming diffidence:
Some positive, persisting fops we know,
Who, if once wrong, will needs be always so;
But you, with pleasure own your errors past,
And make each day a critic on the last.
  'Tis not enough, your counsel still be true;
Blunt truths more mischief than nice falsehoods do;
Men must be taught as if you taught them not,
And things unknown proposed as things forgot.
Without good breeding, truth is disapproved;
That only makes superior sense beloved.

. . . .

The bookful blockhead, ignorantly read,
With loads of learnèd lumber in his head,
With his own tongue still edifies his ears,
And always listening to himself appears.
All books he reads, and all he reads assails,
From Dryden's Fables down to Durfey's Tales.
With him, most authors steal their works, or buy;
Garth did not write his own Dispensary.
Name a new play, and he's the poet's friend,
Nay, showed his faults—but when would poets mend?
No place so sacred from such fops is barred,
Nor is Paul's church more safe than Paul's churchyard:
Nay, fly to altars; there they'll talk you dead:
For fools rush in where angels fear to tread.
Distrustful sense with modest caution speaks,
It still looks home, and short excursions makes;
But rattling nonsense in full volleys breaks,
And never shocked, and never turned aside,
Bursts out, resistless, with a thundering tide.
  But where's the man, who counsel can bestow,
Still pleased to teach, and yet not proud to know?
Unbiassed, or by favour, or by spite;
Not dully prepossessed, nor blindly right;

Though learn'd, well-bred; and though well-bred, sincere,
Modestly bold, and humanly severe:
Who to a friend his faults can freely show,
And gladly praise the merit of a foe?
Blest with a taste exact, yet unconfined;
A knowledge both of books and human kind:
Gen'rous converse; a soul exempt from pride;
And love to praise, with reason on his side?

THE RAPE OF THE LOCK

An Heroi-Comical Poem

CANTO II

Not with more glories, in th' ethereal plain,
The sun first rises o'er the purpled main,
Than, issuing forth, the rival of his beams
Launched on the bosom of the silver Thames.
Fair nymphs, and well-dressed youths around her shone,
But every eye was fixed on her alone.
On her white breast a sparkling cross she wore,
Which Jews might kiss, and infidels adore.
Her lively looks a sprightly mind disclose,
Quick as her eyes, and as unfixed as those;
Favours to none, to all she smiles extends;
Oft she rejects, but never once offends.
Bright as the sun, her eyes the gazers strike,
And, like the sun, they shine on all alike.
Yet graceful ease, and sweetness void of pride,
Might hide her faults, if belles had faults to hide;
If to her share some female errors fall,
Look on her face, and you'll forget 'em all.
 This nymph, to the destruction of mankind,
Nourished two locks, which graceful hung behind
In equal curls, and well conspired to deck
With shining ringlets the smooth ivory neck.
Love in these labyrinths his slaves detains,
And mighty hearts are held in slender chains.
With hairy springes, we the birds betray,
Slight lines of hair surprise the finny prey,

Fair tresses man's imperial race ensnare,
And beauty draws us with a single hair.
  Th' adventurous baron the bright locks admired;
He saw, he wished, and to the prize aspired.
Resolved to win, he meditates the way,
By force to ravish, or by fraud betray;
For when success a lover's toil attends,
Few ask if fraud or force attained his ends.
  For this, ere Phœbus rose, he had implored
Propitious Heaven, and every power adored,
But chiefly Love; to Love an altar built,
Of twelve vast French romances, neatly gilt.
There lay three garters, half a pair of gloves,
And all the trophies of his former loves;
With tender billets-doux he lights the pyre,
And breathes three amorous sighs to raise the fire.
Then prostrate falls, and begs with ardent eyes
Soon to obtain, and long possess the prize.
The powers gave ear, and granted half his prayer;
The rest the winds dispersed in empty air.
  But now secure the painted vessel glides,
The sunbeams trembling on the floating tides;
While melting music steals upon the sky,
And softened sounds along the waters die;
Smooth flow the waves, the zephyrs gently play,
Belinda smiled, and all the world was gay.
All but the sylph—with careful thoughts oppressed,
Th' impending woe sat heavy on his breast.
He summons straight his denizens of air;
The lucid squadrons around the sails repair;
Soft o'er the shrouds aërial whispers breathe,
That seemed but zephyrs to the train beneath.
Some to the sun their insect wings unfold,
Waft on the breeze, or sink in clouds of gold;
Transparent forms, too fine for mortal sight,
Their fluid bodies half dissolved in light.
Loose to the wind their airy garments flew,
Thin glittering textures of the filmy dew,
Dipped in the richest tincture of the skies,
Where light disports in ever-mingling dyes,
While every beam new transient colours flings,
Colours that change whene'er they wave their wings.

Amid the circle, on the gilded mast,
Superior by the head, was Ariel placed;
His purple pinions opening to the sun,
He raised his azure wand, and thus begun:
'Ye sylphs and sylphids, to your chief give ear!
Fays, fairies, genii, elves, and demons, hear!
Ye know the spheres, and various tasks assigned
By laws eternal to th' aërial kind.
Some in the fields of purest æther play,
And bask and whiten in the blaze of day.
Some guide the course of wandering orbs on high,
Or roll the planets through the boundless sky.
Some less refined, beneath the moon's pale light
Pursue the stars that shoot athwart the night,
Or suck the mists in grosser air below,
Or dip their pinions in the painted bow,
Or brew fierce tempests on the wintry main,
Or o'er the glebe distil the kindly rain;
Others on earth o'er human race preside,
Watch all their ways, and all their actions guide:
Of these the chief the care of nations own,
And guard with arms divine the British throne.
'Our humbler province is to tend the fair,
Not a less pleasing, though less glorious care;
To save the powder from too rude a gale,
Nor let th' imprisoned essences exhale;
To draw fresh colours from the vernal flowers;
To steal from rainbows, ere they drop in showers,
A brighter wash; to curl their waving hairs,
Assist their blushes, and inspire their airs;
Nay, oft in dreams, invention we bestow,
To change a flounce, or add a furbelow.
'This day, black omens threat the brightest fair
That e'er deserved a watchful spirit's care;
Some dire disaster, or by force, or sleight;
But what, or where, the fates have wrapped in night.
Whether the nymph shall break Diana's law,
Or some frail china jar receive a flaw;
Or stain her honour, or her new brocade;
Forget her prayers, or miss a masquerade;
Or lose her heart, or necklace, at a ball;
Or whether Heaven has doomed that Shock must fall.

Haste, then, ye spirits! to your charge repair;
The fluttering fan be Zephyretta's care;
The drops to thee, Brillante, we consign;
And, Momentilla, let the watch be thine;
Do thou, Crispissa, tend her favourite lock;
Ariel himself shall be the guard of Shock.
To fifty chosen sylphs, of special note,
We trust th' important charge, the petticoat:
Oft have we known that sevenfold fence to fail,
Though stiff with hoops, and armed with ribs of whale;
Form a strong line about the silver bound,
And guard the wide circumference around.
'Whatever spirit, careless of his charge,
His post neglects, or leaves the fair at large,
Shall feel sharp vengeance soon o'ertake his sins,
Be stopped in vials, or transfixed with pins;
Or plunged in lakes of bitter washes lie,
Or wedged whole ages in a bodkin's eye;
Gums and pomatums shall his flight restrain,
While clogged he beats his silken wings in vain;
Or alum styptics with contracting power
Shrink his thin essence like a rivelled flower;
Or, as Ixion fixed, the wretch shall feel
The giddy motion of the whirling mill,
In fumes of burning chocolate shall glow,
And tremble at the sea that froths below!'
He spoke; the spirits from the sails descend;
Some, orb in orb, around the nymph extend;
Some thrid the mazy ringlets of her hair;
Some hang upon the pendants of her ear;
With beating hearts the dire event they wait,
Anxious, and trembling for the birth of fate.

CANTO III

Close by those meads, forever crowned with flowers,
Where Thames with pride surveys his rising towers,
There stands a structure of majestic frame,
Which from the neighbouring Hampton takes its name.
Here Britain's statesmen oft the fall foredoom
Of foreign tyrants and of nymphs at home;
Here thou, great Anna! whom three realms obey,
Dost sometimes counsel take—and sometimes tea.

Hither the heroes and the nymphs resort,
To taste awhile the pleasures of a court;
In various talk th' instructive hours they passed,
Who gave the ball, or paid the visit last;
One speaks the glory of the British Queen,
And one describes a charming Indian screen;
A third interprets motions, looks, and eyes;
At every word a reputation dies.
Snuff, or the fan, supply each pause of chat,
With singing, laughing, ogling, and all that.
Meanwhile, declining from the noon of day,
The sun obliquely shoots his burning ray;
The hungry judges soon the sentence sign,
And wretches hang that jurymen may dine;
The merchant from th' Exchange returns in peace,
And the long labours of the toilet cease.
Belinda now, whom thirst of fame invites,
Burns to encounter two adventurous knights,
At ombre singly to decide their doom;
And swells her breast with conquests yet to come.
Straight the three bands prepare in arms to join,
Each band the number of the sacred nine.
Soon as she spreads her hand, th' aërial guard
Descend, and sit on each important card:
First, Ariel perched upon a Matadore,
Then each, according to the rank they bore;
For sylphs, yet mindful of their ancient race,
Are, as when women, wondrous fond of place.
Behold, four kings in majesty revered,
With hoary whiskers and a forky beard;
And four fair queens whose hands sustain a flower,
Th' expressive emblem of their softer power;
Four knaves in garbs succinct, a trusty band,
Caps on their heads, and halberts in their hand;
And parti-coloured troops, a shining train,
Draw forth to combat on the velvet plain.
The skilful nymph reviews her force with care:
Let spades be trumps! she said, and trumps they were.
Now moved to war her sable Matadores,
In show like leaders of the swarthy Moors.
Spadillio first, unconquerable lord!
Led off two captive trumps, and swept the board.

As many more Manillio forced to yield
And marched a victor from the verdant field.
Him Basto followed, but his fate more hard
Gained but one trump and one plebeian card.
With his broad sabre next, a chief in years,
The hoary Majesty of Spades appears,
Puts forth one manly leg, to sight revealed,
The rest, his many-coloured robe concealed.
The rebel knave, who dares his prince engage,
Proves the just victim of his royal rage.
Even mighty Pam, that kings and queens o'erthrew,
And mowed down armies in the fights of Loo,
Sad chance of war! now destitute of aid,
Falls undistinguished by the victor spade!
  Thus far both armies to Belinda yield;
Now to the baron fate inclines the field.
His warlike Amazon her host invades,
The imperial consort of the crown of spades;
The club's black tyrant first her victim died,
Spite of his haughty mien, and barbarous pride.
What boots the regal circle on his head,
His giant limbs, in state unwieldy spread;
That long behind he trails his pompous robe,
And, of all monarchs, only grasps the globe?
  The baron now his diamonds pours apace;
Th' embroidered king who shows but half his face,
And his refulgent queen, with powers combined,
Of broken troops an easy conquest find.
Clubs, diamonds, hearts, in wild disorder seen,
With throngs promiscuous strew the level green.
Thus when dispersed a routed army runs,
Of Asia's troops, and Afric's sable sons,
With like confusion different nations fly,
Of various habit, and of various dye,
The pierced battalions disunited fall,
In heaps on heaps; one fate o'erwhelms them all.
  The knave of diamonds tries his wily arts,
And wins (oh shameful chance!) the queen of hearts.
At this the blood the virgin's cheek forsook,
A livid paleness spreads o'er all her look;
She sees, and trembles at th' approaching ill,
Just in the jaws of ruin, and codille.

And now (as oft in some distempered state)
On one nice trick depends the general fate.
An ace of hearts steps forth; the king unseen
Lurked in her hand, and mourned his captive queen:
He springs to vengeance with an eager pace,
And falls like thunder on the prostrate ace.
The nymph exulting fills with shouts the sky;
The walls, the woods, and long canals reply.
Oh thoughtless mortals! ever blind to fate,
Too soon dejected, and too soon elate.
Sudden, these honours shall be snatched away,
And cursed forever this victorious day.
For lo! the board with cups and spoons is crowned,
The berries crackle, and the mill turns round;
On shining altars of Japan they raise
The silver lamp; the fiery spirits blaze;
From silver spouts the grateful liquors glide,
While China's earth receives the smoking tide:
At once they gratify their scent and taste,
And frequent cups prolong the rich repast.
Straight hover round the fair her airy band;
Some, as she sipped, the fuming liquor fanned,
Some o'er her lap their careful plumes displayed,
Trembling, and conscious of the rich brocade.
Coffee (which makes the politician wise,
And see through all things with his half-shut eyes)
Sent up in vapours to the baron's brain
New stratagems the radiant lock to gain.
Ah, cease, rash youth! desist ere 'tis too late,
Fear the just gods, and think of Scylla's fate!
Changed to a bird, and sent to flit in air,
She dearly pays for Nisus' injured hair!
But when to mischief mortals bend their will,
How soon they find fit instruments of ill!
Just then Clarissa drew with tempting grace
A two-edged weapon from her shining case:
So ladies in romance assist their knight,
Present the spear, and arm him for the fight.
He takes the gift with reverence, and extends
The little engine on his fingers' ends;
This just behind Belinda's neck he spread,
As o'er the fragrant steams she bends her head.

Swift to the lock a thousand sprites repair,
A thousand wings, by turns, blow back the hair;
And thrice they twitched the diamond in her ear;
Thrice she looked back, and thrice the foe drew near.
Just in that instant, anxious Ariel sought
The close recesses of the virgin's thought;
As on the nosegay in her breast reclined,
He watched th' ideas rising in her mind,
Sudden he viewed, in spite of all her art,
An earthly lover lurking at her heart.
Amazed, confused, he found his power expired,
Resigned to fate, and with a sigh retired.
  The peer now spreads the glittering forfex wide,
T' inclose the lock; now joins it, to divide.
E'en then, before the fatal engine closed,
A wretched sylph too fondly interposed;
Fate urged the shears, and cut the sylph in twain
(But airy substance soon unites again).
The meeting points the sacred hair dissever
From the fair head, forever, and forever!
  Then flashed the living lightning from her eyes,
And screams of horror rend th' affrighted skies.
Not louder shrieks to pitying Heaven are cast,
When husbands, or when lap-dogs breathe their last;
Or when rich China vessels, fallen from high,
In glittering dust and painted fragments lie!
  'Let wreaths of triumph now my temples twine,'
The victor cried; 'the glorious prize is mine!
While fish in streams, or birds delight in air,
Or in a coach and six the British fair,
As long as Atalantis shall be read,
Or the small pillow grace a lady's bed,
While visits shall be paid on solemn days,
When numerous wax-lights in bright order blaze,
While nymphs take treats, or assignations give,
So long my honour, name, and praise shall live!
What Time would spare, from steel receives its date,
And monuments, like men, submit to fate!
Steel could the labour of the gods destroy,
And strike to dust th' imperial towers of Troy;

Steel could the works of mortal pride confound,
And hew triumphal arches to the ground.
What wonder then, fair nymph! thy hairs should feel,
The conquering force of unresisted steel?'

From TRANSLATION OF THE ILIAD

[THE PARTING OF HECTOR AND ANDROMACHE]

'How would the sons of Troy, in arms renowned,
And Troy's proud dames, whose garments sweep the
ground,
Attaint the lustre of my former name,
Should Hector basely quit the field of fame?
My early youth was bred to martial pains,
My soul impels me to th' embattled plains:
Let me be foremost to defend the throne,
And guard my father's glories and my own.
Yet come it will, the day decreed by fates,
(How my heart trembles while my tongue relates!)
The day when thou, imperial Troy! must bend,
And see thy warriors fall, thy glories end.
And yet no dire presage so wounds my mind,
My mother's death, the ruin of my kind,
Not Priam's hoary hairs defil'd with gore,
Not all my brothers gasping on the shore,
As thine, Andromache! Thy griefs I dread:
I see thee trembling, weeping, captive led,
In Argive looms our battles to design,
And woes of which so large a part was thine!
To bear the victor's hard commands, or bring
The weight of waters from Hyperia's spring!
There, while you groan beneath the load of life,
They cry, "Behold the mighty Hector's wife!"
Some haughty Greek, who lives thy tears to see,
Embitters all thy woes by naming me.
The thoughts of glory past and present shame,
A thousand griefs, shall waken at the name!
May I lie cold before that dreadful day,
Pressed with a load of monumental clay!

Thy Hector, wrapped in everlasting sleep,
Shall neither hear thee sigh, nor see thee weep.'
  Thus having spoke, th' illustrious chief of Troy
Stretched his fond arms to clasp the lovely boy.
The babe clung crying to his nurse's breast,
Scared at the dazzling helm and nodding crest.
With secret pleasure each fond parent smiled,
And Hector hasted to relieve his child;
The glittering terrors from his brows unbound,
And placed the beaming helmet on the ground.
Then kissed the child, and, lifting high in air,
Thus to the gods preferred a father's prayer:
  'O thou! whose glory fills th' ethereal throne,
And all ye deathless powers! protect my son!
Grant him, like me, to purchase just renown,
To guard the Trojans, to defend the crown,
Against his country's foes the war to wage,
And rise the Hector of the future age!
So when, triumphant from successful toils,
Of heroes slain he bears the reeking spoils,
Whole hosts may hail him with deserved acclaim,
And say, "This chief transcends his father's fame":
While pleased, amidst the general shouts of Troy,
His mother's conscious heart o'erflows with joy.'
  He spoke, and fondly gazing on her charms,
Restored the pleasing burthen to her arms;
Soft on her fragrant breast the babe she laid,
Hushed to repose, and with a smile surveyed.
The troubled pleasure soon chastised by fear,
She mingled with the smile a tender tear.
The softened chief with kind compassion viewed,
And dried the falling drops, and thus pursued:
  'Andromache! my soul's far better part,
Why with untimely sorrows heaves thy heart?
No hostile hand can antedate my doom,
Till fate condemns me to the silent tomb.
Fixed is the term to all the race of earth,
And such the hard condition of our birth.
No force can then resist, no flight can save:
All sink alike, the fearful and the brave.
No more—but hasten to thy tasks at home,
There guide the spindle, and direct the loom;

Me glory summons to the martial scene,
The field of combat is the sphere for men.
Where heroes war, the foremost place I claim,
The first in danger as the first in fame.'

From AN ESSAY ON MAN

OF THE NATURE AND STATE OF MAN, WITH RESPECT TO THE UNIVERSE

Awake, my St. John! leave all meaner things
To low ambition, and the pride of kings.
Let us (since life can little more supply
Than just to look about us, and to die)
Expatiate free o'er all this scene of man;
A mighty maze! but not without a plan;
A wild, where weeds and flowers promiscuous shoot;
Or garden, tempting with forbidden fruit.
Together let us beat this ample field,
Try what the open, what the covert yield;
The latent tracts, the giddy heights, explore
Of all who blindly creep, or sightless soar;
Eye Nature's walks, shoot folly as it flies,
And catch the manners living as they rise;
Laugh where we must, be candid where we can,
But vindicate the ways of God to man.
I. Say first, of God above, or man below,
What can we reason, but from what we know?
Of man, what see we but his station here
From which to reason or to which refer?
Through worlds unnumbered though the God be known,
'Tis ours to trace him only in our own.
He, who through vast immensity can pierce,
See worlds on worlds compose one universe,
Observe how system into system runs,
What other planets circle other suns,
What varied being peoples every star,
May tell why Heaven has made us as we are.
But of this frame the bearings, and the ties
The strong connections, nice dependencies,

Gradations just, has thy pervading soul
Looked through? or can a part contain the whole?
Is the great chain, that draws all to agree,
And drawn supports, upheld by God, or thee?
II. Presumptuous man! the reason wouldst thou find,
Why formed so weak, so little, and so blind?
First, if thou canst, the harder reason guess,
Why formed no weaker, blinder, and no less?
Ask of thy mother earth, why oaks are made
Taller or stronger than the weeds they shade?
Or ask of yonder argent fields above,
Why Jove's satellites are less than Jove.
Of systems possible, if 'tis confessed
That wisdom infinite must form the best,
Where all must full or not coherent be,
And all that rises, rise in due degree;
Then, in the scale of reasoning life, 'tis plain,
There must be, somewhere, such a rank as man:
And all the question (wrangle e'er so long)
Is only this, if God has placed him wrong?
Respecting man, whatever wrong we call,
May, must be right, as relative to all.
In human works, though laboured on with pain,
A thousand movements scarce one purpose gain;
In God's, one single can its end produce;
Yet serves to second too some other use.
So man, who here seems principal alone,
Perhaps acts second to some sphere unknown,
Touches some wheel, or verges to some goal;
'Tis but a part we see, and not a whole.
When the proud steed shall know why man restrains
His fiery course, or drives him o'er the plains;
When the dull ox, why now he breaks the clod,
Is now a victim, and now Egypt's god:
Then shall man's pride and dulness comprehend
His actions', passions', being's, use and end;
Why doing, suffering, checked, impelled; and why
This hour a slave, the next a deity.
Then say not man's imperfect, Heaven in fault;
Say rather, man's as perfect as he ought:
His knowledge measured to his state and place,
His time a moment, and a point his space.

If to be perfect in a certain sphere,
What matter, soon or late, or here or there?
The blest to-day is as completely so,
As who began a thousand years ago.

III. Heaven from all creatures hides the book of fate,
All but the page prescribed, their present state:
From brutes what men, from men what spirits know:
Or who could suffer being here below?
The lamb thy riot dooms to bleed to-day,
Had he thy reason, would he skip and play?
Pleased to the last, he crops the flowery food,
And licks the hand just raised to shed his blood.
Oh, blindness to the future! kindly given,
That each may fill the circle marked by Heaven:
Who sees with equal eye, as God of all,
A hero perish, or a sparrow fall,
Atoms or systems into ruin hurled,
And now a bubble burst, and now a world.

Hope humbly then; with trembling pinions soar;
Wait the great teacher Death; and God adore.
What future bliss, he gives not thee to know,
But gives that hope to be thy blessing now.
Hope springs eternal in the human breast:
Man never is, but always to be blessed.
The soul, uneasy and confined from home,
Rests and expatiates in a life to come.

Lo, the poor Indian! whose untutored mind
Sees God in clouds, or hears him in the wind;
His soul, proud science never taught to stray
Far as the solar walk, or milky way;
Yet simple nature to his hope has given,
Behind the cloud-topped hill, an humbler Heaven;
Some safer world in depths of woods embraced,
Some happier island in the watery waste,
Where slaves once more their native land behold,
No fiends torment, no Christians thirst for gold.
To be, contents his natural desire,
He asks no angel's wing, no seraph's fire;
But thinks, admitted to that equal sky,
His faithful dog shall bear him company.

IV. Go, wiser thou! and, in thy scale of sense
Weigh thy opinion against Providence;

Call imperfection what thou fanciest such,
Say, 'Here he gives too little, there too much;'
Destroy all creatures for thy sport or gust,
Yet cry, 'If man's unhappy, God's unjust;'
If man alone engross not Heaven's high care,
Alone made perfect here, immortal there,
Snatch from his hand the balance and the rod,
Rejudge his justice, be the god of God.
In pride, in reasoning pride, our error lies;
All quit their sphere, and rush into the skies.
Pride still is aiming at the blest abodes,
Men would be angels, angels would be gods.
Aspiring to be gods, if angels fell,
Aspiring to be angels, men rebel:
And who but wishes to invert the laws
Of order, sins against the Eternal Cause.
V. Ask for what end the heavenly bodies shine,
Earth for whose use? Pride answers, ''Tis for mine:
For me kind nature wakes her genial power,
Suckles each herb, and spreads out every flower;
Annual for me, the grape, the rose renew
The juice nectareous, and the balmy dew;
For me, the mine a thousand treasures brings;
For me, health gushes from a thousand springs;
Seas roll to waft me, suns to light me rise;
My footstool earth, my canopy the skies.'
But errs not Nature from this gracious end,
From burning suns when livid deaths descend,
When earthquakes swallow, or when tempests sweep
Towns to one grave, whole nations to the deep?
'No ('tis replied), the first Almighty Cause
Acts not by partial, but by general laws;
Th' exceptions few; some change, since all began:
And what created perfect?' Why then man?
If the great end be human happiness,
Then nature deviates; and can man do less?
As much that end a constant course requires
Of showers and sunshine, as of man's desires;
As much eternal springs and cloudless skies,
As men forever temperate, calm, and wise.
If plagues or earthquakes break not Heaven's design,
Why then a Borgia, or a Catiline?

Who knows but He, whose hand the lightning forms,
Who heaves old ocean, and who wings the storms;
Pours fierce ambition in a Cæsar's mind,
Or turns young Ammon loose to scourge mankind?
From pride, from pride, our very reasoning springs.
Account for moral, as for natural things:
Why charge we Heaven in those, in these acquit?
In both, to reason right is to submit.
Better for us, perhaps, it might appear,
Were there all harmony, all virtue here;
That never air or ocean felt the wind;
That never passion discomposed the mind.
But all subsists by elemental strife;
And passions are the elements of life.
The general order, since the whole began,
Is kept in nature, and is kept in man.
VI. What would this man? Now upward will he soar,
And little less than angel, would be more;
Now looking downwards, just as grieved appears
To want the strength of bulls, the fur of bears.
Made for his use all creatures if he call,
Say what their use, had he the powers of all?
Nature to these, without profusion, kind,
The proper organs, proper powers assigned;
Each seeming want compensated of course,
Here with degrees of swiftness, there of force;
All in exact proportion to the state;
Nothing to add, and nothing to abate.
Each beast, each insect, happy in its own:
Is Heaven unkind to man, and man alone?
Shall he alone, whom rational we call,
Be pleased with nothing, if not blessed with all?
The bliss of man (could pride that blessing find)
Is not to act or think beyond mankind;
No powers of body or of soul to share,
But what his nature and his state can bear.
Why has not man a microscopic eye?
For this plain reason, man is not a fly.
Say what the use, were finer optics given,
T' inspect a mite, not comprehend the heaven?
Or touch, if tremblingly alive all o'er,
To smart and agonize at every pore?

Or quick effluvia darting through the brain,
Die of a rose in aromatic pain?
If nature thundered in his opening ears,
And stunned him with the music of the spheres,
How would he wish that Heaven had left him still
The whispering zephyr, and the purling rill?
Who finds not Providence all good and wise,
Alike in what it gives and what denies?
VII. Far as creation's ample range extends,
The scale of sensual, mental power ascends.
Mark how it mounts, to man's imperial race,
From the green myriads in the peopled grass:
What modes of sight betwixt each wide extreme,
The mole's dim curtain, and the lynx's beam:
Of smell, the headlong lioness between
And hound sagacious on the tainted green:
Of hearing, from the life that fills the flood,
To that which warbles through the vernal wood:
The spider's touch, how exquisitely fine!
Feels at each thread, and lives along the line:
In the nice bee, what sense so subtly true
From poisonous herbs extracts the healing dew?
How instinct varies in the grovelling swine,
Compared, half-reasoning elephant, with thine!
'Twixt that and reason, what a nice barrier,
Forever separate, yet forever near!
Remembrance and reflection how allied;
What thin partitions sense from thought divide:
And middle natures, how they long to join,
Yet never pass th' insuperable line!
Without this just gradation, could they be
Subjected, these to those, or all to thee?
The powers of all subdued by thee alone,
Is not thy reason all these powers in one?
VIII. See, through this air, this ocean, and this earth
All matter quick, and bursting into birth.
Above, how high, progressive life may go!
Around, how wide! how deep extend below!
Vast chain of being! which from God began,
Natures ethereal, human, angel, man,
Beast, bird, fish, insect, what no eye can see,
No glass can reach; from infinite to thee,

From thee to nothing.—On superior powers
Were we to pass, inferior might on ours;
Or in the full creation leave a void,
Where, one step broken, the great scale's destroyed:
From nature's chain whatever link you strike,
Tenth, or ten thousandth, breaks the chain alike.
  And, if each system in gradation roll
Alike essential to th' amazing whole,
The least confusion but in one, not all
That system only, but the whole must fall.
Let earth unbalanced from her orbit fly,
Planets and suns run lawless through the sky;
Let ruling angels from their spheres be hurled,
Being on being wrecked, and world on world;
Heaven's whole foundations to their centre nod,
And nature tremble to the throne of God.
All this dread order break—for whom? for thee?
Vile worm!—Oh, madness! pride! impiety!
  IX. What if the foot, ordained the dust to tread,
Or hand, to toil, aspired to be the head?
What if the head, the eye, or ear repined
To serve mere engines to the ruling mind?
Just as absurd for any part to claim
To be another, in this general frame;
Just as absurd, to mourn the tasks or pains,
The great directing Mind of all ordains.
  All are but parts of one stupendous whole,
Whose body nature is, and God the soul;
That, changed through all, and yet in all the same;
Great in the earth, as in th' ethereal frame;
Warms in the sun, refreshes in the breeze,
Glows in the stars, and blossoms in the trees,
Lives through all life, extends through all extent,
Spreads undivided, operates unspent;
Breathes in our soul, informs our mortal part,
As full, as perfect, in a hair as heart;
As full, as perfect, in vile man that mourns,
As the rapt seraph that adores and burns:
To him no high, no low, no great, no small;
He fills, he bounds, connects, and equals all.
  X. Cease then, nor order imperfection name:
Our proper bliss depends on what we blame.

Know thy own point: this kind, this due degree
Of blindness, weakness, Heaven bestows on thee.
Submit.—In this, or any other sphere,
Secure to be as blest as thou canst bear:
Safe in the hand of one disposing Power,
Or in the natal, or the mortal hour.
All nature is but art, unknown to thee;
All chance, direction, which thou canst not see;
All discord, harmony not understood;
All partial evil, universal good:
And, spite of pride, in erring reason's spite,
One truth is clear, *Whatever is, is right.*

[Man's Powers and Frailties]

Know then thyself, presume not God to scan;
The proper study of mankind is Man.
Placed on this isthmus of a middle state,
A being darkly wise, and rudely great:
With too much knowledge for the sceptic side,
With too much weakness for the stoic's pride,
He hangs between; in doubt to act or rest,
In doubt to deem himself a god or beast;
In doubt his mind or body to prefer,
Born but to die, and reasoning but to err;
Alike in ignorance, his reason such
Whether he thinks too little or too much:
Chaos of thought and passion, all confused;
Still by himself abused, or disabused;
Created half to rise, and half to fall;
Great lord of all things, yet a prey to all;
Sole judge of truth, in endless error hurled:
The glory, jest, and riddle of the world!

[Virtue and Happiness]

Oh blind to truth, and God's whole scheme below,
Who fancy bliss to vice, to virtue woe!
Who sees and follows that great scheme the best,
Best knows the blessing, and will most be blessed.
But fools, the good alone unhappy call,
For ills or accidents that chance to all.

See Falkland dies, the virtuous and the just!
See godlike Turenne prostrate on the dust!
See Sidney bleeds amid the martial strife!
Was this their virtue, or contempt of life?
Say, was it virtue, more though Heaven ne'er gave,
Lamented Digby! sunk thee to the grave?
Tell me, if virtue made the son expire,
Why, full of days and honour, lives the sire?
Why drew Marseilles' good bishop purer breath,
When nature sickened, and each gale was death?
Or why so long (in life if long can be)
Lent Heaven a parent to the poor and me?
  What makes all physical or moral ill?
There deviates nature, and here wanders will.
God sends not ill; if rightly understood,
Or partial ill is universal good.
Or change admits, or nature lets it fall,
Short, and but rare, till man improved it all.
We just as wisely might of Heaven complain
That righteous Abel was destroyed by Cain,
As that the virtuous son is ill at ease,
When his lewd father gave the dire disease.
Think we, like some weak prince, th' Eternal Cause
Prone for his favourites to reverse his laws?
  Shall burning Etna, if a sage requires,
Forget to thunder, and recall her fires?
On air or sea new motions be impressed,
Oh blameless Bethel! to relieve thy breast?
When the loose mountain trembles from on high,
Shall gravitation cease, if you go by?
Or some old temple, nodding to its fall,
For Chartres' head reserve the hanging wall?
  But still this world (so fitted for the knave)
Contents us not. A better shall we have?
A kingdom of the just then let it be:
But first consider how those just agree.
The good must merit God's peculiar care;
But who, but God, can tell us who they are?
One thinks on Calvin Heaven's own spirit fell;
Another deems him instrument of hell;
If Calvin feel Heaven's blessing, or its rod.
This cries, there is, and that, there is no God.

What shocks one part will edify the rest,
Nor with one system can they all be blessed.
The very best will variously incline,
And what rewards your virtue, punish mine.
Whatever is, is right.—This world 'tis true
Was made for Cæsar—but for Titus too
And which more blessed? who chained his country, say,
Or he whose virtue sighed to lose a day?
'But sometimes virtue starves, while vice is fed,'
What then? Is the reward of virtue bread?
That, vice may merit, 'tis the price of toil;
The knave deserves it, when he tills the soil,
The knave deserves it when he tempts the main,
Where folly fights for kings, or dives for gain.
The good man may be weak, be indolent:
Nor is his claim to plenty, but content.
But grant him riches, your demand is o'er;
'No—shall the good want health, the good want power?'
Add health, and power, and every earthly thing.
'Why bounded power? why private? why no king?'
Nay, why external for internal given?
Why is not man a god, and earth a Heaven?
Who ask and reason thus, will scarce conceive
God gives enough, while he has more to give:
Immense the power, immense were the demand;
Say, at what part of nature will they stand?
What nothing earthly gives, or can destroy,
The soul's calm sunshine, and the heart-felt joy,
Is virtue's prize: A better would you fix?
Then give humility a coach and six,
Justice a conqueror's sword, or truth a gown,
Or public spirit its great cure, a crown.
Weak, foolish man! will Heaven reward us there
With the same trash mad mortals wish for here?
The boy and man an individual makes,
Yet sigh'st thou now for apples and for cakes?
Go, like the Indian, in another life
Expect thy dog, thy bottle, and thy wife,
As well as dream such trifles are assigned,
As toys and empires, for a god-like mind.
Rewards, that either would to virtue bring
No joy, or be destructive of the thing:

How oft by these at sixty are undone
The virtues of a saint at twenty-one!
To whom can riches give repute, or trust,
Content, or pleasure, but the good and just?
Judges and senates have been bought for gold,
Esteem and love were never to be sold.
Oh fool! to think God hates the worthy mind,
The lover and the love of human-kind,
Whose life is healthful, and whose conscience clear,
Because he wants a thousand pounds a year.
  Honour and shame from no condition rise;
Act well your part, there all the honour lies.
Fortune in men has some small difference made,
One flaunts in rags, one flutters in brocade;
The cobbler aproned, and the parson gowned,
The friar hooded, and the monarch crowned.
'What differ more (you cry) than crown and cowl?'
I'll tell you, friend! a wise man and a fool.
You'll find, if once the monarch acts the monk,
Or, cobbler-like, the parson will be drunk,
Worth makes the man, and want of it the fellow,
The rest is all but leather or prunella.

. . . .

God loves from whole to parts; but human soul
Must rise from individual to whole.
Self-love but serves the virtuous mind to wake,
As the small pebble stirs the peaceful lake;
The centre moved, a circle straight succeeds,
Another still, and still another spreads;
Friend, parent, neighbour, first it will embrace;
His country next; and next all human race;
Wide and more wide, th' o'erflowings of the mind
Take every creature in, of every kind;
Earth smiles around, with boundless bounty blessed,
And Heaven beholds its image in his breast.
  Come then, my friend! my Genius! come along;
Oh master of the poet, and the song!
And while the Muse now stoops, or now ascends,
To man's low passions, or their glorious ends,
Teach me, like thee, in various nature wise,
To fall with dignity, with temper rise;

Formed by thy converse, happily to steer
From grave to gay, from lively to severe;
Correct with spirit, eloquent with ease,
Intent to reason, or polite to please.
Oh! while along the stream of time thy name
Expanded flies, and gathers all its fame,
Say, shall my little bark attendant sail,
Pursue the triumph, and partake the gale?
When statesmen, heroes, kings, in dust repose,
Whose sons shall blush their fathers were thy foes,
Shall then this verse to future age pretend
Thou wert my guide, philosopher, and friend?
That urged by thee, I turned the tuneful art
From sounds to things, from fancy to the heart;
For wit's false mirror held up Nature's light;
Shewed erring pride, *Whatever is, is right;*
That reason, passion, answer one great aim;
That true self-love and social are the same;
That virtue only, makes our bliss below;
And all our knowledge is, *ourselves to know.*

From MORAL ESSAYS

OF THE CHARACTERS OF WOMEN

Nothing so true as what you once let fall,
'Most women have no characters at all.'
Matter too soft a lasting mark to bear,
And best distinguished by black, brown, or fair.
  How many pictures of one nymph we view,
All how unlike each other, all how true!
Arcadia's countess, here in ermined pride,
Is there Pastora by a fountain side;
Here Fannia, leering on her own good man,
And there, a naked Leda with a swan.
Let then the fair one beautifully cry,
In Magdalen's loose hair and lifted eye,
Or dressed in smiles of sweet Cecilia shine,
With simpering angels, palms, and harps divine;
Whether the charmer sinner it, or saint it,
If folly grow romantic, I must paint it.

. . . .

Flavia's a wit, has too much sense to pray;
To toast our wants and wishes, is her way;
Nor asks of God, but of her stars, to give
The mighty blessing, 'while we live, to live.'
Then for all death, that opiate of the soul!
Lucretia's dagger, Rosamonda's bowl.
Say, what can cause such impotence of mind?
A spark too fickle, or a spouse too kind.
Wise wretch! with pleasures too refined to please;
With too much spirit to be e'er at ease;
With too much quickness ever to be taught;
With too much thinking to have common thought:
You purchase pain with all that joy can give,
And die of nothing but a rage to live.
  Turn then from wits; and look on Simo's mate,
No ass so meek, no ass so obstinate;
Or her, that owns her faults, but never mends,
Because she's honest, and the best of friends;
Or her, whose life the Church and scandal share,
Forever in a passion, or a prayer;
Or her, who laughs at hell, but (like her Grace)
Cries, 'Ah! how charming, if there's no such place!'
Or who in sweet vicissitude appears
Of mirth and opium, ratafie and tears,
The daily anodyne, and nightly draught,
To kill those foes to fair ones, time and thought.
Woman and fool are two hard things to hit;
For true no-meaning puzzles more than wit.
  But what are these to great Atossa's mind?
Scarce once herself, by turns all womankind!
Who, with herself, or others, from her birth
Finds all her life one warfare upon earth;
Shines, in exposing knaves, and painting fools,
Yet is, whate'er she hates and ridicules.
No thought advances, but her eddy brain
Whisks it about, and down it goes again.
Full sixty years the world has been her trade,
The wisest fool much time has ever made.
From loveless youth to unrespected age,
No passion gratified except her rage.
So much the fury still outran the wit,
The pleasure missed her, and the scandal hit.

Who breaks with her, provokes revenge from hell,
But he's a bolder man who dares be well.
Her every turn with violence pursued,
Nor more a storm her hate than gratitude:
To that each passion turns, or soon or late;
Love, if it makes her yield, must make her hate:
Superiors? death! and equals? what a curse!
But an inferior not dependent? worse.
Offend her, and she knows not to forgive;
Oblige her, and she'll hate you while you live;
But die, and she'll adore you—then the bust
And temple rise—then fall again to dust.
Last night, her lord was all that's good and great;
A knave this morning, and his will a cheat.
Strange! by the means defeated of the ends,
By spirit robbed of power, by warmth of friends,
By wealth of followers! without one distress,
Sick of herself through very selfishness!
Atossa, cursed with every granted prayer,
Childless with all her children, wants an heir.
To heirs unknown descends th' unguarded store,
Or wanders, Heaven-directed, to the poor.
  Pictures like these, dear Madam, to design,
Asks no firm hand, and no unerring line;
Some wandering touches, some reflected light,
Some flying stroke alone can hit them right:
For how should equal colours do the knack?
Chameleons who can paint in white and black?
  'Yet Chloe sure was formed without a spot'—
Nature in her then erred not, but forgot.
'With every pleasing, every prudent part,
Say, what can Chloe want?'—She wants a heart.
She speaks, behaves, and acts just as she ought;
But never, never, reached one generous thought.
Virtue she finds too painful an endeavour,
Content to dwell in decencies forever.
So very reasonable, so unmoved,
As never yet to love, or to be loved.
She, while her lover pants upon her breast,
Can mark the figures on an Indian chest;
And when she sees her friend in deep despair,
Observes how much a chintz exceeds mohair.

Forbid it Heaven, a favour or a debt
She e'er should cancel—but she may forget.
Safe is your secret still in Chloe's ear;
But none of Chloe's shall you ever hear.
Of all her dears she never slandered one,
But cares not if a thousand are undone.
Would Chloe know if you're alive or dead?
She bids her footman put it in her head.
Chloe is prudent—would you too be wise?
Then never break your heart when Chloe dies.

. . . .

But grant in public men sometimes are shown,
A woman's seen in private life alone:
Our bolder talents in full light displayed;
Your virtues open fairest in the shade.
Bred to disguise, in public 'tis you hide;
There none distinguish 'twixt your shame or pride,
Weakness or delicacy, all so nice,
That each may seem a virtue or a vice.
In men, we various ruling passions find;
In women two almost divide the kind;
Those, only fixed, they first or last obey,
The love of pleasure, and the love of sway.

. . . .

Pleasures the sex, as children birds, pursue,
Still out of reach, yet never out of view;
Sure, if they catch, to spoil the toy at most,
To covet flying, and regret when lost:
At last, to follies youth could scarce defend,
It grows their age's prudence to pretend;
Ashamed to own they gave delight before,
Reduced to feign it, when they give no more:
As hags hold Sabbaths, less for joy than spite,
So these their merry, miserable night;
Still round and round the ghosts of beauty glide,
And haunt the places where their honour died.
See how the world its veterans rewards!
A youth of frolics, an old age of cards;
Fair to no purpose, artful to no end,
Young without lovers, old without a friend;
A fop their passion, but their prize a sot;
Alive, ridiculous, and dead, forgot!

Ah! Friend! to dazzle let the vain design;
To raise the thought and touch the heart be thine!
That charm shall grow, while what fatigues the Ring
Flaunts and goes down, an unregarded thing:
So when the sun's broad beam has tired the sight,
All mild ascends the moon's more sober light,
Serene in virgin modesty she shines,
And unobserved the glaring orb declines.
Oh! blest with temper whose unclouded ray
Can make to-morrow cheerful as to-day;
She, who can love a sister's charms, or hear
Sighs for a daughter with unwounded ear;
She, who ne'er answers till a husband cools,
Or, if she rules him, never shows she rules;
Charms by accepting, by submitting, sways,
Yet has her humour most, when she obeys;
Let fops or fortune fly which way they will;
Disdains all loss of tickets, or codille;
Spleen, vapours, or small-pox, above them all,
And mistress of herself, though china fall.
And yet, believe me, good as well as ill,
Woman's at best a contradiction still.
Heaven, when it strives to polish all it can
Its last best work, but forms a softer man;
Picks from each sex, to make the favourite blest,
Your love of pleasure, our desire of rest:
Blends, in exception to all general rules,
Your taste of follies, with our scorn of fools:
Reserve with frankness, art with truth allied,
Courage with softness, modesty with pride;
Fixed principles, with fancy ever new;
Shakes all together, and produces—You.

From EPISTLE TO DR. ARBUTHNOT

P. Shut, shut the door, good John! fatigued, I said;
Tie up the knocker, say I'm sick, I'm dead.
The Dog-star rages! nay, 'tis past a doubt,
All Bedlam, or Parnassus, is let out:
Fire in each eye, and papers in each hand,
They rave, recite, and madden round the land.

What walls can guard me, or what shades can hide?
They pierce my thickets, through my grot they glide;
By land, by water, they renew the charge;
They stop the chariot, and they board the barge.
No place is sacred, not the church is free;
E'en Sunday shines no Sabbath day to me:
Then from the Mint walks forth the man of rhyme,
Happy to catch me just at dinner-time.
Is there a parson, much demused in beer,
A maudlin poetess, a rhyming peer,
A clerk, foredoomed his father's soul to cross,
Who pens a stanza, when he should engross?
Is there, who, locked from ink and paper, scrawls
With desperate charcoal round his darkened walls?
All fly to Twit'nam, and in humble strain
Apply to me, to keep them mad or vain.
Arthur, whose giddy son neglects the laws,
Imputes to me and my damned works the cause;
Poor Cornus sees his frantic wife elope,
And curses wit, and poetry, and Pope.
Friend to my life! (which did not you prolong,
The world had wanted many an idle song)
What drop or nostrum can this plague remove?
Or which must end me, a fool's wrath or love?
A dire dilemma! either way I'm sped:
If foes, they write, if friends, they read me dead.
Seized and tied down to judge, how wretched I!
Who can't be silent, and who will not lie.
To laugh, were want of goodness and of grace,
And to be grave, exceeds all power of face.
I sit with sad civility, I read
With honest anguish, and an aching head;
And drop at last, but in unwilling ears,
This saving counsel, 'Keep your piece nine years.'
'Nine years!' cries he, who high in Drury Lane,
Lulled by soft zephyrs through the broken pane,
Rhymes ere he wakes, and prints before term ends,
Obliged by hunger, and request of friends:
'The piece, you think, it incorrect? why, take it,
I'm all submission, what you'd have it, make it.'
Three things another's modest wishes bound,
My friendship, and a prologue, and ten pound.

Pitholeon sends to me: 'You know his Grace,
I want a patron; ask him for a place.'
'Pitholeon libelled me' —'But here's a letter
Informs you, sir, 'twas when he knew no better.
Dare you refuse him? Curll invites to dine,
He'll write a journal, or he'll turn divine.'
Bless me! a packet.—' 'Tis a stranger sues,
A virgin tragedy, an orphan Muse.'
If I dislike it, 'Furies, death, and rage!'
If I approve, 'Commend it to the stage.'
There (thank my stars) my whole commission ends,
The players and I are, luckily, no friends.
Fired that the house reject him, ' 'Sdeath I'll print it,
And shame the fools——Your interest, sir, with Lintot!'
'Lintot, dull rogue! will think your price too much:'
'Not, sir, if you revise it, and retouch.'
All my demurs but double his attacks;
At last he whispers, 'Do; and we go snacks.'
Glad of a quarrel, straight I clap the door;
'Sir, let me see your works and you no more.'

. . . .

There are, who to my person pay their court:
I cough like Horace, and, though lean, am short,
Ammon's great son one shoulder had too high,
Such Ovid's nose, and 'Sir! you have an eye'—
Go on, obliging creatures, make me see
All that disgraced my betters, met in me.
Say for my comfort, languishing in bed,
'Just so immortal Maro held his head:'
And when I die, be sure you let me know
Great Homer died three thousand years ago.
Why did I write? what sin to me unknown
Dipped me in ink, my parents', or my own?
As yet a child, nor yet a fool to fame,
I lisped in numbers, for the numbers came.
I left no calling for this idle trade,
No duty broke, no father disobeyed.
The Muse but served to ease some friend, not wife,
To help me through this long disease, my life,
To second, Arbuthnot! thy art and care,
And teach the being you preserved, to bear.

But why then publish? Granville the polite,
And knowing Walsh, would tell me I could write;
Well-natured Garth inflamed with early praise,
And Congreve loved, and Swift endured my lays;
The courtly Talbot, Somers, Sheffield, read;
Even mitred Rochester would nod the head,
And St. John's self (great Dryden's friends before)
With open arms received one poet more.
Happy my studies, when by these approved!
Happier their author, when by these beloved!
From these the world will judge of men and books,
Not from the Burnets, Oldmixons, and Cookes.
Soft were my numbers; who could take offence
While pure description held the place of sense?
Like gentle Fanny's was my flowery theme,
A painted mistress, or a purling stream.
Yet then did Gildon draw his venal quill;—
I wished the man a dinner, and sat still.
Yet then did Dennis rave in furious fret;
I never answered—I was not in debt.
If want provoked, or madness made them print,
I waged no war with Bedlam or the Mint.
Did some more sober critic come aboard;
If wrong, I smiled; if right, I kissed the rod.
Pains, reading, study, are their just pretence,
And all they want is spirit, taste, and sense.
Commas and points they set exactly right,
And 'twere a sin to rob them of their mite;
Yet ne'er one sprig of laurel graced these ribalds,
From slashing Bentley down to piddling Tibbalds.
Each wight, who reads not, and but scans and spells,
Each word-catcher, that lives on syllables,
Even such small critics some regard may claim,
Preserved in Milton's or in Shakespeare's name.
Pretty! in amber to observe the forms
Of hairs, or straws, or dirt, or grubs, or worms!
The things, we know, are neither rich nor rare,
But wonder how the devil they got there.
Were others angry: I excused them too;
Well might they rage, I gave them but their due.
A man's true merit 'tis not hard to find;
But each man's secret standard in his mind,—

That casting-weight pride adds to emptiness,—
This, who can gratify? for who can guess?
The bard whom pilfered Pastorals renown,
Who turns a Persian tale for half a crown,
Just writes to make his barrenness appear,
And strains, from hard-bound brains, eight lines a year;
He, who still wanting, though he lives on theft,
Steals much, spends little, yet has nothing left;
And he, who now to sense, now nonsense leaning,
Means not, but blunders round about a meaning;
And he, whose fustian's so sublimely bad,
It is not poetry, but prose run mad:
All these, my modest satire bade translate,
And owned that nine such poets made a Tate.
How did they fume, and stamp, and roar, and chafe!
And swear, not Addison himself was safe.
  Peace to all such! but were there one whose fires
True genius kindles, and fair fame inspires;
Blessed with each talent and each art to please,
And born to write, converse, and live with ease:
Should such a man, too fond to rule alone,
Bear, like the Turk, no brother near the throne,
View him with scornful, yet with jealous eyes,
And hate for arts that caused himself to rise;
Damn with faint praise, assent with civil leer,
And without sneering, teach the rest to sneer;
Willing to wound, and yet afraid to strike,
Just hint a fault, and hesitate dislike;
Alike reserved to blame, or to commend,
A timorous foe, and a suspicious friend;
Dreading e'en fools, by flatterers besieged,
And so obliging, that he ne'er obliged;
Like Cato, give his little senate laws,
And sit attentive to his own applause;
While wits and Templars every sentence raise,
And wonder with a foolish face of praise—
Who but must laugh, if such a man there be?
Who would not weep, if Atticus were he!

. . . .

Oh, let me live my own, and die so too!
(To live and die is all I have to do:)

Maintain a poet's dignity and ease,
And see what friends, and read what books I please;
Above a patron, though I condescend
Sometimes to call a minister my friend.
I was not born for courts or great affairs;
I pay my debts, believe, and say my prayers;
Can sleep without a poem in my head,
Nor know, if Dennis be alive or dead.
  Why am I asked what next shall see the light?
Heavens! was I born for nothing but to write?
Has life no joys for me? or (to be grave)
Have I no friend to serve, no soul to save?
'I found him close with Swift.'—'Indeed? no doubt,'
Cries prating Balbus, 'something will come out.'
'Tis all in vain, deny it as I will.
'No, such a genius never can lie still;'
And then for mine obligingly mistakes
The first lampoon Sir Will or Bubo makes.
Poor guiltless I! and can I choose but smile,
When every coxcomb knows me by my style?
  Cursed be the verse, how well soe'er it flow,
That tends to make one worthy man my foe,
Give virtue scandal, innocence a fear,
Or from the soft-eyed virgin steal a tear!
But he who hurts a harmless neighbour's peace,
Insults fallen worth, or beauty in distress;
Who loves a lie, lame slander helps about;
Who writes a libel, or who copies out;
That fop, whose pride affects a patron's name,
Yet absent, wounds an author's honest fame;
Who can your merit selfishly approve,
And show the sense of it without the love;
Who has the vanity to call you friend,
Yet wants the honour, injured, to defend;
Who tells whate'er you think, whate'er you say,
And, if he lie not, must at least betray;
Who to the Dean and silver bell can swear,
And sees at Canons what was never there;
Who reads, but with a lust to misapply,
Make satire a lampoon, and fiction, lie:

A lash like mine no honest man shall dread,
But all such babbling blockheads in his stead.

. . . .

Of gentle blood (part shed in honour's cause,
While yet in Britain honour had applause)
Each parent sprung—— *A*. What fortune, pray?—
P. Their own,
And better got, than Bestia's from the throne.
Born to no pride, inheriting no strife,
Nor marrying discord in a noble wife,
Stranger to civil and religious rage,
The good man walked innoxious through his age.
No courts he saw, no suits would ever try,
Nor dared an oath, nor hazarded a lie.
Unlearn'd, he knew no schoolman's subtle art,
No language, but the language of the heart.
By nature honest, by experience wise,
Healthy by temperance, and by exercise;
His life, though long, to sickness passed unknown,
His death was instant, and without a groan.
O grant me thus to live, and thus to die!
Who sprung from kings shall know less joy than I.
O friend! may each domestic bliss be thine!
Be no unpleasing melancholy mine:
Me, let the tender office long engage,
To rock the cradle of reposing age,
With lenient arts extend a mother's breath,
Make languor smile, and smooth the bed of death,
Explore the thought, explain the asking eye,
And keep awhile one parent from the sky!
On cares like these if length of days attend,
May Heaven, to bless those days, preserve my friend,
Preserve him social, cheerful, and serene,
And just as rich as when he served a queen.
A. Whether that blessing be denied or given,
Thus far was right, the rest belongs to Heaven.

From THE FIRST EPISTLE OF THE SECOND BOOK OF HORACE IMITATED

[To George II: On the State of Literature]

To thee, the world its present homage pays
The harvest early, but mature the praise:
Great friend of liberty! in kings a name
Above all Greek, above all Roman fame:
Whose word is truth, as sacred and revered,
As Heaven's own oracles from altars heard.
Wonder of kings! like whom, to mortal eyes
None e'er has risen, and none e'er shall rise.
Just in one instance, be it yet confessed,
Your people, Sir, are partial in the rest:
Foes to all living worth except your own,
And advocates for folly dead and gone.
Authors, like coins, grow dear as they grow old;
It is the rust we value, not the gold.
Chaucer's worst ribaldry is learned by rote,
And beastly Skelton heads of houses quote:
One likes no language but the Faery Queen;
A Scot will fight for Christ's Kirk o' the Green;
And each true Briton is to Ben so civil,
He swears the muses met him at the Devil.
Though justly Greece her eldest sons admires,
Why should not we be wiser than our sires?
In every public virtue we excel,
We build, we paint, we sing, we dance as well.
And learned Athens to our art must stoop,
Could she behold us tumbling through a hoop.
If time improves our wit as well as wine,
Say at what age a poet grows divine?
Shall we, or shall we not, account him so,
Who died, perhaps, a hundred years ago?
End all dispute; and fix the year precise
When British bards begin t' immortalize?
'Who lasts a century can have no flaw,
I hold that wit a classic, good in law.'
Suppose he wants a year, will you compound?
And shall we deem him ancient, right and sound,

Or damn to all eternity at once,
At ninety-nine, a modern and a dunce?
'We shall not quarrel for a year or two;
By courtesy of England, he may do.'
Then, by the rule that made the horse-tail bare,
I pluck out year by year, as hair by hair,
And melt down ancients like a heap of snow:
While you, to measure merits, look in Stowe,
And estimating authors by the year,
Bestow a garland only on a bier.
Shakespeare, (whom you and every play-house bill
Style the divine, the matchless, what you will,)
For gain, not glory, winged his roving flight,
And grew immortal in his own despite.
Ben, old and poor, as little seemed to heed
The life to come, in every poet's creed.
Who now reads Cowley? if he pleases yet,
His moral pleases, not his pointed wit;
Forgot his epic, nay Pindaric art,
But still I love the language of his heart.
'Yet surely, surely, these were famous men!
What boy but hears the sayings of old Ben?
In all debates where critics bear a part,
Not one but nods, and talks of Jonson's art,
Of Shakespeare's nature, and of Cowley's wit;
How Beaumont's judgment checked what Fletcher writ;
How Shadwell hasty, Wycherley was slow;
But, for the passions, Southern sure and Rowe.
These, only these, support the crowded stage,
From eldest Heywood down to Cibber's age.'
All this may be; the people's voice is odd,
It is, and it is not, the voice of God.
To Gammer Gurton if it give the bays,
And yet deny the Careless Husband praise,
Or say our fathers never broke a rule;
Why then, I say, the public is a fool.
But let them own, that greater faults than we
They had, and greater virtues, I'll agree.
Spenser himself affects the obsolete,
And Sidney's verse halts ill on Roman feet:
Milton's strong pinion now not heaven can bound,
Now serpent-like, in prose he sweeps the ground,

In quibbles angel and archangel join,
And God the Father turns a school-divine.
Not that I'd lop the beauties from his book,
Like slashing Bentley with his desperate hook,
Or damn all Shakespeare, like th' affected fool
At court, who hates whate'er he read at school.
But for the wits of either Charles's days,
The mob of gentlemen who wrote with ease;
Sprat, Carew, Sedley, and a hundred more,
(Like twinkling stars the Miscellanies o'er,)
One simile, that solitary shines
In the dry desert of a thousand lines,
Or lengthened thought that gleams through many a page,
Has sanctified whole poems for an age.
I lose my patience, and I owe it too,
When works are censured, not as bad but new;
While if our elders break all reason's laws,
These fools demand not pardon, but applause.
On Avon's bank, where flowers eternal blow,
If I but ask, if any weed can grow;
One tragic sentence if I dare deride
Which Betterton's grave action dignified,
Or well-mouthed Booth with emphasis proclaims,
(Though but, perhaps, a muster-roll of names,)
How will our fathers rise up in a rage,
And swear all shame is lost in George's age!
You'd think no fools disgraced the former reign,
Did not some grave examples yet remain,
Who scorn a lad should teach his father skill,
And, having once been wrong, will be so still.
He, who to seem more deep than you or I,
Extols old bards, or Merlin's prophecy,
Mistake him not; he envies, not admires,
And to debase the sons, exalts the sires.
Had ancient times conspired to disallow
What then was new, what had been ancient now?
Or what remained, so worthy to be read
By learned critics, of the mighty dead?

. . . .

Time was, a sober Englishman would knock
His servants up, and rise by five o'clock,

Instruct his family in every rule,
And send his wife to church, his son to school.
To worship like his fathers, was his care;
To teach their frugal virtues to his heir;
To prove that luxury could never hold;
And place, on good security, his gold.
Now times are changed, and one poetic itch
Has seized the court and city, poor and rich:
Sons, sires, and grandsires, all will wear the bays,
Our wives read Milton, and our daughters plays,
To theatres, and to rehearsals throng,
And all our grace at table is a song.
I, who so oft renounce the muses, lie,
Not ——'s self e'er tells more fibs than I;
When sick of Muse, our follies we deplore,
And promise our best friends to rhyme no more;
We wake next morning in a raging fit,
And call for pen and ink to show our wit.
He served a prenticeship, who sets up shop;
Ward tried on puppies, and the poor, his drop;
Even Radcliffe's doctors travel first to France,
Nor dare to practise till they've learned to dance.
Who builds a bridge that never drove a pile?
(Should Ripley venture, all the world would smile;)
But those who cannot write, and those who can,
All rhyme, and scrawl, and scribble, to a man.
Yet, Sir, reflect, the mischief is not great;
These madmen never hurt the church or state:
Sometimes the folly benefits mankind;
And rarely avarice taints the tuneful mind.
Allow him but his plaything of a pen,
He ne'er rebels, or plots, like other men:
Flight of cashiers, or mobs, he'll never mind;
And knows no losses while the Muse is kind.
To cheat a friend, or ward, he leaves to Peter,
The good man heaps up nothing but mere metre,
Enjoys his garden and his book in quiet;
And then—a perfect hermit in his diet.
Of little use the man you may suppose
Who says in verse what others say in prose;
Yet let me show, a poet's of some weight,
And (though no soldier) useful to the state.

What will a child learn sooner than a song?
What better teach a foreigner the tongue?
What's long or short, each accent where to place,
And speak in public with some sort of grace?
I scarce can think him such a worthless thing,
Unless he praise some monster of a king;
Or virtue, or religion turn to sport,
To please a lewd, or unbelieving Court.
Unhappy Dryden!—In all Charles's days,
Roscommon only boasts unspotted bays;
And in our own (excuse some courtly stains)
No whiter page than Addison remains.
He, from the taste obscene reclaims our youth,
And sets the passions on the side of truth,
Forms the soft bosom with the gentlest art,
And pours each human virtue in the heart.
Let Ireland tell, how wit upheld her cause,
Her trade supported, and supplied her laws;
And leave on Swift this grateful verse engraved,
'The rights a court attacked, a poet saved.'
Behold the hand that wrought a nation's cure,
Stretched to relieve the idiot and the poor,
Proud vice to brand, or injured worth adorn,
And stretch the ray to ages yet unborn.
Not but there are, who merit other palms;
Hopkins and Sternhold glad the heart with psalms:
The boys and girls whom charity maintains,
Implore your help in these pathetic strains:
How could devotion touch the country pews,
Unless the Gods bestowed a proper Muse?
Verse cheers their leisure, verse assists their work,
Verse prays for peace, or sings down Pope and Turk.
The silenced preacher yields to potent strain,
And feels that grace his prayer besought in vain;
The blessing thrills through all the labouring throng,
And Heaven is won by violence of song.
  Our rural ancestors, with little blessed,
Patient of labour when the end was rest,
Indulged the day that housed their annual grain,
With feasts, and offerings, and a thankful strain:
The joy their wives, their sons, and servants share,
Ease of their toil, and partners of their care:

The laugh, the jest, attendants on the bowl,
Smoothed every brow, and opened every soul:
With growing years the pleasing licence grew,
And taunts alternate innocently flew.
But times corrupt, and nature, ill-inclined,
Produced the point that left a sting behind;
Till friend with friend, and families at strife,
Triumphant malice raged through private life.
Who felt the wrong, or feared it, took th' alarm,
Appealed to law, and justice lent her arm.
At length, by wholesome dread of statutes bound,
The poets learned to please, and not to wound:
Most warped to flattery's side; but some, more nice,
Preserved the freedom, and forbore the vice.
Hence satire rose, that just the medium hit,
And heals with morals what it hurts with wit.
We conquered France, but felt our captive's charms;
Her arts victorious triumphed o'er our arms;
Britain to soft refinements less a foe,
Wit grew polite, and numbers learned to flow.
Waller was smooth; but Dryden taught to join
The varying verse, the full-resounding line,
The long majestic march, and energy divine.
Though still some traces of our rustic vein,
And splay-foot verse, remained, and will remain.
Late, very late, correctness grew our care,
When the tired nation breathed from civil war.
Exact Racine, and Corneille's noble fire,
Showed us that France had something to admire.
Not but the tragic spirit was our own,
And full in Shakespeare, fair in Otway shone:
But Otway failed to polish or refine,
And fluent Shakespeare scarce effaced a line.
Even copious Dryden wanted, or forgot,
The last and greatest art, the art to blot.
Some doubt, if equal pains, or equal fire
The humbler muse of comedy require.
But in known images of life, I guess
The labour greater, as th' indulgence less.
Observe how seldom even the best succeed:
Tell me if Congreve's fools are fools indeed?

What pert, low dialogue has Farquhar writ!
How Van wants grace, who never wanted wit!
The stage how loosely does Astræa tread,
Who fairly puts all characters to bed!
And idle Cibber, how he breaks the laws,
To make poor Pinky eat with vast applause!
But fill their purse, our poet's work is done,
Alike to them, by pathos or by pun.

. . . .

Yet lest you think I rally more than teach,
Or praise malignly arts I cannot reach,
Let me for once presume t' instruct the times
To know the poet from the man of rhymes:
'Tis he who gives my breast a thousand pains,
Can make me feel each passion that he feigns;
Enrage, compose, with more than magic art,
With pity, and with terror, tear my heart;
And snatch me, o'er the earth, or through the air,
To Thebes, to Athens, when he will, and where.

From THE EPILOGUE TO THE SATIRES

[The Power of the Satirist]

Yes, I am proud; I must be proud to see
Men not afraid of God, afraid of me:
Safe from the bar, the pulpit, and the throne,
Yet touched and shamed by ridicule alone.
O sacred weapon! left for truth's defense,
Sole dread of folly, vice, and insolence!
To all but Heaven-directed hands denied,
The Muse may give thee, but the gods must guide:
Reverent I touch thee! but with honest zeal,
To rouse the watchmen of the public weal;
To virtue's work provoke the tardy hall,
And goad the prelate slumbering in his stall.
Ye tinsel insects! whom a court maintains,
That counts your beauties only by your stains,
Spin all your cobwebs, o'er the eye of day!
The Muse's wing shall brush you all away.

From THE DUNCIAD

[The College of Dulness]

Close to those walls where Folly holds her throne,
And laughs to think Monroe would take her down,
Where o'er the gates, by his famed father's hand,
Great Cibber's brazen brainless brothers stand,
One cell there is, concealed from vulgar eye,
The cave of Poverty and Poetry.
Keen, hollow winds howl through the bleak recess,
Emblem of music caused by emptiness.
Hence bards, like Proteus long in vain tied down,
Escape in monsters, and amaze the town.
Hence Miscellanies spring, the weekly boast
Of Curll's chaste press and Lintot's rubric post;
Hence hymning Tyburn's elegiac lines;
Hence Journals, Medleys, Mercuries, Magazines,
Sepulchral lies, our holy walls to grace,
And New-year odes, and all the Grub Street race.
  In clouded majesty here Dulness shone.
Four guardian Virtues, round, support her throne:
Fierce champion Fortitude, that knows no fears
Of hisses, blows, or want, or loss of ears;
Calm Temperance, whose blessings those partake
Who hunger and who thirst for scribbling sake;
Prudence, whose glass presents th' approaching jail;
Poetic Justice, with her lifted scale,
Where, in nice balance, truth with gold she weighs,
And solid pudding against empty praise.
Here she beholds the chaos dark and deep,
Where nameless somethings in their causes sleep,
Till genial Jacob or a warm third day
Call forth each mass, a poem or a play:
How hints, like spawn, scarce quick in embryo lie;
How new-born nonsense first is taught to cry;
Maggots, half formed, in rhyme exactly meet,
And learn to crawl upon poetic feet.
Here one poor word an hundred clenches makes,
And ductile Dulness new meanders takes;
There motley images her fancy strike,
Figures ill paired, and similes unlike.

She sees a mob of metaphors advance,
Pleased with the madness of the mazy dance;
How Tragedy and Comedy embrace;
How Farce and Epic get a jumbled race;
How Time himself stands still at her command,
Realms shift their place, and ocean turns to land.
Here gay description Egypt glads with showers,
Or gives to Zembla fruits, to Barca flowers;
Glittering with ice here hoary hills are seen,
There painted valleys of eternal green;
In cold December fragrant chaplets blow,
And heavy harvests nod beneath the snow.
All these and more the cloud-compelling queen
Beholds through fogs, that magnify the scene:
She, tinselled o'er in robes of varying hues,
With self-applause her wild creation views;
Sees momentary monsters rise and fall,
And with her own fools-colours gilds them all.

. . . .

[Cibber as Dulness's Favourite Son]

In each she marks her image full expressed,
But chief in Bays's monster-breeding breast;
Bays, formed by nature stage and town to bless,
And act, and be, a coxcomb with success.
Dulness with transport eyes the lively dunce,
Rememb'ring she herself was Pertness once.
Now (shame to Fortune!) an ill run at play
Blanked his bold visage, and a thin third day:
Swearing and supperless the hero sate,
Blasphemed his gods, the dice, and damned his fate;
Then gnawed his pen, then dashed it on the ground,
Sinking from thought to thought, a vast profound!
Plunged for his sense, but found no bottom there;
Yet wrote and floundered on in mere despair.
Round him much embryo, much abortion lay,
Much future ode, and abdicated play;
Nonsense precipitate, like running lead,
That slipped through cracks and zigzags of the head;
All that on Folly Frenzy could beget,
Fruits of dull heat, and sooterkins of wit.

Next o'er his books his eyes began to roll,
In pleasing memory of all he stole—
How here he sipped, how there he plundered snug,
And sucked all o'er like an industrious bug.
Here lay poor Fletcher's half-eat scenes, and here
The frippery of crucified Molière;
There hapless Shakespeare, yet of Tibbald sore,
Wished he had blotted for himself before.

. . . .

[The Restoration of Night and Chaos]

In vain, in vain—the all-composing hour
Resistless falls: the Muse obeys the power.
She comes! she comes! the sable throne behold
Of Night primeval and of Chaos old!
Before her, Fancy's gilded clouds decay,
And all its varying rainbows die away.
Wit shoots in vain its momentary fires,
The meteor drops, and in a flash expires.
As one by one, at dread Medea's strain,
The sickening stars fade off th' ethereal plain;
As Argus' eyes, by Hermes' wand oppressed,
Closed one by one to everlasting rest:
Thus at her felt approach, and secret might,
Art after art goes out, and all is night.
See skulking Truth to her old cavern fled,
Mountains of casuistry heaped o'er her head!
Philosophy, that leaned on Heaven before,
Shrinks to her second cause, and is no more.
Physic of Metaphysic begs defence,
And Metaphysic calls for aid on Sense!
See Mystery to Mathematics fly!
In vain! they gaze, turn giddy, rave, and die.
Religion blushing veils her sacred fires,
And unawares Morality expires.
Nor public flame, nor private, dares to shine;
Nor human spark is left, nor glimpse divine!
Lo! thy dread empire, Chaos! is restored;
Light dies before thy uncreating word:
Thy hand, great Anarch! lets the curtain fall;
And universal darkness buries all.

LADY WINCHILSEA

TO THE NIGHTINGALE

Exert thy voice, sweet harbinger of Spring!
This moment is thy time to sing,
This moment I attend to praise,
And set my numbers to thy lays.
Free as thine shall be my song;
As thy music, short, or long.
Poets, wild as thee, were born,
Pleasing best when unconfined,
When to please is least designed,
Soothing but their cares to rest;
Cares do still their thoughts molest,
And still th' unhappy poet's breast,
Like thine, when best he sings, is placed against a thorn.
She begins, let all be still!
Muse, thy promise now fulfil!
Sweet, oh! sweet, still sweeter yet!
Can thy words such accents fit?
Canst thou syllables refine,
Melt a sense that shall retain
Still some spirit of the brain,
Till with sounds like these it join?
'Twill not be! then change thy note;
Let division shake thy throat.
Hark! division now she tries;
Yet as far the muse outflies.
Cease then, prithee, cease thy tune;
Trifler, wilt thou sing till June?
Till thy business all lies waste,
And the time of building's past!
Thus we poets that have speech,
Unlike what thy forests teach,
If a fluent vein be shown
That's transcendent to our own,
Criticise, reform, or preach,
Or censure what we cannot reach.

A NOCTURNAL REVERIE

In such a night, when every louder wind
Is to its distant cavern safe confined,
And only gentle Zephyr fans his wings,
And lonely Philomel, still waking, sings;
Or from some tree, famed for the owl's delight,
She hollowing clear, directs the wanderer right;
In such a night, when passing clouds give place,
Or thinly veil the heaven's mysterious face;
When in some river, overhung with green,
The waving moon and trembling leaves are seen;
When freshened grass now bears itself upright,
And makes cool banks to pleasing rest invite,
Whence springs the woodbine and the bramble-rose,
And where the sleepy cowslip sheltered grows;
Whilst now a paler hue the foxglove takes,
Yet chequers still with red the dusky brakes;
When scattered glow-worms, but in twilight fine,
Show trivial beauties watch their hour to shine,
Whilst Salisbury stands the test of every light
In perfect charms and perfect virtue bright;
When odours which declined repelling day
Through temperate air uninterrupted stray;
When darkened groves their softest shadows wear,
And falling waters we distinctly hear;
When through the gloom more venerable shows
Some ancient fabric, awful in repose,
While sunburnt hills their swarthy looks conceal
And swelling haycocks thicken up the vale;
When the loosed horse now, as his pasture leads,
Comes slowly grazing through th' adjoining meads,
Whose stealing pace, and lengthened shade we fear,
Till torn up forage in his teeth we hear;
When nibbling sheep at large pursue their food,
And unmolested kine re-chew the cud;
When curlews cry beneath the village-walls,
And to her straggling brood the partridge calls;
Their shortlived jubilee the creatures keep,
Which but endures whilst tyrant-man does sleep;
When a sedate content the spirit feels,
And no fierce light disturb, whilst it reveals;

But silent musings urge the mind to seek
Something too high for syllables to speak;
Till the free soul to a composedness charmed,
Finding the elements of rage disarmed,
O'er all below a solemn quiet grown,
Joys in th' inferior world and thinks it like her own:
In such a night let me abroad remain
Till morning breaks and all's confused again;
Our cares, our toils, our clamours are renewed,
Or pleasures, seldom reached, again pursued.

JOHN GAY

From RURAL SPORTS

When the ploughman leaves the task of day,
And, trudging homeward, whistles on the way;
When the big-uddered cows with patience stand,
Waiting the strokings of the damsel's hand;
No warbling cheers the woods; the feathered choir,
To court kind slumbers, to their sprays retire;
When no rude gale disturbs the sleeping trees,
Nor aspen leaves confess the gentlest breeze;
Engaged in thought, to Neptune's bounds I stray,
To take my farewell of the parting day:
Far in the deep the sun his glory hides,
A streak of gold the sea and sky divides;
The purple clouds their amber linings show,
And edged with flame rolls every wave below;
Here pensive I behold the fading light,
And o'er the distant billows lose my sight.

From THE SHEPHERD'S WEEK

THURSDAY; OR, THE SPELL

I rue the day, a rueful day I trow,
The woeful day, a day indeed of woe!
When Lubberkin to town his cattle drove:
A maiden fine bedight he happed to love;

The maiden fine bedight his love retains,
And for the village he forsakes the plains.
Return, my Lubberkin! these ditties hear!
Spells will I try, and spells shall ease my care.
With my sharp heel I three times mark the ground,
And turn me thrice around, around, around.

. . . .

Last May Day fair I searched to find a snail
That might my secret lover's name reveal.
Upon a gooseberry-bush a snail I found,
For always snails near sweetest fruit abound.
I seized the vermin, home I quickly sped,
And on the hearth the milk-white embers spread:
Slow crawled the snail, and, if I right can spell,
In the soft ashes marked a curious L.
Oh, may this wondrous omen lucky prove!
For L is found in 'Lubberkin' and 'Love.'
With my sharp heel I three times mark the ground,
And turn me thrice around, around, around.

. . . .

This lady-fly I take from off the grass,
Whose spotted back might scarlet red surpass:
'Fly, lady-bird, north, south, or east, or west!
Fly where the man is found that I love best!'
He leaves my hand: see, to the west he's flown,
To call my true-love from the faithless town.
With my sharp heel I three times mark the ground,
And turn me thrice around, around, around.

This mellow pippin, which I pare around,
My shepherd's name shall flourish on the ground:
I fling th' unbroken paring o'er my head—
Upon the grass a perfect L is read.
Yet on my heart a fairer L is seen
Than what the paring marks upon the green.
With my sharp heel I three times mark the ground,
And turn me thrice around, around, around.

This pippin shall another trial make.
See, from the core two kernels brown I take:

This on my cheek for Lubberkin is worn,
And Boobyclod on t' other side is borne;
But Boobyclod soon drops upon the ground
(A certain token that his love's unsound),
While Lubberkin sticks firmly to the last—
Oh, were his lips to mine but joined so fast!
With my sharp heel I three times mark the ground,
And turn me thrice around, around, around.

As Lubberkin once slept beneath a tree,
I twitched his dangling garter from his knee;
He wist not when the hempen string I drew.
Now mine I quickly doff of inkle blue;
Together fast I tie the garters twain,
And while I knit the knot repeat this strain:
'Three times a true-love's knot I tie secure;
Firm be the knot, firm may his love endure!'
With my sharp heel I three times mark the ground,
And turn me thrice around, around, around.

As I was wont I trudged last market-day
To town, with new-laid eggs preserved in hay.
I made my market long before 't was night;
My purse grew heavy and my basket light:
Straight to the 'pothecary's shop I went,
And in love-powder all my money spent.
Behap what will, next Sunday after prayers,
When to the alehouse Lubberkin repairs,
These golden flies into his mug I'll throw,
And soon the swain with fervent love shall glow.
With my sharp heel I three times mark the ground,
And turn me thrice around, around, around.

But hold! our Lightfoot barks, and cocks his ears:
O'er yonder stile, see, Lubberkin appears!
He comes, he comes! Hobnelia's not bewrayed,
Nor shall she, crowned with willow, die a maid.
He vows, he swears, he'll give me a green gown:
Oh, dear! I fall adown, adown, adown!

From TRIVIA

If clothed in black you tread the busy town,
Or if distinguished by the reverend gown,
Three trades avoid: oft in the mingling press
The barber's apron soils the sable dress;
Shun the perfumer's touch with cautious eye,
Nor let the baker's step advance too nigh.
Ye walkers too that youthful colours wear,
Three sullying trades avoid with equal care:
The little chimney-sweeper skulks along,
And marks with sooty stains the heedless throng;
When 'Small-coal!' murmurs in the hoarser throat,
From smutty dangers guard thy threatened coat;
The dust-man's cart offends thy clothes and eyes,
When through the street a cloud of ashes flies.
But whether black or lighter dyes are worn,
The chandler's basket, on his shoulder borne,
With tallow spots thy coat; resign the way
To shun the surly butcher's greasy tray—
Butchers whose hands are dyed with blood's foul stain,
And always foremost in the hangman's train.
  Let due civilities be strictly paid:
The wall surrender to the hooded maid,
Nor let thy sturdy elbow's hasty rage
Jostle the feeble steps of trembling age;
And when the porter bends beneath his load,
And pants for breath, clear thou the crowded road;
But, above all, the groping blind direct,
And from the pressing throng the lame protect.
You'll sometimes meet a fop, of nicest tread,
Whose mantling peruke veils his empty head;
At every step he dreads the wall to lose
And risks, to save a coach, his red-heeled shoes:
Him, like the miller, pass with caution by,
Lest from his shoulder clouds of powder fly.
But when the bully, with assuming pace,
Cocks his broad hat, edged round with tarnished lace,
Yield not the way; defy his strutting pride,
And thrust him to the muddy kennel's side;
He never turns again nor dares oppose,
But mutters coward curses as he goes.

SWEET WILLIAM'S FAREWELL TO BLACK-EYED SUSAN

All in the Downs the fleet was moored,
  The streamers waving in the wind,
When black-eyed Susan came aboard:
  'Oh, where shall I my true love find?
Tell me, ye jovial sailors, tell me true
If my sweet William sails among the crew?'

William, who high upon the yard
  Rocked with the billow to and fro,
Soon as her well-known voice he heard,
  He sighed and cast his eyes below:
The cord slides swiftly through his glowing hands,
And, quick as lightning, on the deck he stands.

So the sweet lark, high poised in air,
  Shuts close his pinions to his breast,
If chance his mate's shrill call he hear,
  And drops at once into her nest.
The noblest captain in the British fleet
Mighty envy William's lip those kisses sweet.

'O, Susan, Susan, lovely dear,
  My vows shall ever true remain!
Let me kiss off that falling tear:
  We only part to meet again.
Change as ye list, ye winds! my heart shall be
The faithful compass that still points to thee.

'Believe not what the landmen say,
  Who tempt with doubts thy constant mind:
They'll tell thee sailors, when away,
  In every port a mistress find—
Yes, yes, believe them when they tell thee so,
For thou art present wheresoe'er I go.

'If to far India's coast we sail,
  Thy eyes are seen in diamonds bright;
Thy breath is Afric's spicy gale,
  Thy skin is ivory so white.

Thus every beauteous object that I view
Wakes in my soul some charm of lovely Sue.

'Though battle call me from thy arms,
  Let not my pretty Susan mourn;
Though cannons roar, yet, safe from harms,
  William shall to his dear return.
Love turns aside the balls that round me fly,
Lest precious tears should drop from Susan's eye.'

The boatswain gave the dreadful word;
  The sails their swelling bosom spread;
No longer must she stay aboard:
  They kissed—she sighed—he hung his head.
Her lessening boat unwilling rows to land;
'Adieu!' she cries, and waved her lily hand.

MY OWN EPITAPH

Life is a jest, and all things show it:
I thought so once, but now I know it.

SAMUEL CROXALL

From THE VISION

Pensive beneath a spreading oak I stood
That veiled the hollow channel of the flood:
Along whose shelving bank the violet blue
And primrose pale in lovely mixture grew.
High overarched the bloomy woodbine hung,
The gaudy goldfinch from the maple sung;
The little warbling minstrel of the shade
To the gay morn her due devotion paid
Next, the soft linnet echoing to the thrush
With carols filled the smelling briar-bush;
While Philomel attuned her artless throat,
And from the hawthorn breathed a trilling note.

Indulgent Nature smiled in every part,
And filled with joy unknown my ravished heart:
Attent I listened while the feathered throng
Alternate finished and renewed their song.

THOMAS TICKELL

From ON THE DEATH OF MR. ADDISON

Can I forget the dismal night that gave
My soul's best part forever to the grave?
How silent did his old companions tread,
By midnight lamps, the mansions of the dead,
Through breathing statues, then unheeded things,
Through rows of warriors, and through walks of kings!
What awe did the slow solemn knell inspire;
The pealing organ, and the pausing choir;
The duties by the lawn-robed prelate paid;
And the last words, that dust to dust conveyed!
While speechless o'er thy closing grave we bend,
Accept these tears, thou dear departed friend.
Oh, gone forever! take this long adieu;
And sleep in peace next thy loved Montague!
  To strew fresh laurels, let the task be mine,
A frequent pilgrim at thy sacred shrine;
Mine with true sighs thy absence to bemoan,
And grave with faithful epitaphs thy stone.
If e'er from me thy loved memorial part,
May shame afflict this alienated heart;
Of thee forgetful if I form a song,
My lyre be broken, and untuned my tongue,
My griefs be doubled from thy image free,
And mirth a torment, unchastised by thee!
  Oft let me range the gloomy aisles alone,
(Sad luxury to vulgar minds unknown)
Along the walls where speaking marbles show
What worthies form the hallowed mould below;
Proud names, who once the reins of empire held;
In arms who triumphed, or in arts excelled;

Chiefs graced with scars and prodigal of blood;
Stern patriots who for sacred freedom stood;
Just men by whom impartial laws were given;
And saints who taught and led the way to Heaven.
Ne'er to these chambers, where the mighty rest,
Since their foundation came a nobler guest;
Nor e'er was to the bowers of bliss conveyed
A fairer spirit or more welcome shade.

. . . .

That awful form (which, so ye Heavens decree,
Must still be loved and still deplored by me,)
In nightly visions seldom fails to rise,
Or, roused by fancy, meets my waking eyes.
If business calls or crowded courts invite,
Th' unblemished statesman seems to strike my sight;
If in the stage I seek to soothe my care,
I meet his soul which breathes in Cato there;
If pensive to the rural shades I rove,
His shape o'ertakes me in the lonely grove;
'Twas there of just and good he reasoned strong,
Cleared some great truth, or raised some serious song:
There patient showed us the wise course to steer,
A candid censor, and a friend severe;
There taught us how to live, and (oh! too high
The price for knowledge) taught us how to die.

THOMAS PARNELL

From A NIGHT-PIECE ON DEATH

By the blue taper's trembling light,
No more I waste the wakeful night,
Intent with endless view to pore
The schoolmen and the sages o'er;
Their books from wisdom widely stray,
Or point at best the longest way.
I'll seek a readier path, and go
Where wisdom's surely taught below.

How deep yon azure dyes the sky,
Where orbs of gold unnumbered lie,
While through their ranks in silver pride
The nether crescent seems to glide!
The slumbering breeze forgets to breathe,
The lake is smooth and clear beneath,
Where once again the spangled show
Descends to meet our eyes below.
The grounds which on the right aspire,
In dimness from the view retire:
The left presents a place of graves,
Whose wall the silent water laves.
That steeple guides thy doubtful sight
Among the livid gleams of night.
There pass, with melancholy state,
By all the solemn heaps of fate,
And think, as softly-sad you tread
Above the venerable dead,
'Time was, like thee they life possessed,
And time shall be, that thou shalt rest.'

Those graves, with bending osier bound,
That nameless heave the crumbled ground,
Quick to the glancing thought disclose,
Where toil and poverty repose.
The flat smooth stones that bear a name,
The chisel's slender help to fame,
(Which ere our set of friends decay
Their frequent steps may wear away;)
A middle race of mortals own,
Men, half ambitious, all unknown.
The marble tombs that rise on high,
Whose dead in vaulted arches lie,
Whose pillars swell with sculptured stones,
Arms, angels, epitaphs, and bones;
These, all the poor remains of state,
Adorn the rich, or praise the great;
Who while on earth in fame they live,
Are senseless of the fame they give.

Ha! while I gaze, pale Cynthia fades,
The bursting earth unveils the shades!

All slow, and wan, and wrapped with shrouds
They rise in visionary crowds,
And all with sober accent cry,
'Think, mortal, what it is to die.'

Now from yon black and funeral yew
That bathes the charnel house with dew
Methinks I hear a voice begin:
(Ye ravens, cease your croaking din;
Ye tolling clocks, no time resound
O'er the long lake and midnight ground)
It sends a peal of hollow groans
Thus speaking from among the bones:
'When men my scythe and darts supply,
How great a king of fears am I!
They view me like the last of things:
They make, and then they dread, my stings.
Fools! if you less provoked your fears,
No more my spectre-form appears.
Death's but a path that must be trod
If man would ever pass to God,
A port of calms, a state of ease
From the rough rage of swelling seas.'

A HYMN OF CONTENTMENT

Lovely, lasting peace of mind!
Sweet delight of humankind!
Heavenly-born, and bred on high,
To crown the favourites of the sky
With more of happiness below
Than victors in a triumph know!
Whither, O whither art thou fled,
To lay thy meek, contented head?
What happy region dost thou please
To make the seat of calms and ease?

Ambition searches all its sphere
Of pomp and state, to meet thee there.
Increasing Avarice would find
Thy presence in its gold enshrined.

The bold adventurer ploughs his way,
Through rocks amidst the foaming sea,
To gain thy love; and then perceives
Thou wert not in the rocks and waves.
The silent heart which grief assails,
Treads soft and lonesome o'er the vales,
Sees daisies open, rivers run,
And seeks, as I have vainly done,
Amusing thought; but learns to know
That solitude's the nurse of woe.
No real happiness is found
In trailing purple o'er the ground;
Or in a soul exalted high,
To range the circuit of the sky,
Converse with stars above, and know
All nature in its forms below;
The rest it seeks, in seeking dies,
And doubts at last, for knowledge, rise.

Lovely, lasting peace, appear!
This world itself, if thou art here,
Is once again with Eden blest,
And man contains it in his breast.

'Twas thus, as under shade I stood,
I sung my wishes to the wood,
And lost in thought, no more perceived
The branches whisper as they waved:
It seemed, as all the quiet place
Confess'd the presence of the Grace.
When thus she spoke—'Go rule thy will,
Bid thy wild passions all be still,
Know God, and bring thy heart to know
The joys which from religion flow;
Then every grace shall prove its guest,
And I'll be there to crown the rest.'

Oh! by yonder mossy seat,
In my hours of sweet retreat,
Might I thus my soul employ,
With sense of gratitude and joy!

Raised as ancient prophets were,
In heavenly vision, praise, and prayer;
Pleasing all men, hurting none,
Pleased and blessed with God alone;
Then while the gardens take my sight,
With all the colours of delight;
While silver waters glide along,
To please my ear, and court my song;
I'll lift my voice, and tune my string,
And thee, great Source of nature, sing.

The sun that walks his airy way,
To light the world, and give the day;
The moon that shines with borrowed light;
The stars that gild the gloomy night;
The seas that roll unnumbered waves;
The wood that spreads its shady leaves;
The field whose ears conceal the grain,
The yellow treasure of the plain;
All of these, and all I see,
Should be sung, and sung by me:
They speak their Maker as they can,
But want and ask the tongue of man.

Go search among your idle dreams,
Your busy or your vain extremes;
And find a life of equal bliss,
Or own the next begun in this.

ALLAN RAMSAY

FROM THE GENTLE SHEPHERD

PATIE AND ROGER

Beneath the south side of a craigy bield,
Where crystal springs the halesome waters yield,
Twa youthfu' shepherds on the gowans lay,
Tenting their flocks ae bonny morn of May.

Poor Roger granes, till hollow echoes ring;
But blither Patie likes to laugh and sing.

Patie. My Peggy is a young thing,
Just entered in her teens,
Fair as the day, and sweet as May,
Fair as the day, and always gay;
My Peggy is a young thing,
And I'm not very auld,
Yet well I like to meet her at
The wauking of the fauld.

My Peggy speaks sae sweetly
Whene'er we meet alane,
I wish nae mair to lay my care,
I wish nae mair of a' that's rare;
My Peggy speaks sae sweetly,
To a' the lave I'm cauld,
But she gars a' my spirits glow
At wauking of the fauld.

My Peggy smiles sae kindly
Whene'er I whisper love,
That I look down on a' the town,
That I look down upon a crown;
My Peggy smiles sae kindly,
It makes me blythe and bauld,
And naething gi'es me sic delight
At wauking of the fauld.

My Peggy sings sae saftly
When on my pipe I play,
By a' the rest it is confest,
By a' the rest, that she sings best;
My Peggy sings sae saftly,
And in her sangs are tauld
With innocence the wale of sense,
At wauking of the fauld.

This sunny morning, Roger, chears my blood,
And puts all Nature in a jovial mood.
How hartsome is't to see the rising plants,
To hear the birds chirm o'er their pleasing rants!

How halesom 'tis to snuff the cauler air,
And all the sweets it bears, when void of care!
What ails thee, Roger, then? what gars thee grane?
Tell me the cause of thy ill-seasoned pain.
Roger. I'm born, O Patie, to a thrawart fate;
I'm born to strive with hardships sad and great!
Tempests may cease to jaw the rowan flood,
Corbies and tods to grein for lambkins' blood;
But I, oppressed with never-ending grief,
Maun ay despair of lighting on relief.

. . . .

You have sae saft a voice and slid a tongue,
You are the darling of baith auld and young:
If I but ettle at a sang or speak,
They dit their lugs, syne up their leglens cleek,
And jeer me hameward frae the loan or bught,
While I'm confused with mony a vexing thought;
Yet I am tall, and as well built as thee,
Nor mair unlikely to a lass's eye;
For ilka sheep ye have I'll number ten,
And should, as ane may think, come farer ben.

. . . .

Patie. Daft gowk! leave aff that silly whinging way!
Seem careless: there's my hand ye'll win the day.
Hear how I served my lass I love as weel
As ye do Jenny and with heart as leel.
Last morning I was gay and early out;
Upon a dyke I leaned, glowring about.
I saw my Meg come linkan o'er the lea;
I saw my Meg, but Peggy saw na me,
For yet the sun was wading thro' the mist,
And she was close upon me e'er she wist:
Her coats were kiltit, and did sweetly shaw
Her straight bare legs, that whiter were than snaw.
Her cockernony snooded up fou sleek,
Her haffet-locks hang waving on her cheek;
Her cheeks sae ruddy, and her een sae clear;
And, oh, her mouth's like ony hinny pear;
Neat, neat she was in bustine waistcoat clean,
As she came skiffing o'er the dewy green.
Blythesome I cried, 'My bonnie Meg, come here!
I ferly wherefore ye're sae soon asteer,

But I can guess ye're gawn to gather dew.'
She scoured awa, and said, 'What's that to you?'
'Then fare ye weel, Meg Dorts, and e'en's ye like,'
I careless cried, and lap in o'er the dyke.
I trow when that she saw, within a crack
She came with a right thieveless errand back:
Misca'd me first; then bade me hound my dog,
To wear up three waff ewes strayed on the bog.
I leugh, an sae did she: then with great haste
I clasped my arms about her neck and waist,
About her yielding waist, and took a fourth
Of sweetest kisses frae her glowing mouth;
While hard and fast I held her in my grips,
My very saul came louping to my lips;
Sair, sair she flet wi' me 'tween ilka smack,
But weel I kenned she meant nae as she spak.
Dear Roger, when your jo puts on her gloom,
Do ye sae too and never fash your thumb:
Seem to forsake her, soon she'll change her mood;
Gae woo anither, and she'll gang clean wood.

Dear Roger, if your Jenny geck,
  And answer kindness with a slight,
Seem unconcerned at her neglect;
  For women in a man delight,
But them despise who're soon defeat
  And with a simple face give way
To a repulse: then be not blate;
  Push bauldly on, and win the day.

When maidens, innocently young,
  Say aften what they never mean,
Ne'er mind their pretty lying tongue,
  But tent the language of their een:
If these agree, and she persist
  To answer all your love with hate,
Seek elsewhere to be better blest,
  And let her sigh when 'tis too late.

Roger. Kind Patie, now fair fa' your honest heart!
Ye're ay sae cadgy, and have sic an art

To hearten ane; for now, as clean's a leek,
Ye've cherished me since ye began to speak.
Sae, for your pains, I'll mak ye a propine
(My mother, rest her saul! she made it fine)—
A tartan plaid, spun of good hawslock woo,
Scarlet and green the sets, the borders blue,
With spraings like gowd and siller crossed with black;
I never had it yet upon my back:
Weel are ye wordy o' 't, what have sae kind
Red up my reveled doubts and cleared my mind.

AMBROSE PHILIPS

TO MISS CHARLOTTE PULTENEY, IN HER MOTHER'S ARMS

Timely blossom, infant fair,
Fondling of a happy pair,
Every morn and every night
Their solicitous delight;
Sleeping, waking, still at ease,
Pleasing, without skill to please;
Little gossip, blithe and hale,
Tattling many a broken tale,
Singing many a tuneless song,
Lavish of a heedless tongue.
Simple maiden, void of art,
Babbling out the very heart,
Yet abandoned to thy will,
Yet imagining no ill,
Yet too innocent to blush;
Like the linnet in the bush,
To the mother-linnet's note
Moduling her slender throat,
Chirping forth thy pretty joys;
Wanton in the change of toys,
Like the linnet green, in May,
Flitting to each bloomy spray;

Wearied then, and glad of rest,
Like the linnet in the nest.
This thy present happy lot,
This, in time, will be forgot;
Other pleasures, other cares,
Ever-busy Time prepares;
And thou shalt in thy daughter see
This picture once resembled thee.

JOHN DYER

GRONGAR HILL

Silent Nymph, with curious eye!
Who, the purple evening, lie
On the mountain's lonely van,
Beyond the noise of busy man;
Painting fair the form of things,
While the yellow linnet sings;
Or the tuneful nightingale
Charms the forest with her tale;
Come, with all thy various hues,
Come, and aid thy sister Muse;
Now while Phœbus riding high
Gives lustre to the land and sky!
Grongar Hill invites my song,
Draw the landscape bright and strong;
Grongar, in whose mossy cells
Sweetly musing Quiet dwells;
Grongar, in whose silent shade,
For the modest Muses made,
So oft I have, the evening still,
At the fountain of a rill,
Sate upon a flowery bed,
With my hand beneath my head;
While strayed my eyes o'er Towy's flood,
Over mead, and over wood,
From house to house, from hill to hill,
'Till Contemplation had her fill.

About his chequered sides I wind,
And leave his brooks and meads behind,
And groves, and grottoes where I lay,
And vistas shooting beams of day:
Wide and wider spreads the vale,
As circles on a smooth canal:
The mountains round—unhappy fate!
Sooner or later, of all height,
Withdraw their summits from the skies,
And lessen as the others rise:
Still the prospect wider spreads,
Adds a thousand woods and meads;
Still it widens, widens still,
And sinks the newly-risen hill.
Now I gain the mountain's brow,
What a landscape lies below!
No clouds, no vapours intervene,
But the gay, the open scene
Does the face of nature shew,
In all the hues of heaven's bow!
And, swelling to embrace the light,
Spreads around beneath the sight.
Old castles on the cliffs arise,
Proudly towering in the skies!
Rushing from the woods, the spires
Seem from hence ascending fires!
Half his beams Apollo sheds
On the yellow mountain-heads!
Gilds the fleeces of the flocks,
And glitters on the broken rocks!
Below me trees unnumbered rise,
Beautiful in various dyes:
The gloomy pine, the poplar blue,
The yellow beech, the sable yew,
The slender fir, that taper grows,
The sturdy oak with broad-spread boughs;
And beyond the purple grove,
Haunt of Phillis, queen of love!
Gaudy as the opening dawn,
Lies a long and level lawn
On which a dark hill, steep and high,
Holds and charms the wandering eye!

Deep are his feet in Towy's flood,
His sides are clothed with waving wood,
And ancient towers crown his brow,
That cast an awful look below;
Whose ragged walls the ivy creeps,
And with her arms from falling keeps;
So both a safety from the wind
On mutual dependence find.
'Tis now the raven's bleak abode;
'Tis now th' apartment of the toad;
And there the fox securely feeds;
And there the poisonous adder breeds
Concealed in ruins, moss, and weeds;
While, ever and anon, there falls
Huge heaps of hoary mouldered walls.
Yet time has seen, that lifts the low,
And level lays the lofty brow,
Has seen this broken pile complete,
Big with the vanity of state;
But transient is the smile of fate!
A little rule, a little sway,
A sunbeam in a winter's day,
Is all the proud and mighty have
Between the cradle and the grave.
And see the rivers how they run,
Through woods and meads, in shade and sun,
Sometimes swift, sometimes slow,
Wave succeeding wave, they go
A various journey to the deep,
Like human life to endless sleep!
Thus is nature's vesture wrought,
To instruct our wandering thought;
Thus she dresses green and gay,
To disperse our cares away.
Ever charming, ever new,
When will the landscape tire the view!
The fountain's fall, the river's flow,
The woody valleys warm and low;
The windy summit, wild and high,
Roughly rushing on the sky;
The pleasant seat, the ruined tower,
The naked rock, the shady bower;

The town and village, dome and farm,
Each gives each a double charm,
As pearls upon an Æthiop's arm.
  See, on the mountain's southern side,
Where the prospect opens wide,
Where the evening gilds the tide;
How close and small the hedges lie!
What streaks of meadows cross the eye!
A step methinks may pass the stream,
So little distant dangers seem;
So we mistake the future's face,
Eyed through Hope's deluding glass;
As yon summits soft and fair
Clad in colours of the air,
Which to those who journey near,
Barren, brown, and rough appear;
Still we tread the same coarse way;
The present's still a cloudy day.
  O may I with myself agree,
And never covet what I see:
Content me with an humble shade,
My passions tamed, my wishes laid;
For while our wishes wildly roll,
We banish quiet from the soul:
'Tis thus the busy beat the air;
And misers gather wealth and care.
  Now, even now, my joys run high,
As on the mountain-turf I lie;
While the wanton Zephyr sings,
And in the vale perfumes his wings;
While the waters murmur deep;
While the shepherd charms his sheep;
While the birds unbounded fly,
And with music fill the sky,
Now, even now, my joys run high.
  Be full, ye courts, be great who will;
Search for Peace with all your skill:
Open wide the lofty door,
Seek her on the marble floor,
In vain ye search, she is not there;
In vain ye search the domes of Care!

Grass and flowers Quiet treads,
On the meads, and mountain-heads,
Along with Pleasure, close allied,
Ever by each other's side:
And often, by the murmuring rill,
Hears the thrush, while all is still,
Within the groves of Grongar Hill.

GEORGE BERKELEY

VERSES ON THE PROSPECT OF PLANTING ARTS AND LEARNING IN AMERICA

The Muse, disgusted at an age and clime
  Barren of every glorious theme,
In distant lands now waits a better time,
  Producing subjects worthy fame:

In happy climes where from the genial sun
  And virgin earth such scenes ensue,
The force of art in nature seems outdone,
  And fancied beauties by the true:

In happy climes, the seat of innocence,
  Where nature guides and virtue rules,
Where men shall not impose for truth and sense
  The pedantry of courts and schools.

There shall be sung another golden age,
  The rise of empire and of arts,
The good and great inspiring epic rage,
  The wisest heads and noblest hearts.

Not such as Europe breeds in her decay;
  Such as she bred when fresh and young,
When heavenly flame did animate her clay,
  By future poets shall be sung.

Westward the course of empire takes its way;
The four first acts already past,
A fifth shall close the drama with the day;
Time's noblest offspring is the last.

JAMES THOMSON

THE SEASONS

From WINTER

[Hardships and Benevolence]

The keener tempests come; and, fuming dun
From all the livid east or piercing north,
Thick clouds ascend, in whose capacious womb
A vapoury deluge lies, to snow congealed.
Heavy they roll their fleecy world along,
And the sky saddens with the gathered storm.
Through the hushed air the whitening shower descends,
At first thin wavering, till at last the flakes
Fall broad and wide and fast, dimming the day
With a continual flow. The cherished fields
Put on their winter robe of purest white;
'Tis brightness all, save where the new snow melts
Along the mazy current; low the woods
Bow their hoar head; and ere the languid sun
Faint from the west emits his evening ray,
Earth's universal face, deep-hid and chill,
Is one wild dazzling waste, that buries wide
The works of man. Drooping, the labourer-ox
Stands covered o'er with snow, and then demands
The fruit of all his toil. The fowls of heaven,
Tamed by the cruel season, crowd around
The winnowing store, and claim the little boon
Which Providence assigns them. One alone,
The redbreast, sacred to the household gods,
Wisely regardful of th' embroiling sky,
In joyless fields and thorny thickets leaves

His shivering mates, and pays to trusted man
His annual visit: half-afraid, he first
Against the window beats; then brisk alights
On the warm hearth; then, hopping o'er the floor,
Eyes all the smiling family askance,
And pecks, and starts, and wonders where he is,
Till, more familiar grown, the table-crumbs
Attract his slender feet. The foodless wilds
Pour forth their brown inhabitants. The hare,
Though timorous of heart and hard beset
By death in various forms—dark snares, and dogs,
And more unpitying men,—the garden seeks,
Urged on by fearless want. The bleating kind
Eye the black heaven, and next the glistening earth,
With looks of dumb despair; then, sad dispersed,
Dig for the withered herb through heaps of snow.
  Now, shepherds, to your helpless charge be kind:
Baffle the raging year, and fill their pens
With food at will; lodge them below the storm,
And watch them strict, for from the bellowing east,
In this dire season, oft the whirlwind's wing
Sweeps up the burthen of whole wintry plains
At one wide waft, and o'er the hapless flocks,
Hid in the hollow of two neighbouring hills,
The billowy tempest whelms, till, upward urged,
The valley to a shining mountain swells,
Tipped with a wreath high-curling in the sky.
  As thus the snows arise, and foul and fierce
All Winter drives along the darkened air,
In his own loose-revolving fields the swain
Disastered stands; sees other hills ascend,
Of unknown, joyless brow, and other scenes,
Of horrid prospect, shag the trackless plain;
Nor finds the river nor the forest, hid
Beneath the formless wild, but wanders on
From hill to dale, still more and more astray,
Impatient flouncing through the drifted heaps,
Stung with the thoughts of home. The thoughts of home
Rush on his nerves, and call their vigour forth
In many a vain attempt. How sinks his soul,
What black despair, what horror fills his heart,
When, for the dusky spot which fancy feigned

His tufted cottage rising through the snow,
He meets the roughness of the middle waste,
Far from the track and blest abode of man,
While round him night resistless closes fast,
And every tempest, howling o'er his head,
Renders the savage wilderness more wild!
Then throng the busy shapes into his mind
Of covered pits unfathomably deep
(A dire descent!), beyond the power of frost;
Of faithless bogs; of precipices huge,
Smoothed up with snow; and—what is land unknown,
What water—of the still unfrozen spring,
In the loose marsh or solitary lake,
Where the fresh fountain from the bottom boils.
These check his fearful steps; and down he sinks
Beneath the shelter of the shapeless drift,
Thinking o'er all the bitterness of death,
Mixed with the tender anguish nature shoots
Through the wrung bosom of the dying man—
His wife, his children, and his friends unseen.
In vain for him th' officious wife prepares
The fire fair-blazing and the vestment warm;
In vain his little children, peeping out
Into the mingling storm, demand their sire,
With tears of artless innocence. Alas!
Nor wife nor children more shall he behold,
Nor friends nor sacred home: on every nerve
The deadly Winter seizes, shuts up sense,
And, o'er his inmost vitals creeping cold,
Lays him along the snows a stiffened corse,
Stretched out and bleaching in the northern blast.
Ah, little think the gay licentious proud
Whom pleasure, power, and affluence surround;
They who their thoughtless hours in giddy mirth,
And wanton, often cruel, riot waste;
Ah, little think they, while they dance along,
How many feel, this very moment, death
And all the sad variety of pain:
How many sink in the devouring flood,
Or more devouring flame; how many bleed,
By shameful variance betwixt man and man;
How many pine in want, and dungeon glooms,

Shut from the common air, and common use
Of their own limbs; how many drink the cup
Of baleful grief, or eat the bitter bread
Of misery; sore pierced by wintry winds,
How many shrink into the sordid hut
Of cheerless poverty; how many shake
With all the fiercer tortures of the mind,
Unbounded passion, madness, guilt, remorse;
Whence tumbled headlong from the height of life,
They furnish matter for the tragic Muse;
Even in the vale, where wisdom loves to dwell,
With friendship, peace, and contemplation joined,
How many, racked with honest passions, droop
In deep retired distress; how many stand
Around the deathbed of their dearest friends,
And point the parting anguish. Thought fond man
Of these, and all the thousand nameless ills,
That one incessant struggle render life,
One scene of toil, of suffering, and of fate,
Vice in his high career would stand appalled,
And heedless rambling impulse learn to think;
The conscious heart of charity would warm,
And her wide wish benevolence dilate;
The social tear would rise, the social sigh;
And into clear perfection, gradual bliss,
Refining still, the social passions work.

From SUMMER

[Life's Meaning to the Generous Mind]

Forever running an enchanted round,
Passes the day, deceitful vain and void,
As fleets the vision o'er the formful brain,
This moment hurrying wild th' impassioned soul,
The next in nothing lost. 'Tis so to him,
The dreamer of this earth, an idle blank;
A sight of horror to the cruel wretch,
Who all day long in sordid pleasure rolled,
Himself an useless load, has squandered vile,
Upon his scoundrel train, what might have cheered
A drooping family of modest worth.

But to the generous still-improving mind,
That gives the hopeless heart to sing for joy,
Diffusing kind beneficence around,
Boastless,—as now descends the silent dew,—
To him the long review of ordered life
Is inward rapture, only to be felt.

FROM SPRING

[THE DIVINE FORCE IN SPRING]

Come, gentle Spring, ethereal mildness, come!
And from the bosom of yon dropping cloud,
While music wakes around, veiled in a shower
Of shadowing roses, on our plains descend!
  O Hertford, fitted or to shine in courts
With unaffected grace, or walk the plain
With Innocence and Meditation joined
In soft assemblage, listen to my song,
Which thy own season paints, when nature all
Is blooming and benevolent, like thee.
  And see where surly Winter passes off,
Far to the north, and calls his ruffian blasts:
His blasts obey, and quit the howling hill,
The shattered forest, and the ravaged vale;
While softer gales succeed, at whose kind touch—
Dissolving snows in livid torrents lost—
The mountains lift their green heads to the sky.
As yet the trembling year is unconfirmed,
And Winter oft at eve resumes the breeze,
Chills the pale morn, and bids his driving sleets
Deform the day delightless; so that scarce
The bittern knows his time, with bill engulfed,
To shake the sounding marsh, or from the shore
The plovers when to scatter o'er the heath
And sing their wild notes to the listening waste.
At last from Aries rolls the bounteous sun,
And the bright Bull receives him. Then no more
Th' expansive atmosphere is cramped with cold,
But, full of life and vivifying soul,
Lifts the light clouds sublime and spreads them thin,
Fleecy and white, o'er all-surrounding heaven;

Forth fly the tepid airs, and, unconfined,
Unbinding earth, the moving softness strays.
Joyous, th' impatient husbandman perceives
Relenting nature, and his lusty steers
Drives from their stalls, to where the well-used plough
Lies in the furrow, loosened from the frost;
There, unrefusing, to the harnessed yoke
They lend their shoulder, and begin their toil,
Cheered by the simple song and soaring lark;
Meanwhile incumbent o'er the shining share
The master leans, removes th' obstructing clay,
Winds the whole work, and sidelong lays the glebe.
White through the neighbouring fields the sower stalks,
With measured step, and liberal throws the grain
Into the faithful bosom of the ground;
The harrow follows harsh, and shuts the scene.
  Be gracious, Heaven! for now laborious man
Has done his part. Ye fostering breezes, blow!
Ye softening dews, ye tender showers, descend!
And temper all, thou world-reviving sun,
Into the perfect year! Nor ye who live
In luxury and ease, in pomp and pride,
Think these lost themes unworthy of your ear.
Such themes as these the rural Maro sung
To wide-imperial Rome, in the full height
Of elegance and taste, by Greece refined.
In ancient times, the sacred plough employed
The kings and awful fathers of mankind;
And some, with whom compared your insect tribes
Are but the beings of a summer's day,
Have held the scale of empire, ruled the storm
Of mighty war, then with victorious hand,
Disdaining little delicacies, seized
The plough, and, greatly independent, scorned
All the vile stores corruption can bestow.
Ye generous Britons, venerate the plough;
And o'er your hills and long-withdrawing vales
Let Autumn spread his treasures to the sun,
Luxuriant and unbounded! As the sea,
Far through his azure, turbulent domain,
Your empire owns, and from a thousand shores
Wafts all the pomp of life into your ports,

So with superior boon may your rich soil,
Exuberant, Nature's better blessings pour
O'er every land, the naked nations clothe,
And be th' exhaustless granary of a world.
  Nor only through the lenient air this change,
Delicious, breathes: the penetrative sun,
His force deep-darting to the dark retreat
Of vegetation, sets the steaming power
At large, to wander o'er the verdant earth,
In various hues—but chiefly thee, gay green!
Thou smiling Nature's universal robe,
United light and shade, where the sight dwells
With growing strength and ever new delight.
From the moist meadow to the withered hill,
Led by the breeze, the vivid verdure runs,
And swells and deepens to the cherished eye.
The hawthorn whitens; and the juicy groves
Put forth their buds, unfolding by degrees,
Till the whole leafy forest stands displayed
In full luxuriance to the sighing gales,
Where the deer rustle through the twining brake,
And the birds sing concealed. At once, arrayed
In all the colours of the flushing year
By Nature's swift and secret-working hand,
The garden glows, and fills the liberal air
With lavished fragrance, while the promised fruit
Lies yet a little embryo, unperceived,
Within its crimson folds. Now from the town,
Buried in smoke and sleep and noisome damps,
Oft let me wander o'er the dewy fields,
Where freshness breathes, and dash the trembling
    drops
From the bent bush, as through the verdant maze
Of sweet-briar hedges I pursue my walk;
Or taste the smell of dairy; or ascend
Some eminence, Augusta, in thy plains,
And see the country, far diffused around,
One boundless blush, one white-empurpled shower
Of mingled blossoms, where the raptured eye
Hurries from joy to joy, and, hid beneath
The fair profusion, yellow Autumn spies.

. . . .

What is this mighty breath, ye sages, say,
That in a powerful language, felt not heard,
Instructs the fowl of heaven, and through their
breast
These arts of love diffuses? What but God?
Inspiring God! who boundless spirit all,
And unremitting energy, pervades,
Adjusts, sustains, and agitates the whole.
He ceaseless works alone, and yet alone
Seems not to work; with such perfection framed
Is this complex, stupendous scheme of things.
But, though concealed, to every purer eye
Th' informing author in his works appears:
Chief, lovely Spring, in thee, and thy soft scenes,
The smiling God is seen; while water, earth,
And air attest his bounty; which exalts
The brute creation to this finer thought,
And annual melts their undesigning hearts
Profusely thus in tenderness and joy.
Still let my song a nobler note assume,
And sing th' infusive force of Spring on man,
When heaven and earth, as if contending, vie
To raise his being, and serene his soul.
Can he forbear to join the general smile
Of nature? Can fierce passions vex his breast,
While every gale is peace, and every grove
Is melody? Hence from the bounteous walks
Of flowing Spring, ye sordid sons of earth,
Hard, and unfeeling of another's woe;
Or only lavish to yourselves; away!
But come, ye generous minds, in whose wide
thought,
Of all his works, creative bounty burns
With warmest beam!

From AUTUMN

[The Pleasing Sadness of the Declining Year]

But see! the fading many-coloured woods,
Shade deepening over shade, the country round
Imbrown, a crowded umbrage, dusk and dun,

Of every hue from wan declining green
To sooty dark. These now the lonesome Muse,
Low-whispering, lead into their leaf-strown walks,
And give the season in its latest view.
Meantime, light-shadowing all, a sober calm
Fleeces unbounded ether, whose least wave
Stands tremulous, uncertain where to turn
The gentle current, while, illumined wide,
The dewy-skirted clouds imbibe the sun,
And through their lucid veil his softened force
Shed o'er the peaceful world. Then is the time,
For those whom wisdom and whom nature charm,
To steal themselves from the degenerate crowd,
And soar above this little scene of things,
To tread low-thoughted Vice beneath their feet,
To soothe the throbbing passions into peace,
And woo lone Quiet in her silent walks.
Thus solitary, and in pensive guise,
Oft let me wander o'er the russet mead
And through the saddened grove, where scarce is
heard
One dying strain to cheer the woodman's toil.
Haply some widowed songster pours his plaint,
Far, in faint warblings, through the tawny copse;
While congregated thrushes, linnets, larks,
And each wild throat whose artless strains so late
Swelled all the music of the swarming shades,
Robbed of their tuneful souls, now shivering sit
On the dead tree, a dull despondent flock,
With not a brightness waving o'er their plumes,
And naught save chattering discord in their note.
Oh, let not, aimed from some inhuman eye,
The gun the music of the coming year
Destroy, and harmless, unsuspecting harm,
Lay the weak tribes a miserable prey,
In mingled murder fluttering on the ground!
The pale descending year, yet pleasing still,
A gentler mood inspires: for now the leaf
Incessant rustles from the mournful grove,
Oft startling such as, studious, walk below,
And slowly circles through the waving air;
But should a quicker breeze amid the boughs

Sob, o'er the sky the leafy deluge streams,
Till, choked and matted with the dreary shower,
The forest walks, at every rising gale,
Roll wide the withered waste and whistle bleak.
Fled is the blasted verdure of the fields,
And, shrunk into their beds, the flowery race
Their sunny robes resign; even what remained
Of stronger fruits fall from the naked tree;
And woods, fields, gardens, orchards, all around,
The desolated prospect thrills the soul.

A HYMN

[Concluding the Seasons]

These, as they change, Almighty Father, these,
Are but the varied God. The rolling year
Is full of Thee. Forth in the pleasing Spring
Thy beauty walks, thy tenderness and love.
Wide-flush the fields; the softening air is balm;
Echo the mountains round; the forest smiles;
And every sense, and every heart is joy.
Then comes thy glory in the summer-months,
With light and heat refulgent. Then thy sun
Shoots full perfection through the swelling year:
And oft thy voice in dreadful thunder speaks;
And oft at dawn, deep noon, or falling eve,
By brooks and groves, in hollow-whispering gales.
Thy bounty shines in autumn unconfined,
And spreads a common feast for all that lives.
In winter awful thou! with clouds and storms
Around thee thrown, tempest o'er tempest rolled
Majestic darkness! on the whirlwind's wing,
Riding sublime, thou bidst the world adore,
And humblest nature with thy northern blast.
  Mysterious round! what skill, what force Divine,
Deepfelt, in these appear! a simple train,
Yet so delightful mixed, with such kind art,
Such beauty and beneficence combined:
Shade, unperceived, so softening into shade;
And all so forming an harmonious whole;

That, as they still succeed, they ravish still.
But wandering oft, with brute unconscious gaze,
Man marks not Thee, marks not the mighty hand;
That, ever-busy, wheels the silent spheres;
Works in the secret deep; shoots, steaming, thence
The fair profusion that o'erspreads the spring:
Flings from the sun direct the flaming day;
Feeds every creature; hurls the tempest forth;
And, as on earth this grateful change revolves,
With transport touches all the springs of life.
  Nature, attend! join every living soul,
Beneath the spacious temple of the sky,
In adoration join; and ardent raise
One general song! To Him, ye vocal gales,
Breathe soft, whose spirit in your freshness
    breathes.
Oh, talk of Him in solitary glooms
Where o'er the rock the scarcely waving pine
Fills the brown shade with a religious awe;
And ye, whose bolder note is heard afar,
Who shake the astonished world, lift high to
    heaven
Th' impetuous song, and say from whom you rage.
His praise, ye brooks, attune, ye trembling rills;
And let me catch it as I muse along.
Ye headlong torrents, rapid and profound;
Ye softer floods, that lead the humid maze
Along the vale; and thou, majestic main,
A secret world of wonders in thyself,
Sound His stupendous praise, whose greater voice
Or bids you roar, or bids your roarings fall.
So roll your incense, herbs, and fruits, and flowers,
In mingled clouds to Him, whose sun exalts,
Whose breath perfumes you, and whose pencil
    paints.
Ye forests, bend, ye harvests, wave to Him;
Breathe your still song into the reaper's heart,
As home he goes beneath the joyous moon.
Ye that keep watch in Heaven, as earth asleep
Unconscious lies, effuse your mildest beams;
Ye constellations, while your angels strike,
Amid the spangled sky, the silver lyre.

Great source of day! blest image here below
Of thy Creator, ever pouring wide,
From world to world, the vital ocean round,
On nature write with every beam His praise.
The thunder rolls: be hushed the prostrate world,
While cloud to cloud returns the solemn hymn.
Bleat out afresh, ye hills; ye mossy rocks,
Retain the sound; the broad responsive low,
Ye valleys, raise; for the Great Shepherd reigns,
And his unsuffering kingdom yet will come.
Ye woodlands, all awake; a boundless song
Burst from the groves; and when the restless day,
Expiring, lays the warbling world asleep,
Sweetest of birds! sweet Philomela, charm
The listening shades, and teach the night His
praise.
Ye chief, for whom the whole creation smiles;
At once the head, the heart, the tongue of all,
Crown the great hymn! in swarming cities vast,
Assembled men to the deep organ join
The long resounding voice, oft breaking clear,
At solemn pauses, through the swelling base;
And, as each mingling flame increases each,
In one united ardour rise to Heaven.
Or if you rather choose the rural shade,
And find a fane in every sacred grove,
There let the shepherd's lute, the virgin's lay,
The prompting seraph, and the poet's lyre,
Still sing the God of Seasons as they roll.
For me, when I forget the darling theme,
Whether the blossom blows, the Summer ray
Russets the plain, inspiring Autumn gleams,
Or Winter rises in the blackening east—
Be my tongue mute, my fancy paint no more,
And, dead to joy, forget my heart to beat.
Should Fate command me to the furthest verge
Of the green earth, to distant barbarous climes,
Rivers unknown to song; where first the sun
Gilds Indian mountains, or his setting beam
Flames on the Atlantic isles, 'tis nought to me;
Since God is ever present, ever felt,
In the void waste as in the city full;

And where He vital breathes, there must be joy.
When even at last the solemn hour shall come,
And wing my mystic flight to future worlds,
I cheerfully will obey; there with new powers,
Will rising wonders sing. I cannot go
Where Universal Love not smiles around,
Sustaining all yon orbs, and all their suns;
From seeming evil still educing good,
And better thence again, and better still,
In infinite progression. But I lose
Myself in Him, in Light ineffable!
Come, then, expressive silence, muse His praise.

[RULE, BRITANNIA]

An Ode: From Alfred, a Masque

When Britain first, at Heaven's command,
  Arose from out the azure main,
This was the charter of the land,
  And guardian angels sang this strain:
    Rule, Britannia, Britannia rules the waves!
    Britons never will be slaves!

The nations not so blest as thee,
  Must in their turns to tyrants fall,
Whilst thou shalt flourish great and free,
  The dread and envy of them all.
    Rule, Britannia, etc.

Still more majestic shalt thou rise,
  More dreadful from each foreign stroke;
As the loud blast that tears the skies,
  Serves but to root thy native oak.
    Rule, Britannia, etc.

Thee haughty tyrants ne'er shall tame;
  And their attempts to bend thee down
Will but arouse thy generous flame,
  But work their woe and thy renown.
    Rule, Britannia, etc.

To thee belongs the rural reign;
  Thy cities shall with commerce shine;
All thine shall be the subject main,
  And every shore it circles thine.
    Rule, Britannia, etc.

The Muses, still with freedom found,
  Shall to thy happy coast repair;
Blest isle, with matchless beauty crowned,
  And manly hearts to guard the fair!
    Rule, Britannia, etc.

From THE CASTLE OF INDOLENCE

O mortal man, who livest here by toil,
Do not complain of this thy hard estate:
That like an emmet thou must ever moil
Is a sad sentence of an ancient date;
And, certes, there is for it reason great,
For though sometimes it makes thee weep and wail,
And curse thy star, and early drudge and late,
Withouten that would come an heavier bale—
Loose life, unruly passions, and diseases pale.

In lowly dale, fast by a river's side,
With woody hill o'er hill encompassed round,
A most enchanting wizard did abide,
Than whom a fiend more fell is nowhere found.
It was, I ween, a lovely spot of ground;
And there a season atween June and May,
Half prankt with spring, with summer half imbrowned,
A listless climate made, where, sooth to say,
No living wight could work, ne carèd even for play.

Was naught around but images of rest:
Sleep-soothing groves, and quiet lawns between;
And flowery beds that slumbrous influence kest,
From poppies breathed; and beds of pleasant green,
Where never yet was creeping creature seen.
Meantime unnumbered glittering streamlets played,
And hurlèd everywhere their waters sheen,

That, as they bickered through the sunny glade,
Though restless still themselves, a lulling murmur made.

Joined to the prattle of the purling rills,
Were heard the lowing herds along the vale,
And flocks loud-bleating from the distant hills,
And vacant shepherds piping in the dale;
And now and then sweet Philomel would wail,
Or stock doves 'plain amid the forest deep,
That drowsy rustled to the sighing gale;
And still a coil the grasshopper did keep:
Yet all these sounds, yblent, inclinèd all to sleep.

Full in the passage of the vale, above,
A sable, silent, solemn forest stood,
Where naught but shadowy forms was seen to move,
As Idless fancied in her dreaming mood;
And up the hills, on either side, a wood
Of blackening pines, aye waving to and fro,
Sent forth a sleepy horror through the blood;
And where this valley winded out, below,
The murmuring main was heard, and scarcely heard, to flow.

A pleasing land of drowsyhed it was:
Of dreams that wave before the half-shut eye;
And of gay castles in the clouds that pass,
Forever flushing round a summer sky.
There eke the soft delights, that witchingly
Instil a wanton sweetness through the breast,
And the calm pleasures, always hovered nigh;
But whate'er smacked of 'noyance or unrest
Was far, far off expelled from this delicious nest.

The landskip such, inspiring perfect ease,
Where Indolence (for so the wizard hight)
Close-hid his castle mid embowering trees,
That half shut out the beams of Phœbus bright,
And made a kind of checkered day and night.
Meanwhile, unceasing at the massy gate,
Beneath a spacious palm, the wicked wight
Was placed; and, to his lute, of cruel fate
And labour harsh complained, lamenting man's estate.

Thither continual pilgrims crowded still,
From all the roads of earth that pass there by;
For, as they chaunced to breathe on neighbouring hill,
The freshness of this valley smote their eye,
And drew them ever and anon more nigh,
Till clustering round th' enchanter false they hung,
Ymolten with his syren melody,
While o'er th' enfeebling lute his hand he flung,
And to the trembling chords these tempting verses sung:

'Behold, ye pilgrims of this earth, behold!
See all but man with unearned pleasure gay!
See her bright robes the butterfly unfold,
Broke from her wintry tomb in prime of May.
What youthful bride can equal her array?
Who can with her for easy pleasure vie?
From mead to mead with gentle wing to stray,
From flower to flower on balmy gales to fly,
Is all she has to do beneath the radiant sky.

'Behold the merry minstrels of the morn,
The swarming songsters of the careless grove,
Ten thousand throats that, from the flowering thorn,
Hymn their good God and carol sweet of love,
Such grateful kindly raptures them emove!
They neither plough nor sow; ne, fit for flail,
E'er to the barn the nodding sheaves they drove;
Yet theirs each harvest dancing in the gale,
Whatever crowns the hill or smiles along the vale.

'Outcast of Nature, man! the wretched thrall
Of bitter-dropping sweat, of sweltry pain,
Of cares that eat away thy heart with gall,
And of the vices, an inhuman train,
That all proceed from savage thirst of gain:
For when hard-hearted Interest first began
To poison earth, Astræa left the plain;
Guile, violence, and murder seized on man,
And, for soft milky streams, with blood the rivers ran.'

. . . .

He ceased. But still their trembling ears retained
The deep vibrations of his 'witching song,
That, by a kind of magic power, constrained
To enter in, pell-mell, the listening throng:
Heaps poured on heaps, and yet they slipped along
In silent ease; as when beneath the beam
Of summer moons, the distant woods among,
Or by some flood all silvered with the gleam,
The soft-embodied fays through airy portal stream.

. . . .

Of all the gentle tenants of the place,
There was a man of special grave remark;
A certain tender gloom o'erspread his face,
Pensive, not sad; in thought involved, not dark;
As soote this man could sing as morning lark,
And teach the noblest morals of the heart;
But these his talents were yburied stark:
Of the fine stores he nothing would impart,
Which or boon Nature gave, or nature-painting Art.

To noontide shades incontinent he ran,
Where purls the brook with sleep-inviting sound,
Or when Dan Sol to slope his wheels began,
Amid the broom he basked him on the ground,
Where the wild thyme and camomil are found;
There would he linger, till the latest ray
Of light sate trembling on the welkin's bound,
Then homeward through the twilight shadows stray,
Sauntering and slow: so had he passèd many a day.

Yet not in thoughtless slumber were they passed;
For oft the heavenly fire, that lay concealed
Beneath the sleeping embers, mounted fast,
And all its native light anew revealed;
Oft as he traversed the cerulean field,
And marked the clouds that drove before the wind,
Ten thousand glorious systems would he build,
Ten thousand great ideas filled his mind:
But with the clouds they fled, and left no trace behind.

EDWARD YOUNG

From LOVE OF FAME

ON WOMEN

Such blessings Nature pours,
O'erstocked mankind enjoy but half her stores:
In distant wilds, by human eyes unseen,
She rears her flowers, and spreads her velvet green:
Pure, gurgling rills the lonely desert trace,
And waste their music on the savage race.
Is Nature then a niggard of her bliss?
Repine we guiltless in a world like this?
But our lewd tastes her lawful charms refuse,
And painted art's depraved allurements choose.
Such Fulvia's passion for the town; fresh air
(An odd effect!) gives vapours to the fair;
Green fields, and shady groves, and crystal springs,
And larks, and nightingales, are odious things;
But smoke, and dust, and noise, and crowds, delight;
And to be pressed to death, transports her quite:
Where silver rivulets play through flowery meads,
And woodbines give their sweets, and limes their shades,
Black kennels' absent odours she regrets,
And stops her nose at beds of violets.

. . . .

Few to good-breeding make a just pretense;
Good-breeding is the blossom of good-sense;
The last result of an accomplished mind,
With outward grace, the body's virtue, joined.
A violated decency now reigns;
And nymphs for failings take peculiar pains.
With Chinese painters modern toasts agree,
The point they aim at is deformity:
They throw their persons with a hoyden air
Across the room, and toss into the chair.
So far their commerce with mankind is gone,
They, for our manners, have exchanged their own.

The modest look, the castigated grace,
The gentle movement, and slow-measured pace,
For which her lovers died, her parents prayed,
Are indecorums with the modern maid.

. . . .

What swarms of amorous grandmothers I see!
And misses, ancient in iniquity!
What blasting whispers, and what loud declaiming!
What lying, drinking, bawding, swearing, gaming!
Friendship so cold, such warm incontinence;
Such griping avarice, such profuse expense;
Such dead devotion, such a zeal for crimes;
Such licensed ill, such masquerading times;
Such venal faith, such misapplied applause;
Such flattered guilt, and such inverted laws!
  Such dissolution through the whole I find,
'Tis not a world, but chaos of mankind.
Since Sundays have no balls, the well-dressed belle
Shines in the pew, but smiles to hear of Hell;
And casts an eye of sweet disdain on all
Who listen less to Collins than St. Paul.
Atheists have been but rare; since Nature's birth
Till now, she-atheists ne'er appeared on earth.
Ye men of deep researches, say, whence springs
This daring character, in timorous things?
Who start at feathers, from an insect fly,
A match for nothing—but the Deity.
But, not to wrong the fair, the Muse must own
In this pursuit they court not fame alone;
But join to that a more substantial view,
'From thinking free, to be free agents, too.'
  They strive with their own hearts, and keep them down,
In complaisance to all the fools in town.
O how they tremble at the name of prude!
And die with shame at thought of being good!
For, what will Artimis, the rich and gay,
What will the wits, that is, the coxcombs, say?
They Heaven defy, to earth's vile dregs a slave;
Through cowardice, most execrably brave.
With our own judgments durst we to comply,
In virtue should we live, in glory die.

Rise then, my Muse, in honest fury rise;
They dread a satire who defy the skies.
  Atheists are few: most nymphs a Godhead own;
And nothing but his attributes dethrone.
From atheists far, they steadfastly believe
God is, and is almighty—to forgive.
His other excellence they'll not dispute;
But mercy, sure, is his chief attribute.
Shall pleasures of a short duration chain
A lady's soul in everlasting pain?
Will the great Author us poor worms destroy,
For now and then a sip of transient joy?
No; he's forever in a smiling mood;
He's like themselves; or how could he be good?
And they blaspheme, who blacker schemes suppose.
Devoutly, thus, Jehovah they depose,
The pure! the just! and set up, in his stead,
A deity that's perfectly well-bred.
  'Dear Tillotson! be sure the best of men;
Nor thought he more than thought great Origen.
Though once upon a time he misbehaved,
Poor Satan! doubtless, he'll at length be saved.
Let priests do something for their one in ten;
It is their trade; so far they're honest men.
Let them cant on, since they have got the knack,
And dress their notions, like themselves, in black;
Fright us, with terrors of a world unknown,
From joys of this, to keep them all their own.
Of earth's fair fruits, indeed, they claim a fee;
But then they leave our untithed virtue free.
Virtue's a pretty thing to make a show:
Did ever mortal write like Rochefoucauld?'
Thus pleads the Devil's fair apologist,
And, pleading, safely enters on his list.

NIGHT-THOUGHTS

[MAN'S MARVELLOUS NATURE]

How poor, how rich, how abject, how august,
How complicate, how wonderful is man!
How passing wonder He who made him such,
Who centred in our make such strange extremes!
From different natures marvellously mixed,
Connection exquisite of distant worlds!
Distinguished link in being's endless chain!
Midway from nothing to the Deity!
A beam ethereal, sullied and absorbed!
Though sullied and dishonoured, still divine!
Dim miniature of greatness absolute!
An heir of glory! A frail child of dust!
Helpless immortal! insect infinite!
A worm! A god!—I tremble at myself,
And in myself am lost. At home a stranger,
Thought wanders up and down, surprised, aghast
And wondering at her own. How reason reels!
O what a miracle to man is man,
Triumphantly distressed; what joy! what dread!
Alternately transported and alarmed!
What can preserve my life? or what destroy?
An angel's arm can't snatch me from the grave;
Legions of angels can't confine me there.

[SATIETY IN THIS WORLD]

Live ever here, Lorenzo? Shocking thought!
So shocking, they who wish disown it, too;
Disown from shame what they from folly crave.
Live ever in the womb nor see the light?
For what live ever here? With labouring step
To tread our former footsteps? pace the round
Eternal? to climb life's worn, heavy wheel,
Which draws up nothing new? to beat, and beat
The beaten track? to bid each wretched day
The former mock? to surfeit on the same,
And yawn our joys? or thank a misery
For change, though sad? to see what we have seen;

Hear, till unheard, the same old slabbered tale?
To taste the tasted, and at each return
Less tasteful? o'er our palates to decant
Another vintage? strain a flatter year,
Through loaded vessels and a laxer tone?
Crazy machines, to grind earth's wasted fruits!

[God Just as Well as Merciful]

Thou most indulgent, most tremendous Power!
Still more tremendous for thy wondrous love!
That arms, with awe more awful, thy commands;
And foul transgression dips in sevenfold guilt!
How our hearts tremble at thy love immense!
In love immense, inviolably just!
Thou, rather than thy justice should be stained,
Didst stain the cross; and, work of wonders far
The greatest, that thy dearest far might bleed.
Bold thought! shall I dare speak it, or repress?
Should man more execrate, or boast, the guilt
Which roused such vengeance? which such love inflamed?
Our guilt (how mountainous!) with outstretched arms,
Stern justice and soft-smiling love embrace,
Supporting, in full majesty, thy throne,
When seemed its majesty to need support,
Or that, or man, inevitably lost;
What, but the fathomless of thought divine,
Could labour such expedient from despair,
And rescue both? both rescue! both exalt!
O how are both exalted by the deed!
The wondrous deed! or shall I call it more
A wonder in Omnipotence itself!
A mystery no less to gods than men!
Not thus our infidels th' Eternal draw,—
A God all o'er, consummate, absolute,
Full-orbed, in his whole round of rays complete.
They set at odds Heaven's jarring attributes,
And, with one excellence, another wound;
Maim Heaven's perfection, break its equal beams,
Bid mercy triumph over—God himself,
Undeified by their opprobrious praise;
A God all mercy, is a God unjust.

[MAN'S NATURE PROVES HIS IMMORTALITY]

In man, the more we dive, the more we see
Heaven's signet stamping an immortal make.
Dive to the bottom of the soul, the base
Sustaining all, what find we? Knowledge, love.
As light and heat essential to the sun,
These to the soul. And why, if souls expire?
How little lovely here! How little known!
Small knowledge we dig up with endless toil;
And love unfeigned may purchase perfect hate.
Why starved on earth our angel appetites,
While brutal are indulged their fulsome fill?
Were then capacities divine conferred
As a mock diadem, in savage sport,
Rank insult of our pompous poverty,
Which reaps but pain from seeming claims so fair?
In future age lies no redress? And shuts
Eternity the door on our complaint?
If so, for what strange ends were mortals made!
The worst to wallow, and the best to weep;
The man who merits most, must most complain:
Can we conceive a disregard in Heaven
What the worst perpetrate or best endure?
This cannot be. To love, and know, in man
Is boundless appetite, and boundless power:
And these demonstrate boundless objects, too.
Objects, powers, appetites, Heaven suits in all;
Nor, nature through, e'er violates this sweet
Eternal concord, on her tuneful string.
Is man the sole exception from her laws?
Eternity struck off from human hope,
(I speak with truth, but veneration too)
Man is a monster, the reproach of Heaven,
A stain, a dark impenetrable cloud
On Nature's beauteous aspect; and deforms
(Amazing blot!) deforms her with her lord.
If such is man's allotment, what is Heaven?
Or own the soul immortal, or blaspheme.
Or own the soul immortal, or invert
All order. Go, mock-majesty! go, man!
And bow to thy superiors of the stall;

Through every scene of sense superior far:
They graze the turf untilled; they drink the stream
Unbrewed, and ever full, and unembittered
With doubts, fears, fruitless hopes, regrets, despair.
Mankind's peculiar! reason's precious dower!
No foreign clime they ransack for their robes,
No brother cite to the litigious bar.
Their good is good entire, unmixed, unmarred;
They find a paradise in every field,
On boughs forbidden, where no curses hang:
Their ill no more than strikes the sense, unstretched
By previous dread or murmur in the rear;
When the worst comes, it comes unfeared; one stroke
Begins and ends their woe: they die but once;
Blessed incommunicable privilege! for which
Proud man, who rules the globe and reads the stars,
Philosopher or hero, sighs in vain.
Account for this prerogative in brutes:
No day, no glimpse of day, to solve the knot
But what beams on it from eternity.
O sole and sweet solution! that unties
The difficult, and softens the severe;
The cloud on Nature's beauteous face dispels,
Restores bright order, casts the brute beneath,
And re-enthrones us in supremacy
Of joy, e'en here. Admit immortal life,
And virtue is knight-errantry no more:
Each virtue brings in hand a golden dower
Far richer in reversion: Hope exults,
And, though much bitter in our cup is thrown,
Predominates and gives the taste of Heaven.

ANONYMOUS

THE HAPPY SAVAGE

Oh, happy he who never saw the face
Of man, nor heard the sound of human voice!
But soon as born was carried and exposed
In some vast desert, suckled by the wolf
Or shaggy bear, more kind than our fell race;
Who with his fellow brutes can range around
The echoing forest. His rude artless mind
Uncultivated as the soil, he joins
The dreadful harmony of howling wolves,
And the fierce lion's roar; while far away
Th' affrighted traveller retires and trembles.
Happy the lonely savage! nor deceived,
Nor vexed, nor grieved; in every darksome cave,
Under each verdant shade, he takes repose.
Sweet are his slumbers: of all human arts
Happily ignorant, nor taught by wisdom
Numberless woes, nor polished into torment.

SOAME JENYNS

From AN ESSAY ON VIRTUE

Were once these maxims fixed, that God's our friend,
Virtue our good, and happiness our end,
How soon must reason o'er the world prevail,
And error, fraud, and superstition fail!
None would hereafter then with groundless fear
Describe th' Almighty cruel and severe,
Predestinating some without pretence
To Heaven, and some to Hell for no offence;
Inflicting endless pains for transient crimes,
And favouring sects or nations, men or times.

To please him none would foolishly forbear
Or food, or rest, or itch in shirts of hair,
Or deem it merit to believe or teach
What reason contradicts, within its reach;
None would fierce zeal for piety mistake,
Or malice for whatever tenet's sake,
Or think salvation to one sect confined,
And Heaven too narrow to contain mankind.

. . . .

No servile tenets would admittance find
Destructive of the rights of humankind;
Of power divine, hereditary right,
And non-resistance to a tyrant's might.
For sure that all should thus for one be cursed,
Is but great nature's edict just reversed.
No moralists then, righteous to excess,
Would show fair Virtue in so black a dress,
That they, like boys, who some feigned sprite array,
First from the spectre fly themselves away:
No preachers in the terrible delight,
But choose to win by reason, not affright;
Not, conjurors like, in fire and brimstone dwell,
And draw each moving argument from Hell.

. . . .

No more applause would on ambition wait,
And laying waste the world be counted great,
But one good-natured act more praises gain,
Than armies overthrown, and thousands slain;
No more would brutal rage disturb our peace,
But envy, hatred, war, and discord cease;
Our own and others' good each hour employ,
And all things smile with universal joy;
Virtue with Happiness, her consort, joined,
Would regulate and bless each human mind,
And man be what his Maker first designed.

PHILIP DODDRIDGE

SURSUM

Ye golden lamps of heaven, farewell,
With all your feeble light;
Farewell, thou ever-changing moon,
Pale empress of the night.

And thou refulgent orb of day,
In brighter flames arrayed;
My soul that springs beyond thy sphere,
No more demands thine aid.

Ye stars are but the shining dust
Of my divine abode,
The pavement of those heavenly courts
Where I shall reign with God.

The Father of eternal light
Shall there His beams display;
Nor shall one moment's darkness mix
With that unvaried day.

No more the drops of piercing grief
Shall swell into mine eyes;
Nor the meridian sun decline
Amidst those brighter skies.

WILLIAM SOMERVILLE

From THE CHASE

Here on this verdant spot, where nature kind,
With double blessings crowns the farmer's hopes;
Where flowers autumnal spring, and the rank mead
Affords the wandering hares a rich repast;
Throw off thy ready pack. See, where they spread

And range around, and dash the glittering dew.
If some staunch hound, with his authentic voice,
Avow the recent trail, the justling tribe
Attend his call, then with one mutual cry,
The welcome news confirm, and echoing hills
Repeat the pleasing tale. See how they thread
The brakes, and up yon furrow drive along!
But quick they back recoil, and wisely check
Their eager haste; then o'er the fallowed ground
How leisurely they work, and many a pause
Th' harmonious concert breaks; till more assured
With joy redoubled the low valleys ring.
What artful labyrinths perplex their way!
Ah! there she lies; how close! she pants, she doubts
If now she lives; she trembles as she sits,
With horror seized. The withered grass that clings
Around her head of the same russet hue
Almost deceived my sight, had not her eyes
With life full-beaming her vain wiles betrayed.
At distance draw thy pack, let all be hushed,
No clamour loud, no frantic joy be heard,
Lest the wild hound run gadding o'er the plain
Untractable, nor hear thy chiding voice.
Now gently put her off; see how direct
To her known mew she flies! Here, huntsman, bring
(But without hurry) all thy jolly hounds,
And calmly lay them in. How low they stoop,
And seem to plough the ground! then all at once
With greedy nostrils snuff the fuming steam
That glads their fluttering hearts. As winds let loose
From the dark caverns of the blustering god,
They burst away, and sweep the dewy lawn.
Hope gives them wings, while she's spurred on by fear;
The welkin rings; men, dogs, hills, rocks, and woods
In the full concert join. Now, my brave youths,
Stripped for the chase, give all your souls to joy!
See how their coursers, than the mountain roe
More fleet, the verdant carpet skim; thick clouds
Snorting they breathe; their shining hoofs scarce print
The grass unbruised; when emulation fired,
They strain to lead the field, top the barred gate,
O'er the deep ditch exulting bound, and brush

The thorny-twining hedge; the riders bend
O'er their arched necks; with steady hands, by turns
Indulge their speed, or moderate their rage.
Where are their sorrows, disappointments, wrongs,
Vexations, sickness, cares? All, all are gone,
And with the panting winds lag far behind.

HENRY BROOKE

From UNIVERSAL BEAUTY

[The Deity in Every Atom]

Thus beauty, mimicked in our humbler strains,
Illustrious through the world's great poem reigns!
The One grows sundry by creative power,
Th' eternal's found in each revolving hour;
Th' immense appears in every point of space,
Th' unchangeable in nature's varying face;
Th' invisible conspicuous to our mind,
And Deity in every atom shrined.

[Nature Superior to Civilization]

O Nature, whom the song aspires to scan!
O Beauty, trod by proud insulting man,
This boasted tyrant of thy wondrous ball,
This mighty, haughty, little lord of all;
This king o'er reason, but this slave to sense,
Of wisdom careless, but of whim immense;
Towards thee incurious, ignorant, profane,
But of his own, dear, strange productions vain!
Then with this champion let the field be fought,
And nature's simplest arts 'gainst human wisdom brought.
Let elegance and bounty here unite—
There kings beneficent and courts polite;
Here nature's wealth—there chemist's golden dreams;
Her texture here—and there the statesman's schemes;

Conspicuous here let sacred truth appear—
The courtier's word, and lordling's honour, there;
Here native sweets in boon profusion flow—
There smells that scented nothing of a beau;
Let justice here unequal combat wage—
Nor poise the judgment of the law-learned sage;
Though all-proportioned with exactest skill,
Yet gay as woman's wish, and various as her will.
O say ye pitied, envied, wretched great,
Who veil pernicion with the mask of state!
Whence are those domes that reach the mocking skies,
And vainly emulous of nature rise?
Behold the swain projected o'er the vale!
See slumbering peace his rural eyelids seal;
Earth's flowery lap supports his vacant head,
Beneath his limbs her broidered garments spread;
Aloft her elegant pavilion bends,
And living shade of vegetation lends,
With ever propagated bounty blessed,
And hospitably spread for every guest:
No tinsel here adorns a tawdry woof,
Nor lying wash besmears a varnished roof;
With native mode the vivid colours shine,
And Heaven's own loom has wrought the weft divine,
Where art veils art, and beauties' beauties close,
While central grace diffused throughout the system flows.

[The Splendour of Insects]

Gemmed o'er their heads the mines of India gleam,
And heaven's own wardrobe has arrayed their frame;
Each spangled back bright sprinkling specks adorn,
Each plume imbibes the rosy-tinctured morn;
Spread on each wing, the florid seasons glow,
Shaded and verged with the celestial bow,
Where colours blend an ever-varying dye,
And wanton in their gay exchanges vie.
Not all the glitter fops and fair ones prize,
The pride of fools, and pity of the wise;
Not all the show and mockery of state,
The little, low, fine follies of the great;

Not all the wealth which eastern pageants wore,
What still our idolizing worlds adore;
Can boast the least inimitable grace
Which decks profusive this illustrious race.

[Moral Lessons from Animal Life]

Ye self-sufficient sons of reasoning pride,
Too wise to take Omniscience for your guide,
Those rules from insects, birds, and brutes discern
Which from the Maker you disdain to learn!
The social friendship, and the firm ally,
The filial sanctitude, and nuptial tie,
Patience in want, and faith to persevere,
Th' endearing sentiment, and tender care,
Courage o'er private interest to prevail,
And die all Decii for the public weal.

[Promptings of Divine Instinct]

Dispersed through every copse or marshy plain,
Where hunts the woodcock or the annual crane,
Where else encamped the feathered legions spread
Or bathe incumbent on their oozy bed,
The brimming lake thy smiling presence fills,
And waves the banners of a thousand hills.
Thou speed'st the summons of thy warning voice:
Winged at thy word, the distant troops rejoice,
From every quarter scour the fields of air,
And to the general rendezvous repair;
Each from the mingled rout disporting turns,
And with the love of kindred plumage burns.
Thy potent will instinctive bosoms feel,
And here arranging semilunar, wheel;
Or marshalled here the painted rhomb display
Or point the wedge that cleaves th' aërial way:
Uplifted on thy wafting breath they rise;
Thou pav'st the regions of the pathless skies,
Through boundless tracts support'st the journeyed host
And point'st the voyage to the certain coast,—
Thou the sure compass and the sea they sail,
The chart, the port, the steerage, and the gale!

PROLOGUE TO 'GUSTAVUS VASA'

Britons! this night presents a state distressed:
Though brave, yet vanquished; and though great, oppressed.
Vice, ravening vulture, on her vitals preyed;
Her peers, her prelates, fell corruption swayed:
Their rights, for power, the ambitious weakly sold:
The wealthy, poorly, for superfluous gold.
Hence wasting ills, hence severing factions rose,
And gave large entrance to invading foes:
Truth, justice, honour, fled th' infected shore;
For freedom, sacred freedom, was no more.
  Then, greatly rising in his country's right,
Her hero, her deliverer sprung to light:
A race of hardy northern sons he led,
Guiltless of courts, untainted, and unread;
Whose inborn spirit spurned th' ignoble fee,
Whose hands scorned bondage, for their hearts were free.
  Ask ye what law their conquering cause confessed?—
Great Nature's law, the law within the breast:
Formed by no art, and to no sect confined,
But stamped by Heaven upon th' unlettered mind.
  Such, such of old, the first born natives were
Who breathed the virtues of Britannia's air,
Their realm when mighty Cæsar vainly sought,
For mightier freedom against Cæsar fought,
And rudely drove the famed invader home,
To tyrannize o'er polished—venal Rome.
  Our bard, exalted in a freeborn flame,
To every nation would transfer this claim:
He to no state, no climate, bounds his page,
But bids the moral beam through every age.
Then be your judgment generous as his plan;
Ye sons of freedom! save the friend of man.

From CONRADE, A FRAGMENT

What do I love—what is it that mine eyes
Turn round in search of—that my soul longs after,
But cannot quench her thirst?—'Tis Beauty, Phelin!

I see it wide beneath the arch of heaven,
When the stars peep upon their evening hour,
And the moon rises on the eastern wave,
Housed in a cloud of gold! I see it wide
In earth's autumnal taints of various landscape
When the first ray of morning tips the trees,
And fires the distant rock! I hear its voice
When thy hand sends the sound along the gale,
Swept from the silver strings or on mine ear
Drops the sweet sadness! At my heart I feel
Its potent grasp, I melt beneath the touch,
When the tale pours upon my sense humane
The woes of other times! What art thou, Beauty?
Thou art not colour, fancy, sound, nor form—
These but the conduits are, whence the soul quaffs
The liquor of its heaven. Whate'er thou art,
Nature, or Nature's spirit, thou art all
I long for! Oh, descend upon my thoughts!
To thine own music tune, thou power of grace,
The cordage of my heart! Fill every shape
That rises to my dream or wakes to vision;
And touch the threads of every mental nerve,
With all thy sacred feelings!

MATTHEW GREEN

From THE SPLEEN

To cure the mind's wrong bias, spleen,
Some recommend the bowling-green;
Some, hilly walks; all, exercise;
Fling but a stone, the giant dies.
Laugh and be well. Monkeys have been
Extreme good doctors for the spleen;
And kitten, if the humour hit,
Has harlequined away the fit.
  Since mirth is good in this behalf,
At some particulars let us laugh:

Witlings, brisk fools, cursed with half-sense,
That stimulates their impotence;
Who buzz in rhyme, and, like blind flies,
Err with their wings for want of eyes;
Poor authors worshipping a calf,
Deep tragedies that make us laugh,
A strict dissenter saying grace,
A lecturer preaching for a place,
Folks, things prophetic to dispense,
Making the past the future tense,
The popish dubbing of a priest,
Fine epitaphs on knaves deceased.

. . . .

Forced by soft violence of prayer,
The blithesome goddess soothes my care,
I feel the deity inspire,
And thus she models my desire.
Two hundred pounds half-yearly paid,
Annuity securely made,
A farm some twenty miles from town,
Small, tight, salubrious, and my own;
Two maids, that never saw the town,
A serving-man not quite a clown,
A boy to help to tread the mow,
And drive, while t'other holds the plough;
A chief, of temper formed to please,
Fit to converse, and keep the keys;
And better to preserve the peace,
Commissioned by the name of niece;
With understandings of a size
To think their master very wise.

WILLIAM SHENSTONE

From THE SCHOOLMISTRESS

Her cap, far whiter than the driven snow,
Emblem right meet of decency does yield:
Her apron dyed in grain, as blue, I trow,
As is the harebell that adorns the field;

And in her hand, for sceptre, she does wield
Tway birchen sprays; with anxious fear entwined,
With dark distrust, and sad repentance filled;
And steadfast hate, and sharp affliction joined,
And fury uncontrolled, and chastisement unkind.

. . . .

A russet stole was o'er her shoulders thrown;
A russet kirtle fenced the nipping air;
'Twas simple russet, but it was her own;
'Twas her own country bred the flock so fair!
'Twas her own labour did the fleece prepare;
And, sooth to say, her pupils ranged around,
Through pious awe, did term it passing rare;
For they in gaping wonderment abound,
And think, no doubt, she been the greatest wight on ground.

. . . .

Lo, now with state she utters the command!
Eftsoons the urchins to their tasks repair;
Their books of stature small they take in hand,
Which with pellucid horn securèd are;
To save from finger wet the letters fair:
The work so gay, that on their back is seen,
St. George's high achievements does declare;
On which thilk wight that has y-gazing been
Kens the forth-coming rod, unpleasing sight, I ween!

Ah, luckless he, and born beneath the beam
Of evil star! it irks me whilst I write!
As erst the bard by Mulla's silver stream,
Oft, as he told of deadly dolorous plight,
Sighed as he sung, and did in tears indite.
For brandishing the rod, she doth begin
To loose the brogues, the stripling's late delight!
And down they drop; appears his dainty skin,
Fair as the furry coat of whitest ermilin.

O ruthful scene! when from a nook obscure,
His little sister doth his peril see:
All playful as she sate, she grows demure;
She finds full soon her wonted spirits flee;
She meditates a prayer to set him free:

Nor gentle pardon could this dame deny,
(If gentle pardon could with dames agree)
To her sad grief that swells in either eye,
And wrings her so that all for pity she could die.

. . . .

The other tribe, aghast, with sore dismay,
Attend, and conn their tasks with mickle care:
By turns, astonied, every twig survey,
And, from their fellow's hateful wounds, beware;
Knowing, I wist, how each the same may share;
Till fear has taught them a performance meet,
And to the well-known chest the dame repairs;
Whence oft with sugared cates she doth 'em greet,
And ginger-bread y-rare; now, certes, doubly sweet!

. . . .

Yet nursed with skill, what dazzling fruits appear!
Even now sagacious foresight points to show
A little bench of heedless bishops here,
And there a chancellor in embryo,
Or bard sublime, if bard may e'er be so,
As Milton, Shakespeare, names that ne'er shall die!
Though now he crawl along the ground so low,
Nor weeting how the muse should soar on high,
Wisheth, poor starveling elf! his paper kite may fly.

WRITTEN AT AN INN AT HENLEY

To thee, fair freedom! I retire
From flattery, cards, and dice, and din;
Nor art thou found in mansions higher
Than the low cot, or humble inn.

'Tis here with boundless power I reign;
And every health which I begin,
Converts dull port to bright champagne;
Such freedom crowns it, at an inn.

I fly from pomp, I fly from plate!
I fly from falsehood's specious grin!
Freedom I love, and form I hate,
And choose my lodgings at an inn.

Here, waiter! take my sordid ore,
  Which lacqueys else might hope to win;
It buys, what courts have not in store;
  It buys me freedom, at an inn.

Whoe'er has travelled life's dull round,
  Where'er his stages may have been,
May sigh to think he still has found
  The warmest welcome at an inn.

JONATHAN SWIFT

From THE BEASTS' CONFESSION

When beasts could speak, (the learned say
They still can do so every day,)
It seems they had religion then,
As much as now we find in men.
It happened, when a plague broke out,
(Which therefore made them more devout,)
The king of brutes (to make it plain,
Of quadrupeds I only mean)
By proclamation gave command
That every subject in the land
Should to the priest confess their sins;
And thus the pious Wolf begins:—
'Good father, I must own with shame,
That often I have been to blame:
I must confess, on Friday last,
Wretch that I was! I broke my fast:
But I defy the basest tongue
To prove I did my neighbour wrong;
Or ever went to seek my food,
By rapine, theft, or thirst of blood.'
  The Ass approaching next, confessed
That in his heart he loved a jest:
A wag he was, he needs must own,
And could not let a dunce alone:

Sometimes his friend he would not spare,
And might perhaps be too severe:
But yet the worst that could be said,
He was a wit both born and bred;
And, if it be a sin and shame,
Nature alone must bear the blame:
One fault he has, is sorry for't,
His ears are half a foot too short;
Which could he to the standard bring,
He'd show his face before the king:
Then for his voice, there's none disputes
That he's the nightingale of brutes.
  The Swine with contrite heart allowed
His shape and beauty made him proud:
In diet was perhaps too nice,
But gluttony was ne'er his vice:
In every turn of life content,
And meekly took what fortune sent:
Inquire through all the parish round,
A better neighbour ne'er was found;
His vigilance might some displease;
'Tis true, he hated sloth like pease.
  The mimic Ape began his chatter,
How evil tongues his life bespatter;
Much of the censuring world complained,
Who said, his gravity was feigned:
Indeed, the strictness of his morals
Engaged him in a hundred quarrels:
He saw, and he was grieved to see 't,
His zeal was sometimes indiscreet:
He found his virtues too severe
For our corrupted times to bear;
Yet such a lewd licentious age
Might well excuse a stoic's rage.
  The Goat advanced with decent pace,
And first excused his youthful face;
Forgiveness begged that he appeared
('Twas Nature's fault) without a beard.
'Tis true, he was not much inclined
To fondness for the female kind:
Not, as his enemies object,
From chance, or natural defect;

Not by his frigid constitution;
But through a pious resolution:
For he had made a holy vow
Of chastity, as monks do now:
Which he resolved to keep for ever hence
And strictly too, as doth his reverence.
Apply the tale, and you shall find,
How just it suits with human kind.
Some faults we own; but can you guess?
—Why, virtues carried to excess,
Wherewith our vanity endows us,
Though neither foe nor friend allows us.
The Lawyer swears (you may rely on't)
He never squeezed a needy client;
And this he makes his constant rule,
For which his brethren call him fool;
His conscience always was so nice,
He freely gave the poor advice;
By which he lost, he may affirm,
A hundred fees last Easter term;
While others of the learned robe,
Would break the patience of a Job.
No pleader at the bar could match
His diligence and quick dispatch;
Ne'er kept a cause, he well may boast,
Above a term or two at most.
The cringing Knave, who seeks a place
Without success, thus tells his case:
Why should he longer mince the matter?
He failed, because he could not flatter;
He had not learned to turn his coat,
Nor for a party give his vote:
His crime he quickly understood;
Too zealous for the nation's good:
He found the ministers resent it,
Yet could not for his heart repent it.
The Chaplain vows, he cannot fawn,
Though it would raise him to the lawn:
He passed his hours among his books;
You find it in his meagre looks:
He might, if he were worldly wise,
Preferment get, and spare his eyes;

But owns he had a stubborn spirit,
That made him trust alone to merit;
Would rise by merit to promotion;
Alas! a mere chimeric notion.
  The Doctor, if you will believe him,
Confessed a sin; (and God forgive him!)
Called up at midnight, ran to save
A blind old beggar from the grave:
But see how Satan spreads his snares;
He quite forgot to say his prayers.
He cannot help it, for his heart,
Sometimes to act the parson's part:
Quotes from the Bible many a sentence,
That moves his patients to repentance;
And, when his medicines do no good,
Supports their minds with heavenly food:
At which, however well intended,
He hears the clergy are offended;
And grown so bold behind his back,
To call him hypocrite and quack.

. . . .

I own the moral not exact,
Besides, the tale is false, in fact;
And so absurd, that could I raise up,
From fields Elysian, fabling Æsop,
I would accuse him to his face,
For libelling the four-foot race.
Creatures of every kind but ours
Well comprehend their natural powers,
While we, whom reason ought to sway,
Mistake our talents every day.
The Ass was never known so stupid
To act the part of Tray or Cupid;
Nor leaps upon his master's lap,
There to be stroked, and fed with pap,
As Æsop would the world persuade;
He better understands his trade:
Nor comes whene'er his lady whistles,
But carries loads, and feeds on thistles.
Our author's meaning, I presume, is
A creature *bipes et implumis;*

Wherein the moralist designed
A compliment on human kind;
For here he owns, that now and then
Beasts may degenerate into men.

FROM VERSES ON THE DEATH OF DR. SWIFT

Vain human kind! fantastic race!
Thy various follies who can trace?
Self-love, ambition, envy, pride,
Their empire in our hearts divide.
Give others riches, power, and station,
'Tis all on me a usurpation.
I have no title to aspire;
Yet, when you sink, I seem the higher.
In Pope I cannot read a line
But with a sigh I wish it mine;
When he can in one couplet fix
More sense than I can do in six,
It gives me such a jealous fit
I cry, 'Pox take him and his wit!'
I grieve to be outdone by Gay
In my own humorous biting way.
Arbuthnot is no more my friend,
Who dares to irony pretend,
Which I was born to introduce,
Refined it first, and showed its use.
St. John, as well as Pultney, knows,
That I had some repute for prose;
And, till they drove me out of date,
Could maul a minister of state.
If they have mortified my pride,
And made me throw my pen aside:
If with such talents Heaven has blessed 'em,
Have I not reason to detest 'em?

. . . .

Suppose me dead; and then suppose
A club assembled at the Rose;
Where, from discourse of this and that,
I grow the subject of their chat.

And while they toss my name about,
With favour some, and some without,
One, quite indifferent in the cause,
My character impartial draws:
'The Dean, if we believe report,
Was never ill-received at court.
As for his works in verse and prose,
I own myself no judge of those;
Nor can I tell what critics thought 'em,
But this I know, all people bought 'em.
As with a moral view designed
To cure the vices of mankind,
His vein, ironically grave,
Exposed the fool, and lashed the knave.
To steal a hint was never known,
But what he writ was all his own.
'He never thought an honour done him,
Because a duke was proud to own him;
Would rather slip aside and choose
To talk with wits in dirty shoes;
Despised the fools with stars and garters,
So often seen caressing Chartres.
He never courted men in station,
Nor persons held in admiration;
Of no man's greatness was afraid,
Because he sought for no man's aid.
Though trusted long in great affairs,
He gave himself no haughty airs.
Without regarding private ends,
Spent all his credit for his friends;
And only chose the wise and good;
No flatterers; no allies in blood:
But succoured virtue in distress,
And seldom failed of good success;
As numbers in their hearts must own,
Who, but for him, had been unknown.

. . . .

'Perhaps I may allow the Dean
Had too much satire in his vein;
And seemed determined not to starve it,
Because no age could more deserve it.

Yet malice never was his aim;
He lashed the vice, but spared the name;
No individual could resent,
Where thousands equally were meant;
His satire points at no defect,
But what all mortals may correct;
For he abhorred that senseless tribe
Who call it humour when they gibe:
He spared a hump, or crooked nose,
Whose owners set not up for beaux.
True genuine dulness moved his pity,
Unless it offered to be witty.
Those who their ignorance confessed,
He never offended with a jest;
But laughed to hear an idiot quote
A verse from Horace learned by rote.
'He knew a hundred pleasing stories,
With all the turns of Whigs and Tories:
Was cheerful to his dying day;
And friends would let him have his way.
'He gave the little wealth he had
To build a house for fools and mad;
And showed by one satiric touch,
No nation wanted it so much.'

CHARLES WESLEY

FOR CHRISTMAS-DAY

Hark! how all the welkin rings
'Glory to the King of kings!
Peace on earth, and mercy mild,
God and sinners reconciled!'

Joyful, all ye nations, rise,
Join the triumph of the skies;
Universal nature say,
'Christ the Lord is born to-day!'

Christ, by highest Heaven adored;
Christ, the everlasting Lord;
Late in time behold Him come,
Offspring of a virgin's womb!

Veiled in flesh the Godhead see;
Hail, th' incarnate Deity,
Pleased as man with men to appear,
Jesus, our Immanuel here!

Hail! the heavenly Prince of Peace!
Hail! the Sun of Righteousness!
Light and life to all He brings,
Risen with healing in His wings.

Mild He lays His glory by,
Born that man no more may die,
Born to raise the sons of earth,
Born to give them second birth.

Come, Desire of Nations, come,
Fix in us Thy humble home!
Rise, the Woman's conquering Seed,
Bruise in us the Serpent's head!

Now display Thy saving power,
Ruined nature now restore,
Now in mystic union join
Thine to ours, and ours to Thine!

Adam's likeness, Lord, efface;
Stamp Thy image in its place;
Second Adam from above,
Reinstate us in Thy love!

Let us Thee, though lost, regain,
Thee, the Life, the Inner Man:
O! to all Thyself impart,
Formed in each believing heart!

FOR EASTER-DAY

'Christ the Lord is risen to-day,'
Sons of men and angels say:
Raise your joys and triumphs high,
Sing, ye heavens, and earth reply.

Love's redeeming work is done,
Fought the fight, the battle won:
Lo! our Sun's eclipse is o'er;
Lo! He sets in blood no more.

Vain the stone, the watch, the seal;
Christ hath burst the gates of hell!
Death in vain forbids His rise;
Christ hath opened Paradise!

Lives again our glorious King:
Where, O Death, is now thy sting?
Dying once, He all doth save:
Where thy victory, O Grave?

Soar we now where Christ has led,
Following our exalted Head;
Made like Him, like Him we rise;
Ours the Cross, the grave, the skies.

What though once we perished all,
Partners in our parents' fall?
Second life we all receive,
In our Heavenly Adam live.

Risen with Him, we upward move;
Still we seek the things above;
Still pursue, and kiss the Son
Seated on His Father's Throne.

Scarce on earth a thought bestow,
Dead to all we leave below;
Heaven our aim, and loved abode,
Hid our life with Christ in God:

Hid, till Christ our Life appear
Glorious in His members here;
Joined to Him, we then shall shine,
All immortal, all divine.

Hail the Lord of Earth and Heaven!
Praise to Thee by both be given!
Thee we greet triumphant now!
Hail, the Resurrection Thou!

King of glory, Soul of bliss!
Everlasting life is this,
Thee to know, Thy power to prove,
Thus to sing, and thus to love!

IN TEMPTATION

Jesu, lover of my soul,
  Let me to Thy bosom fly,
While the nearer waters roll,
  While the tempest still is high!
Hide me, O my Saviour, hide,
  Till the storm of life is past,
Safe into the haven guide;
  O receive my soul at last!

Other refuge have I none;
  Hangs my helpless soul on Thee;
Leave, ah! leave me not alone,
  Still support and comfort me!
All my trust on Thee is stayed,
  All my help from Thee I bring:
Cover my defenceless head
  With the shadow of Thy wing!

Wilt Thou not regard my call?
  Wilt Thou not accept my prayer?
Lo! I sink, I faint, I fall!
  Lo! on Thee I cast my care!

Reach me out Thy gracious hand!
  While I of Thy strength receive,
Hoping against hope I stand,
  Dying, and behold I live!

Thou, O Christ, art all I want;
  More than all in Thee I find:
Raise the fallen, cheer the faint,
  Heal the sick, and lead the blind!
Just and holy is Thy Name;
  I am all unrighteousness;
False and full of sin I am,
  Thou art full of truth and grace.

Plenteous grace with Thee is found,
  Grace to cover all my sin;
Let the healing streams abound;
  Make and keep me pure within!
Thou of Life the Fountain art,
Freely let me take of Thee;
Spring Thou up within my heart!
  Rise to all eternity!

WRESTLING JACOB

Come, O thou Traveller unknown,
  Whom still I hold, but cannot see;
My company before is gone,
  And I am left alone with Thee;
With Thee all night I mean to stay,
And wrestle till the break of day.

I need not tell Thee who I am,
  My misery or sin declare;
Thyself hast called me by my name;
  Look on Thy hands, and read it there!
But who, I ask Thee, who art Thou?
Tell me Thy name, and tell me now.

In vain Thou strugglest to get free,
  I never will unloose my hold;
Art Thou the Man that died for me?
  The secret of Thy love unfold.

Wrestling, I will not let Thee go,
Till I Thy name, Thy nature know.

Wilt Thou not yet to me reveal
  Thy new, unutterable name?
Tell me, I still beseech Thee, tell:
  To know it now, resolved I am:
Wrestling, I will not let Thee go,
Till I Thy name, Thy nature know.

'Tis all in vain to hold Thy tongue,
  Or touch the hollow of my thigh;
Though every sinew be unstrung,
  Out of my arms Thou shalt not fly;
Wrestling, I will not let Thee go,
Till I Thy name, Thy nature know.

What though my shrinking flesh complain,
  And murmur to contend so long?
I rise superior to my pain;
  When I am weak, then I am strong:
And when my all of strength shall fail,
I shall with the God-Man prevail.

My strength is gone; my nature dies;
  I sink beneath Thy weighty hand,
Faint to revive, and fall to rise;
  I fall, and yet by faith I stand:
I stand, and will not let Thee go,
Till I Thy name, Thy nature know.

Yield to me now, for I am weak,
  But confident in self-despair;
Speak to my heart, in blessings speak,
  Be conquered by my instant prayer!
Speak, or Thou never hence shalt move,
And tell me, if Thy name is Love?

'Tis Love! 'tis Love! Thou diedst for me!
  I hear Thy whisper in my heart!
The morning breaks, the shadows flee;
  Pure universal Love Thou art!

To me, to all, Thy bowels move;
Thy nature, and Thy name, is Love!

My prayer hath power with God; the grace
  Unspeakable I now receive;
Through faith I see Thee face to face,
  I see Thee face to face, and live:
In vain I have not wept and strove;
Thy nature, and Thy name, is Love.

I know Thee, Saviour, who Thou art;
  Jesus, the feeble sinner's friend!
Nor wilt Thou with the night depart,
  But stay, and love me to the end!
Thy mercies never shall remove,
Thy nature, and Thy name, is Love!

The Sun of Righteousness on me
  Hath rose, with healing in His wings;
Withered my nature's strength, from Thee
  My soul its life and succour brings;
My help is all laid up above;
Thy nature, and Thy name, is Love.

Contented now upon my thigh
  I halt, till life's short journey end;
All helplessness, all weakness, I
  On Thee alone for strength depend;
Nor have I power from Thee to move;
Thy nature, and Thy name, is Love.

Lame as I am, I take the prey,
  Hell, earth, and sin, with ease o'ercome;
I leap for joy, pursue my way,
  And as a bounding hart fly home!
Through all eternity to prove,
Thy nature, and Thy name, is Love!

ROBERT BLAIR

From THE GRAVE

See yonder hallowed fane;—the pious work
Of names once famed, now dubious or forgot,
And buried midst the wreck of things which were;
There lie interred the more illustrious dead.
The wind is up: hark! how it howls! Methinks
Till now I never heard a sound so dreary:
Doors creak, and windows clap, and night's foul bird,
Rooked in the spire, screams loud: the gloomy aisles,
Black-plastered, and hung round with shreds of 'scutcheons
And tattered coats of arms, send back the sound
Laden with heavier airs, from the low vaults,
The mansions of the dead.—Roused from their slumbers,
In grim array the grisly spectres rise,
Grin horrible, and, obstinately sullen,
Pass and repass, hushed as the foot of night.
Again the screech-owl shrieks: ungracious sound!
I'll hear no more; it makes one's blood run chill.

. . . .

Oft in the lone churchyard at night I've seen,
By glimpse of moonshine chequering through the trees,
The school-boy, with his satchel in his hand,
Whistling aloud to bear his courage up,
And lightly tripping o'er the long flat stones,
(With nettles skirted, and with moss o'ergrown,)
That tell in homely phrase who lie below.
Sudden he starts, and hears, or thinks he hears,
The sound of something purring at his heels;
Full fast he flies, and dares not look behind him,
Till out of breath he overtakes his fellows;
Who gather round, and wonder at the tale
Of horrid apparition, tall and ghastly,
That walks at dead of night, or takes his stand
O'er some new-opened grave; and (strange to tell!)
Evanishes at crowing of the cock.

The new-made widow, too, I've sometimes spied,
Sad sight! slow moving o'er the prostrate dead:
Listless, she crawls along in doleful black,
Whilst bursts of sorrow gush from either eye,
Fast falling down her now untasted cheek:
Prone on the lowly grave of the dear man
She drops; whilst busy, meddling memory,
In barbarous succession musters up
The past endearments of their softer hours,
Tenacious of its theme. Still, still she thinks
She sees him, and indulging the fond thought,
Clings yet more closely to the senseless turf,
Nor heeds the passenger who looks that way.

. . . .

When the dread trumpet sounds, the slumbering dust,
Not unattentive to the call, shall wake,
And every joint possess its proper place
With a new elegance of form unknown
To its first state. Nor shall the conscious soul
Mistake its partner, but, amidst the crowd
Singling its other half, into its arms
Shall rush with all the impatience of a man
That's new come home, who having long been absent
With haste runs over every different room
In pain to see the whole. Thrice happy meeting!
Nor time nor death shall part them ever more.
'Tis but a night, a long and moonless night,
We make the grave our bed, and then are gone.

Thus at the shut of even the weary bird
Leaves the wide air and, in some lonely brake,
Cowers down and dozes till the dawn of day,
Then claps his well-fledged wings and bears away.

WILLIAM WHITEHEAD

From ON RIDICULE

Our mirthful age, to all extremes a prey,
Even courts the lash, and laughs her pains away,
Declining worth imperial wit supplies,
And Momus triumphs, while Astræa flies.
No truth so sacred, banter cannot hit,
No fool so stupid but he aims at wit.
Even those whose breasts ne'er planned one virtuous deed,
Nor raised a thought beyond the earth they tread:
Even those can censure, those can dare deride
A Bacon's avarice, or a Tully's pride;
And sneer at human checks by Nature given.
To curb perfection e'er it rival Heaven:
Nay, chiefly such in these low arts prevail,
Whose want of talents leaves them time to raid.
Born for no end, they worse than useless grow,
(As waters poison, if they cease to flow;)
And pests become, whom kinder fate designed
But harmless expletives of human kind.
See with what zeal th' insidious task they ply!
Where shall the prudent, where the virtuous fly?
Lurk as ye can, if they direct the ray,
The veriest atoms in the sunbeams play.
No venial slip their quick attention 'scapes;
They trace each Proteus through his hundred shapes;
To Mirth's tribunal drag the caitiff train,
Where Mercy sleeps, and Nature pleads in vain.

. . . .

Here then we fix, and lash without control
These mental pests, and hydras of the soul;
Acquired ill-nature, ever prompt debate,
A zeal for slander, and deliberate hate:
These court contempt, proclaim the public foe,
And each, Ulysses like, should aim the blow.
Yet sure, even here, our motives should be known:
Rail we to check his spleen, or ease our own?

Does injured virtue every shaft supply,
Arm the keen tongue, and flush th' erected eye?
Or do we from ourselves ourselves disguise?
And act, perhaps, the villain we chastise?
Hope we to mend him? hopes, alas, how vain!
He feels the lash, not listens to the rein.
'Tis dangerous too, in these licentious times,
Howe'er severe the smile, to sport with crimes.
Vices when ridiculed, experience says,
First lose that horror which they ought to raise,
Grow by degrees approved, and almost aim at praise.

. . . .

[The] fear of man, in his most mirthful mood,
May make us hypocrites, but seldom good.

. . . .

Besides, in men have varying passions made
Such nice confusions, blending light with shade,
That eager zeal to laugh the vice away
May hurt some virtue's intermingling ray.

. . . .

Then let good-nature every charm exert,
And while it mends it, win th' unfolding heart.
Let moral mirth a face of triumph wear,
Yet smile unconscious of th' extorted tear.
See with what grace instructive satire flows,
Politely keen, in Clio's numbered prose!
That great example should our zeal excite,
And censors learn from Addison to write.
So, in our age, too prone to sport with pain,
Might soft humanity resume her reign;
Pride without rancour feel th' objected fault,
And folly blush, as willing to be taught;
Critics grow mild, life's witty warfare cease,
And true good-nature breathe the balm of peace.

THE ENTHUSIAST

Once—I remember well the day,
'Twas ere the blooming sweets of May
  Had lost their freshest hues,
When every flower on every hill,
In every vale, had drank its fill
  Of sunshine and of dews.

In short, 'twas that sweet season's prime
When Spring gives up the reins of time
To Summer's glowing hand,
And doubting mortals hardly know
By whose command the breezes blow
  Which fan the smiling land.

'Twas then, beside a greenwood shade
Which clothed a lawn's aspiring head,
  I urged my devious way,
With loitering steps regardless where,
So soft, so genial was the air,
  So wondrous bright the day.

And now my eyes with transport rove
O'er all the blue expanse above,
  Unbroken by a cloud!
And now beneath delighted pass,
Where winding through the deep-green grass
  A full-brimmed river flowed.

I stop, I gaze; in accents rude,
To thee, serenest Solitude,
  Bursts forth th' unbidden lay;
'Begone vile world! the learned, the wise,
The great, the busy, I despise,
  And pity even the gay.

'These, these are joys alone, I cry,
'Tis here, divine Philosophy,
  Thou deign'st to fix thy throne!
Here contemplation points the road
Through nature's charms to nature's God!
  These, these are joys alone!

'Adieu, ye vain low-thoughted cares,
Ye human hopes, and human fears,
  Ye pleasures and ye pains!'
While thus I spake, o'er all my soul
A philosophic calmness stole,
  A stoic stillness reigns.

The tyrant passions all subside,
Fear, anger, pity, shame, and pride,
  No more my bosom move;
Yet still I felt, or seemed to feel
A kind of visionary zeal
  Of universal love.

When lo! a voice, a voice I hear!
'Twas Reason whispered in my ear
  These monitory strains:
'What mean'st thou, man? wouldst thou unbind
The ties which constitute thy kind,
  The pleasures and the pains?

'The same Almighty Power unseen,
Who spreads the gay or solemn scene
  To contemplation's eye,
Fixed every movement of the soul,
Taught every wish its destined goal,
  And quickened every joy.

'He bids the tyrant passions rage,
He bids them war eternal wage,
  And combat each his foe:
Till from dissensions concords rise,
And beauties from deformities,
  And happiness from woe.

'Art thou not man, and dar'st thou find
A bliss which leans not to mankind?
  Presumptuous thought and vain
Each bliss unshared is unenjoyed,
Each power is weak unless employed
  Some social good to gain.

'Shall light and shade, and warmth and air,
With those exalted joys compare
  Which active virtue feels,
When on she drags, as lawful prize,
Contempt, and Indolence, and Vice,
  At her triumphant wheels?

'As rest to labour still succeeds,
To man, whilst virtue's glorious deeds
  Employ his toilsome day,
This fair variety of things
Are merely life's refreshing springs,
  To sooth him on his way.

'Enthusiast go, unstring thy lyre,
In vain thou sing'st if none admire,
  How sweet soe'er the strain.
And is not thy o'erflowing mind,
Unless thou mixest with thy kind,
  Benevolent in vain?

'Enthusiast go, try every sense,
If not thy bliss, thy excellence,
  Thou yet hast learned to scan;
At least thy wants, thy weakness know,
And see them all uniting show
  That man was made for man.'

MARK AKENSIDE

From THE PLEASURES OF IMAGINATION

[The Æsthetic and Moral Influence of Nature]

Fruitless is the attempt,
By dull obedience and by creeping toil
Obscure, to conquer the severe ascent
Of high Parnassus. Nature's kindling breath
Must fire the chosen genius; Nature's hand

Must string his nerves, and imp his eagle-wings,
Impatient of the painful steep, to soar
High as the summit, there to breathe at large
Ethereal air, with bards and sages old,
Immortal sons of praise.

. . . .

Even so did Nature's hand
To certain species of external things
Attune the finer organs of the mind:
So the glad impulse of congenial powers,
Or of sweet sounds, or fair-proportioned form,
The grace of motion, or the bloom of light,
Thrills through imagination's tender frame,
From nerve to nerve; all naked and alive
They catch the spreading rays, till now the soul
At length discloses every tuneful spring,
To that harmonious movement from without
Responsive.

. . . .

What then is taste, but these internal powers
Active, and strong, and feelingly alive
To each fine impulse? a discerning sense
Of decent and sublime, with quick disgust
From things deformed, or disarranged, or gross
In species? This, nor gems, nor stores of gold,
Nor purple state, nor culture can bestow;
But God alone, when first his active hand
Imprints the secret bias of the soul.
He, mighty parent wise and just in all,
Free as the vital breeze or light of heaven,
Reveals the charms of nature. Ask the swain
Who journey's homeward from a summer day's
Long labour, why, forgetful of his toils
And due repose, he loiters to behold
The sunshine gleaming as through amber clouds
O'er all the western sky; full soon, I ween,
His rude expression and untutored airs,
Beyond the power of language, will unfold
The form of beauty smiling at his heart—
How lovely! how commanding!

. . . .

Oh! blest of Heaven, whom not the languid songs
Of Luxury, the siren! nor the bribes
Of sordid Wealth, nor all the gaudy spoils
Of pageant Honour, can seduce to leave
Those ever-blooming sweets which, from the store
Of Nature, fair Imagination culls
To charm th' enlivened soul! What though not all
Of mortal offspring can attain the heights
Of envied life, though only few possess
Patrician treasures or imperial state;
Yet Nature's care, to all her children just,
With richer treasure and an ampler state,
Endows at large whatever happy man
Will deign to use them. His the city's pomp;
The rural honours his. Whate'er adorns
The princely dome, the column and the arch,
The breathing marbles and the sculptured gold,
Beyond the proud possessor's narrow claim,
His tuneful breast enjoys. For him the Spring
Distils her dews, and from the silken gem
Its lucid leaves unfolds; for him the hand
Of Autumn tinges every fertile branch
With blooming gold, and blushes like the morn.
Each passing hour sheds tribute from her wings;
And still new beauties meet his lonely walk,
And loves unfelt attract him. Not a breeze
Flies o'er the meadow, not a cloud imbibes
The setting sun's effulgence, not a strain
From all the tenants of the warbling shade
Ascends, but whence his bosom can partake
Fresh pleasure unreproved. Nor thence partakes
Fresh pleasure only; for th' attentive mind,
By this harmonious action on her powers,
Becomes herself harmonious: wont so oft
In outward things to meditate the charm
Of sacred order, soon she seeks at home
To find a kindred order, to exert
Within herself this elegance of love,
This fair-inspired delight; her tempered powers
Refine at length, and every passion wears
A chaster, milder, more attractive mien.
  But if to ampler prospects, if to gaze

On Nature's form where, negligent of all
These lesser graces, she assumes the part
Of that Eternal Majesty that weighed
The world's foundations, if to these the mind
Exalts her daring eye; then mightier far
Will be the change, and nobler. Would the forms
Of servile custom cramp her generous powers?
Would sordid policies, the barbarous growth
Of ignorance and rapine, bow her down
To tame pursuits, to indolence and fear?
Lo! she appeals to Nature, to the winds
And rolling waves, the sun's unwearied course,
The elements and seasons: all declare
For what th' Eternal Maker has ordained
The powers of man: we feel within ourselves
His energy divine: he tells the heart
He meant, he made us, to behold and love
What he beholds and loves, the general orb
Of life and being; to be great like him,
Beneficent and active. Thus the men
Whom nature's works can charm, with God himself
Hold converse; grow familiar, day by day,
With his conceptions; act upon his plan;
And form to his, the relish of their souls.

JOSEPH WARTON

From THE ENTHUSIAST; OR, THE LOVER OF NATURE

Ye green-robed Dryads, oft at dusky eve
By wondering shepherds seen, to forests brown
To unfrequented meads, and pathless wilds,
Lead me from gardens decked with art's vain pomps.
Can gilt alcoves, can marble-mimic gods,
Parterres embroidered, obelisks, and urns
Of high relief; can the long, spreading lake,
Or vista lessening to the sight; can Stow,

With all her Attic fanes, such raptures raise,
As the thrush-haunted copse, where lightly leaps
The fearful fawn the rustling leaves along,
And the brisk squirrel sports from bough to bough,
While from an hollow oak, whose naked roots
O'erhang a pensive rill, the busy bees
Hum drowsy lullabies? The bards of old,
Fair Nature's friends, sought such retreats, to charm
Sweet Echo with their songs; oft too they met
In summer evenings, near sequestered bowers,
Or mountain nymph, or Muse, and eager learnt
The moral strains she taught to mend mankind.

. . . .

Rich in her weeping country's spoils, Versailles
May boast a thousand fountains, that can cast
The tortured waters to the distant heavens:
Yet let me choose some pine-topped precipice
Abrupt and shaggy, whence a foamy stream,
Like Anio, tumbling roars; or some bleak heath,
Where straggling stands the mournful juniper,
Or yew-tree scathed; while in clear prospect round
From the grove's bosom spires emerge, and smoke
In bluish wreaths ascends, ripe harvests wave,
Low, lonely cottages, and ruined tops
Of Gothic battlements appear, and streams
Beneath the sunbeams twinkle.

. . . .

Happy the first of men, ere yet confined
To smoky cities; who in sheltering groves,
Warm caves, and deep-sunk valleys lived and loved,
By cares unwounded; what the sun and showers,
And genial earth untillaged, could produce,
They gathered grateful, or the acorn brown
Or blushing berry; by the liquid lapse
Of murmuring waters called to slake their thirst,
Or with fair nymphs their sun-brown limbs to bathe;
With nymphs who fondly clasped their favourite youths,
Unawed by shame, beneath the beechen shade,
Nor wiles nor artificial coyness knew.
Then doors and walls were not; the melting maid
Nor frown of parents feared, nor husband's threats;

Nor had cursed gold their tender hearts allured:
Then beauty was not venal. Injured Love,
Oh! whither, god of raptures, art thou fled?

. . . .

What are the lays of artful Addison,
Coldly correct, to Shakespeare's warblings wild?
Whom on the winding Avon's willowed banks
Fair Fancy found, and bore the smiling babe
To a close cavern (still the shepherds show
The sacred place, whence with religious awe
They hear, returning from the field at eve,
Strange whisperings of sweet music through the air).
Here, as with honey gathered from the rock,
She fed the little prattler, and with songs
Oft soothed his wandering ears; with deep delight
On her soft lap he sat, and caught the sounds.
Oft near some crowded city would I walk,
Listening the far-off noises, rattling cars,
Loud shouts of joy, sad shrieks of sorrow, knells
Full slowly tolling, instruments of trade,
Striking my ears with one deep-swelling hum.
Or wandering near the sea, attend the sounds
Of hollow winds and ever-beating waves.
Even when wild tempests swallow up the plains,
And Boreas' blasts, big hail, and rains combine
To shake the groves and mountains, would I sit,
Pensively musing on th' outrageous crimes
That wake Heaven's vengeance: at such solemn hours,
Demons and goblins through the dark air shriek,
While Hecat, with her black-browed sisters nine,
Rides o'er the Earth, and scatters woes and death.
Then, too, they say, in drear Egyptian wilds
The lion and the tiger prowl for prey
With roarings loud! The listening traveller
Starts fear-struck, while the hollow echoing vaults
Of pyramids increase the deathful sounds.
But let me never fail in cloudless nights,
When silent Cynthia in her silver car
Through the blue concave slides, when shine the hills,
Twinkle the streams, and woods look tipped with gold,
To seek some level mead, and there invoke

Old Midnight's sister, Contemplation sage,
(Queen of the rugged brow and stern-fixt eye,)
To lift my soul above this little earth,
This folly-fettered world: to purge my ears,
That I may hear the rolling planets' song,
And tuneful turning spheres: if this be barred
The little fays, that dance in neighbouring dales,
Sipping the night-dew, while they laugh and love,
Shall charm me with aërial notes.—As thus
I wander musing, lo, what awful forms
Yonder appear! sharp-eyed Philosophy
Clad in dun robes, an eagle on his wrist,
First meets my eye; next, virgin Solitude
Serene, who blushes at each gazer's sight;
Then Wisdom's hoary head, with crutch in hand,
Trembling, and bent with age; last Virtue's self,
Smiling, in white arrayed, who with her leads
Sweet Innocence, that prattles by her side,
A naked boy!—Harassed with fear I stop,
I gaze, when Virtue thus—'Whoe'er thou art,
Mortal, by whom I deign to be beheld
In these my midnight walks; depart, and say,
That henceforth I and my immortal train
Forsake Britannia's isle; who fondly stoops
To vice, her favourite paramour.' She spoke,
And as she turned, her round and rosy neck,
Her flowing train, and long ambrosial hair,
Breathing rich odours, I enamoured view.
  O who will bear me then to western climes,
Since virtue leaves our wretched land, to fields
Yet unpolluted with Iberian swords,
The isles of innocence, from mortal view
Deeply retired, beneath a plantain's shade,
Where happiness and quiet sit enthroned,
With simple Indian swains, that I may hunt
The boar and tiger through savannahs wild,
Through fragrant deserts and through citron groves?
There fed on dates and herbs, would I despise
The far-fetched cates of luxury, and hoards
Of narrow-hearted avarice; nor heed
The distant din of the tumultuous world.

JOHN GILBERT COOPER

From THE POWER OF HARMONY

THE HARMONY OF NATURE

Hail, thrice hail!
Ye solitary seats, where Wisdom seeks
Beauty and Good, th' unseparable pair,
Sweet offspring of the sky, those emblems fair
Of the celestial cause, whose tuneful word
From discord and from chaos raised this globe
And all the wide effulgence of the day.
From him begins this beam of gay delight,
When aught harmonious strikes th' attentive mind;
In him shall end; for he attuned the frame
Of passive organs with internal sense,
To feel an instantaneous glow of joy,
When Beauty from her native seat of Heaven,
Clothed in ethereal wildness, on our plains
Descends, ere Reason with her tardy eye
Can view the form divine; and through the world
The heavenly boon to every being flows.

. . . .

Nor less admire those things, which viewed apart
Uncouth appear, or horrid; ridges black
Of shagged rocks, which hang tremendous o'er
Some barren heath; the congregated clouds
Which spread their sable skirts, and wait the wind
To burst th' embosomed storm; a leafless wood,
A mouldering ruin, lightning-blasted fields;
Nay, e'en the seat where Desolation reigns
In brownest horror; by familiar thought
Connected to this universal frame,
With equal beauty charms the tasteful soul
As the gold landscapes of the happy isles
Crowned with Hesperian fruit: for Nature formed
One plan entire, and made each separate scene

Co-operate with the general of all
In that harmonious contrast.

. . . .

From these sweet meditations on the charms
Of things external, on the genuine forms
Which blossom in creation, on the scene
Where mimic art with emulative hue
Usurps the throne of Nature unreproved,
On the just concord of mellifluent sounds;
The soul, and all the intellectual train
Of fond desires, gay hopes, or threatening fears,
Through this habitual intercourse of sense
Is harmonized within, till all is fair
And perfect; till each moral power perceives
Its own resemblance, with fraternal joy,
In every form complete, and smiling feels
Beauty and Good the same.

WILLIAM COLLINS

ODE

WRITTEN IN THE BEGINNING OF THE YEAR 1746

How sleep the brave who sink to rest
By all their country's wishes blest!
When Spring, with dewy fingers cold,
Returns to deck their hallowed mould,
She there shall dress a sweeter sod
Than Fancy's feet have ever trod.

By fairy hands their knell is rung,
By forms unseen their dirge is sung;
There Honour comes, a pilgrim grey,
To bless the turf that wraps their clay;
And Freedom shall awhile repair,
To dwell a weeping hermit there!

ODE TO EVENING

If aught of oaten stop or pastoral song
May hope, chaste Eve, to soothe thy modest ear,
Like thy own solemn springs,
Thy springs and dying gales,

O nymph reserved, while now the bright-haired sun
Sits in yon western tent, whose cloudy skirts,
With brede ethereal wove,
O'erhang his wavy bed:

Now air is hushed, save where the weak-eyed bat,
With short, shrill shriek, flits by on leathern wing;
Or where the beetle winds
His small but sullen horn,

As oft he rises 'midst the twilight path,
Against the pilgrim borne in heedless hum:
Now teach me, maid composed,
To breathe some softened strain,

Whose numbers, stealing through thy darkening vale,
May not unseemly with its stillness suit,
As, musing slow, I hail
Thy genial loved return!

For when thy folding-star, arising, shows
His paly circlet, at his warning lamp
The fragrant Hours, and elves
Who slept in flowers the day,

And many a nymph who wreathes her brows with sedge,
And sheds the freshening dew, and, lovelier still,
The pensive Pleasures sweet,
Prepare thy shadowy car.

Then lead, calm votaress, where some sheety lake
Cheers the lone heath, or some time-hallowed pile
Or upland fallows grey
Reflect its last cool gleam.

But when chill blustering winds or driving rain
Forbid my willing feet, be mine the hut
    That from the mountain's side
    Views wilds, and swelling floods,

And hamlets brown, and dim-discovered spires,
And hears their simple bell, and marks o'er all
    Thy dewy fingers draw
    The gradual dusky veil.

While Spring shall pour his showers, as oft he wont,
And bathe thy breathing tresses, meekest Eve;
    While Summer loves to sport
    Beneath thy lingering light;

While sallow Autumn fills thy lap with leaves;
Or Winter, yelling through the troublous air,
    Affrights thy shrinking train,
    And rudely rends thy robes;

So long, sure-found beneath the sylvan shed,
Shall Fancy, Friendship, Science, rose-lipped Health,
    Thy gentlest influence own,
    And hymn thy favourite name!

ODE ON THE POETICAL CHARACTER

STROPHE

As once— if not with light regard
I read aright that gifted bard
(Him whose school above the rest
His loveliest Elfin Queen has blest)—
One, only one, unrivalled fair
Might hope the magic girdle wear,
At solemn tourney hung on high,
The wish of each love-darting eye;
Lo! to each other nymph in turn applied,
As if, in air unseen, some hovering hand,
Some chaste and angel friend to virgin fame,
With whispered spell had burst the starting band,

It left unblest her loathed, dishonoured side;
Happier, hopeless fair, if never
Her baffled hand, with vain endeavour,
Had touched that fatal zone to her denied!
Young Fancy thus, to me divinest name,
To whom, prepared and bathed in heaven,
The cest of amplest power is given,
To few the godlike gift assigns
To gird their blest, prophetic loins,
And gaze her visions wild, and feel unmixed her flame!

EPODE

The band, as fairy legends say,
Was wove on that creating day
When He who called with thought to birth
Yon tented sky, this laughing earth,
And dressed with springs and forests tall,
And poured the main engirting all,
Long by the loved enthusiast wooed,
Himself in some diviner mood,
Retiring, sate with her alone,
And placed her on his sapphire throne,
The whiles, the vaulted shrine around,
Seraphic wires were heard to sound,
Now sublimest triumph swelling,
Now on love and mercy dwelling;
And she, from out the veiling cloud,
Breathed her magic notes aloud,
And thou, thou rich-haired Youth of Morn,
And all thy subject life, was born!
The dangerous passions kept aloof,
Far from the sainted growing woof:
But near it sate ecstatic Wonder,
Listening the deep applauding thunder;
And Truth, in sunny vest arrayed,
By whose the tarsel's eyes were made;
All the shadowy tribes of mind,
In braided dance, their murmurs joined,
And all the bright uncounted powers
Who feed on heaven's ambrosial flowers.
Where is the bard whose soul can now
Its high presuming hopes avow?

Where he who thinks, with rapture blind,
This hallowed work for him designed?

ANTISTROPHE

High on some cliff, to heaven up-piled,
Of rude access, of prospect wild,
Where, tangled round the jealous steep,
Strange shades o'erbrow the valleys deep,
And holy genii guard the rock,
Its glooms embrown, its springs unlock,
While on its rich ambitious head
An Eden, like his own, lies spread,
I view that oak, the fancied glades among,
By which as Milton lay, his evening ear,
From many a cloud that dropped ethereal dew,
Nigh sphered in heaven, its native strains could hear,
On which that ancient trump he reached was hung:
Thither oft, his glory greeting,
From Waller's myrtle shades retreating,
With many a vow from Hope's aspiring tongue,
My trembling feet his guiding steps pursue;
In vain—such bliss to one alone
Of all the sons of soul was known,
And Heaven and Fancy, kindred powers,
Have now o'erturned th' inspiring bowers,
Or curtained close such scene from every future view.

THE PASSIONS

AN ODE FOR MUSIC

When Music, heavenly maid, was young,
While yet in early Greece she sung,
The Passions oft, to hear her shell,
Thronged around her magic cell,
Exulting, trembling, raging, fainting,
Possessed beyond the Muse's painting;
By turns they felt the glowing mind
Disturbed, delighted, raised, refined:

Till once, 'tis said, when all were fired,
Filled with fury, rapt, inspired,
From the supporting myrtles round
They snatched her instruments of sound;
And, as they oft had heard apart
Sweet lessons of her forceful art,
Each (for madness ruled the hour)
Would prove his own expressive power.

First Fear in hand, its skill to try,
Amid the chords bewildered laid,
And back recoiled, he knew not why,
Even at the sound himself had made.

Next Anger rushed: his eyes, on fire,
In lightnings owned his secret stings;
In one rude clash he struck the lyre,
And swept with hurried hand the strings.

With woeful measures wan Despair
Low, sullen sounds his grief beguiled;
A solemn, strange, and mingled air—
'Twas sad by fits, by starts 'twas wild.

But thou, O Hope, with eyes so fair,
What was thy delightful measure?
Still it whispered promised pleasure,
And bade the lovely scenes at distance hail!
Still would her touch the strain prolong;
And from the rocks, the woods, the vale,
She called on Echo still, through all the song;
And where her sweetest theme she chose,
A soft responsive voice was heard at every close,
And Hope, enchanted, smiled, and waved her golden hair.

And longer had she sung—but with a frown
Revenge impatient rose;
He threw his blood-stained sword in thunder down,
And with a withering look
The war-denouncing trumpet took,
And blew a blast so loud and dread,
Were ne'er prophetic sounds so full of woe.

And ever and anon he beat
The doubling drum with furious heat;
And though sometimes, each dreary pause between,
Dejected Pity, at his side,
Her soul-subduing voice applied,
Yet still he kept his wild unaltered mien,
While each strained ball of sight seemed bursting from his head.
Thy numbers, Jealousy, to naught were fixed,
Sad proof of thy distressful state;
Of differing themes the veering song was mixed,
And now it courted Love, now raving called on Hate.

With eyes upraised, as one inspired,
Pale Melancholy sate retired,
And from her wild sequestered seat,
In notes by distance made more sweet,
Poured through the mellow horn her pensive soul;
And, dashing soft from rocks around,
Bubbling runnels joined the sound:
Through glades and glooms the mingled measure stole,
Or o'er some haunted stream, with fond delay,
Round an holy calm diffusing,
Love of peace and lonely musing,
In hollow murmurs died away.

But O how altered was its sprightlier tone,
When Cheerfulness, a nymph of healthiest hue,
Her bow across her shoulder flung,
Her buskins gemmed with morning dew,
Blew an inspiring air, that dale and thicket rung,
The hunter's call, to faun and dryad known!
The oak-crowned sisters, and their chaste-eyed queen,
Satyrs, and sylvan boys, were seen,
Peeping from forth their alleys green;
Brown Exercise rejoiced to hear;
And Sport leaped up, and seized his beechen spear.
Last came Joy's ecstatic trial:
He, with viny crown advancing,
First to the lively pipe his hand addressed;
But soon he saw the brisk awakening viol,
Whose sweet entrancing voice he loved the best.

They would have thought, who heard the strain,
They saw in Tempe's vale her native maids,
Amidst the festal-sounding shades,
To some unwearied minstrel dancing,
While, as his flying fingers kissed the strings,
Love framed with Mirth a gay fantastic round;
Loose were her tresses seen, her zone unbound,
And he, amidst his frolic play,
As if he would the charming air repay,
Shook thousand odours from his dewy wings.

O Music! sphere-descended maid!
Friend of Pleasure, Wisdom's aid!
Why, goddess, why, to us denied,
Lay'st thou thy ancient lyre aside?
As in that loved Athenian bower
You learned an all-commanding power,
Thy mimic soul, O nymph endeared,
Can well recall what then it heard.
Where is thy native simple heart,
Devote to Virtue, Fancy, Art?
Arise as in that elder time,
Warm, energic, chaste, sublime!
Thy wonders, in that godlike age,
Fill thy recording sister's page:
'Tis said, and I believe the tale,
Thy humblest reed could more prevail,
Had more of strength, diviner rage,
Than all which charms this laggard age,
E'en all at once together found,
Cecilia's mingled world of sound.
O bid our vain endeavours cease:
Revive the just designs of Greece;
Return in all thy simple state;
Confirm the tales her sons relate!

ODE ON THE POPULAR SUPERSTITIONS OF THE HIGHLANDS OF SCOTLAND

Considered as the Subject of Poetry

I

H——, thou return'st from Thames, whose naiads long
 Have seen thee lingering, with a fond delay,
 'Mid those soft friends, whose hearts, some future day,
Shall melt, perhaps, to hear thy tragic song.
Go, not unmindful of that cordial youth
 Whom, long-endeared, thou leav'st by Levant's side;
Together let us wish him lasting truth,
 And joy untâinted, with his destined bride.
Go! nor regardless, while these numbers boast
 My short-lived bliss, forget my social name;
But think, far off, how on the Southern coast
 I met thy friendship with an equal flame!
Fresh to that soil thou turn'st, whose every vale
 Shall prompt the poet, and his song demand:
To thee thy copious subjects ne'er shall fail;
 Thou need'st but take the pencil to thy hand,
And paint what all believe who own thy genial land.

II

There must thou wake perforce thy Doric quill;
 'Tis Fancy's land to which thou sett'st thy feet,
 Where still, 'tis said, the fairy people meet
Beneath each birken shade on mead or hill.
There each trim lass that skims the milky store
 To the swart tribes their creamy bowl allots;
By night they sip it round the cottage door,
 While airy minstrels warble jocund notes.
There every herd, by sad experience, knows
 How, winged with fate, their elf-shot arrows fly;
When the sick ewe her summer food foregoes,
 Or, stretched on earth, the heart-smit heifers lie.
Such airy beings awe th' untutored swain:
 Nor thou, though learn'd, his homelier thoughts neglect;
Let thy sweet Muse the rural faith sustain:
 These are the themes of simple, sure effect,

That add new conquests to her boundless reign,
And fill, with double force, her heart-commanding strain.

III

Even yet preserved, how often may'st thou hear,
  Where to the pole the boreal mountains run,
  Taught by the father to his listening son,
Strange lays, whose power had charmed a Spenser's ear.
At every pause, before thy mind possessed,
  Old Runic bards shall seem to rise around,
With uncouth lyres, in many-coloured vest,
  Their matted hair with boughs fantastic crowned:
Whether thou bid'st the well-taught hind repeat
  The choral dirge that mourns some chieftain brave,
When every shrieking maid her bosom beat,
  And strewed with choicest herbs his scented grave;
Or whether, sitting in the shepherd's shiel,
  Thou hear'st some sounding tale of war's alarms,
When, at the bugle's call, with fire and steel,
  The sturdy clans poured forth their bony swarms,
And hostile brothers met to prove each other's arms.

IV

'Tis thine to sing, how, framing hideous spells,
  In Skye's lone isle the gifted wizard seer,
  Lodged in the wintry cave with [Fate's fell spear;]
Or in the depth of Uist's dark forests dwells:
How they whose sight such dreary dreams engross,
  With their own visions oft astonished droop,
When o'er the watery strath or quaggy moss
  They see the gliding ghosts unbodied troop;
Or if in sports, or on the festive green,
  Their [destined] glance some fated youth descry,
Who, now perhaps in lusty vigour seen
  And rosy health, shall soon lamented die.
For them the viewless forms of air obey,
  Their bidding heed, and at their beck repair.
They know what spirit brews the stormful day,
  And, heartless, oft like moody madness stare
To see the phantom train their secret work prepare.

V

[To monarchs dear, some hundred miles astray,
Oft have they seen Fate give the fatal blow!
The seer, in Skye, shrieked as the blood did flow,
When headless Charles warm on the scaffold lay!
As Boreas threw his young Aurora forth,
In the first year of the first George's reign,
And battles raged in welkin of the North,
They mourned in air, fell, fell Rebellion slain!
And as, of late, they joyed in Preston's fight,
Saw at sad Falkirk all their hopes near crowned,
They raved, divining, through their second sight,
Pale, red Culloden, where these hopes were drowned!
Illustrious William! Britain's guardian name!
One William saved us from a tyrant's stroke;
He, for a sceptre, gained heroic fame;
But thou, more glorious, Slavery's chain hast broke,
To reign a private man, and bow to Freedom's yoke!

VI

These, too, thou'lt sing! for well thy magic Muse
Can to the topmost heaven of grandeur soar!
Or stoop to wail the swain that is no more!
Ah, homely swains! your homeward steps ne'er lose;
Let not dank Will mislead you to the heath:
Dancing in mirky night, o'er fen and lake,
He glows, to draw you downward to your death,
In his bewitched, low, marshy willow brake!]
What though far off, from some dark dell espied,
His glimmering mazes cheer th' excursive sight,
Yet turn, ye wanderers, turn your steps aside,
Nor trust the guidance of that faithless light;
For, watchful, lurking 'mid th' unrustling reed,
At those mirk hours the wily monster lies,
And listens oft to hear the passing steed,
And frequent round him rolls his sullen eyes,
If chance his savage wrath may some weak wretch surprise.

VII

Ah, luckless swain, o'er all unblest indeed!
Whom, late bewildered in the dank, dark fen,
Far from his flocks and smoking hamlet then,
To that sad spot [where hums the sedgy weed:]

On him, enraged, the fiend, in angry mood,
Shall never look with Pity's kind concern,
But instant, furious, raise the whelming flood
O'er its drowned bank, forbidding all return.
Or, if he meditate his wished escape
To some dim hill that seems uprising near,
To his faint eye the grim and grisly shape,
In all its terrors clad, shall wild appear.
Meantime, the watery surge shall round him rise,
Poured sudden forth from every swelling source.
What now remains but tears and hopeless sighs?
His fear-shook limbs have lost their youthly force,
And down the waves he floats, a pale and breathless corse.

VIII

For him, in vain, his anxious wife shall wait,
Or wander forth to meet him on his way;
For him, in vain, at to-fall of the day,
His babes shall linger at th' unclosing gate.
Ah, ne'er shall he return! Alone, if night
Her travelled limbs in broken slumbers steep,
With dropping willows dressed, his mournful sprite
Shall visit sad, perchance, her silent sleep:
Then he, perhaps, with moist and watery hand,
Shall fondly seem to press her shuddering cheek,
And with his blue-swoln face before her stand,
And, shivering cold, these piteous accents speak:
'Pursue, dear wife, thy daily toils pursue
At dawn or dusk, industrious as before;
Nor e'er of me one hapless thought renew,
While I lie weltering on the oziered shore,
Drowned by the kelpie's wrath, nor e'er shall aid thee more!'

IX

Unbounded is thy range; with varied style
Thy Muse may, like those feathery tribes which spring
From their rude rocks, extend her skirting wing
Round the moist marge of each cold Hebrid isle
To that hoar pile which still its ruin shows:
In whose small vaults a pigmy-folk is found,
Whose bones the delver with his spade upthrows,
And culls them, wondering, from the hallowed ground!

Or thither, where, beneath the showery West,
  The mighty kings of three fair realms are laid:
Once foes, perhaps, together now they rest;
  No slaves revere them, and no wars invade:
Yet frequent now, at midnight's solemn hour,
  The rifted mounds their yawning cells unfold,
And forth the monarchs stalk with sovereign power,
  In pageant robes, and wreathed with sheeny gold,
And on their twilight tombs aërial council hold.

X

But oh, o'er all, forget not Kilda's race,
  On whose bleak rocks, which brave the wasting tides,
  Fair Nature's daughter, Virtue, yet abides.
Go, just as they, their blameless manners trace!
Then to my ear transmit some gentle song
  Of those whose lives are yet sincere and plain,
Their bounded walks the rugged cliffs along,
  And all their prospect but the wintry main.
With sparing temperance, at the needful time,
  They drain the sainted spring, or, hunger-pressed,
Along th' Atlantic rock undreading climb,
  And of its eggs despoil the solan's nest.
Thus blest in primal innocence they live,
  Sufficed and happy with that frugal fare
Which tasteful toil and hourly danger give.
  Hard is their shallow soil, and bleak and bare;
Nor ever vernal bee was heard to murmur there!

XI

Nor need'st thou blush, that such false themes engage
  Thy gentle mind, of fairer stores possessed;
  For not alone they touch the village breast,
But filled in elder time th' historic page.
There Shakespeare's self, with every garland crowned,—
  [Flew to those fairy climes his fancy sheen!]—
In musing hour, his wayward Sisters found,
  And with their terrors dressed the magic scene.
From them he sung, when, 'mid his bold design,
  Before the Scot afflicted and aghast,
The shadowy kings of Banquo's fated line
  Through the dark cave in gleamy pageant passed.

Proceed, nor quit the tales which, simply told,
  Could once so well my answering bosom pierce;
Proceed! in forceful sounds and colours bold,
  The native legends of thy land rehearse;
To such adapt thy lyre and suit thy powerful verse.

XII

In scenes like these, which, daring to depart
  From sober truth, are still to nature true,
  And call forth fresh delight to Fancy's view,
Th' heroic muse employed her Tasso's art!
How have I trembled, when, at Tancred's stroke,
  Its gushing blood the gaping cypress poured;
When each live plant with mortal accents spoke,
  And the wild blast upheaved the vanished sword!
How have I sat, when piped the pensive wind,
  To hear his harp, by British Fairfax strung,—
Prevailing poet, whose undoubting mind
  Believed the magic wonders which he sung!
Hence at each sound imagination glows;
  [*The MS. lacks a line here.*]
Hence his warm lay with softest sweetness flows;
  Melting it flows, pure, numerous, strong, and clear,
And fills th' impassioned heart, and wins th' harmonious
    ear.

XIII

All hail, ye scenes that o'er my soul prevail,
  Ye [splendid] friths and lakes which, far away,
  Are by smooth Annan fill'd, or pastoral Tay,
Or Don's romantic springs; at distance, hail!
The time shall come when I, perhaps, may tread
  Your lowly glens, o'erhung with spreading broom,
Or o'er your stretching heaths by fancy led
[Or o'er your mountains creep, in awful gloom:]
Then will I dress once more the faded bower.
  Where Jonson sat in Drummond's [classic] shade,
Or crop from Teviot's dale each [lyric flower]
  And mourn on Yarrow's banks [where Willy's laid!]

Meantime, ye Powers that on the plains which bore
  The cordial youth, on Lothian's plains, attend,
Where'er he dwell, on hill or lowly muir,
  To him I lose your kind protection lend,
And, touched with love like mine, preserve my absent
    friend!

THOMAS WARTON

From THE PLEASURES OF MELANCHOLY

Beneath yon ruined abbey's moss-grown piles
Oft let me sit, at twilight hour of eve,
Where through some western window the pale moon
Pours her long-levelled rule of streaming light,
While sullen, sacred silence reigns around,
Save the lone screech-owl's note, who builds his bower
Amid the mouldering caverns dark and damp,
Or the calm breeze that rustles in the leaves
Of flaunting ivy, that with mantle green
Invests some wasted tower. Or let me tread
Its neighbouring walk of pines, where mused of old
The cloistered brothers: through the gloomy void
That far extends beneath their ample arch
As on I pace, religious horror wraps
My soul in dread repose. But when the world
Is clad in midnight's raven-coloured robe,
'Mid hollow charnel let me watch the flame
Of taper dim, shedding a livid glare
O'er the wan heaps, while airy voices talk
Along the glimmering walls, or ghostly shape,
At distance seen, invites with beckoning hand
My lonesome steps through the far-winding vaults.
Nor undelightful is the solemn noon
Of night, when, haply wakeful, from my couch
I start: lo, all is motionless around!
Roars not the rushing wind; the sons of men
And every beast in mute oblivion lie;
All nature's hushed in silence and in sleep:

O then how fearful is it to reflect
That through the still globe's awful solitude
No being wakes but me! till stealing sleep
My drooping temples bathes in opiate dews.
Nor then let dreams, of wanton folly born,
My senses lead through flowery paths of joy:
But let the sacred genius of the night
Such mystic visions send as Spenser saw
When through bewildering Fancy's magic maze,
To the fell house of Busyrane, he led
Th' unshaken Britomart; or Milton knew,
When in abstracted thought he first conceived
All Heaven in tumult, and the seraphim
Come towering, armed in adamant and gold.

. . . .

Through Pope's soft song though all the Graces breathe,
And happiest art adorn his Attic page,
Yet does my mind with sweeter transport glow,
As, at the root of mossy trunk reclined,
In magic Spenser's wildly-warbled song
I see deserted Una wander wide
Through wasteful solitudes and lurid heaths,
Weary, forlorn, than when the fated fair
Upon the bosom bright of silver Thames
Launches in all the lustre of brocade,
Amid the splendours of the laughing sun:
The gay description palls upon the sense,
And coldly strikes the mind with feeble bliss.

. . . .

The tapered choir, at the late hour of prayer,
Oft let me tread, while to th' according voice
The many-sounding organ peals on high
The clear slow-dittied chant or varied hymn,
Till all my soul is bathed in ecstasies
And lapped in Paradise. Or let me sit
Far in sequestered aisles of the deep dome;
There lonesome listen to the sacred sounds,
Which, as they lengthen through the Gothic vaults,
In hollow murmurs reach my ravished ear.
Nor when the lamps, expiring, yield to night,

And solitude returns, would I forsake
The solemn mansion, but attentive mark
The due clock swinging slow with sweepy sway,
Measuring Time's flight with momentary sound.

From THE GRAVE OF KING ARTHUR

[The Passing of the King]

O'er Cornwall's cliffs the tempest roared,
High the screaming sea-mew soared;
On Tintagel's topmost tower
Darksome fell the sleety shower;
Round the rough castle shrilly sung
The whirling blast, and wildly flung
On each tall rampart's thundering side
The surges of the tumbling tide:
When Arthur ranged his red-cross ranks
On conscious Camlan's crimsoned banks:
By Mordred's faithless guile decreed
Beneath a Saxon spear to bleed!
Yet in vain a paynim foe
Armed with fate the mighty blow;
For when he fell, an Elfin Queen
All in secret, and unseen,
O'er the fainting hero threw
Her mantle of ambrosial blue;
And bade her spirits bear him far,
In Merlin's agate-axled car,
To her green isle's enamelled steep
Far in the navel of the deep.
O'er his wounds she sprinkled dew
From flowers that in Arabia grew:
On a rich enchanted bed
She pillowed his majestic head;
O'er his brow, with whispers bland,
Thrice she waved an opiate wand;
And to soft music's airy sound,
Her magic curtains closed around.
There, renewed the vital spring,
Again he reigns a mighty king;

And many a fair and fragrant clime,
Blooming in immortal prime,
By gales of Eden ever fanned,
Owns the monarch's high command:
Thence to Britain shall return
(If right prophetic rolls I learn),
Born on Victory's spreading plume,
His ancient sceptre to resume;
Once more, in old heroic pride,
His barbèd courser to bestride;
His knightly table to restore,
And brave the tournaments of yore.

SONNET WRITTEN IN A BLANK LEAF OF DUGDALE'S 'MONASTICON'

Deem not devoid of elegance the sage,
By Fancy's genuine feelings unbeguiled,
Of painful pedantry the poring child,
Who turns, of these proud domes, th' historic page,
Now sunk by Time, and Henry's fiercer rage.
Think'st thou the warbling Muses never smiled
On his lone hours? Ingenuous views engage
His thoughts, on themes, unclassic falsely styled,
Intent. While cloistered Piety displays
Her mouldering roll, the piercing eye explores
New manners, and the pomp of elder days,
Whence culls the pensive bard his pictured stores.
Nor rough nor barren are the winding ways
Of hoar antiquity, but strown with flowers.

SONNET WRITTEN AT STONEHENGE

Thou noblest monument of Albion's isle!
Whether by Merlin's aid from Scythia's shore,
To Amber's fatal plain Pendragon bore,
Huge frame of giant-hands, the mighty pile,
T' entomb his Britons slain by Hengist's guile:
Or Druid priests, sprinkled with human gore,
Taught 'mid thy massy maze their mystic lore:

Or Danish chiefs, enriched with savage spoil,
To Victory's idol vast, an unhewn shrine,
Reared the rude heap: or, in thy hallowed round,
Repose the kings of Brutus' genuine line;
Or here those kings in solemn state were crowned:
Studious to trace thy wondrous origin,
We muse on many an ancient tale renowned.

SONNET TO THE RIVER LODON

Ah! what a weary race my feet have run,
Since first I trod thy banks with alders crowned,
And thought my way was all through fairy ground,
Beneath thy azure sky and golden sun,
Where first my Muse to lisp her notes begun!
While pensive Memory traces back the round,
Which fills the varied interval between;
Much pleasure, more of sorrow, marks the scene.
Sweet native stream! those skies and suns so pure
No more return, to cheer my evening road!
Yet still one joy remains: that not obscure
Nor useless, all my vacant days have flowed,
From youth's gay dawn to manhood's prime mature;
Nor with the Muse's laurel unbestowed.

THOMAS GRAY

ODE ON A DISTANT PROSPECT OF ETON COLLEGE

Ye distant spires, ye antique towers,
  That crown the watery glade,
Where grateful Science still adores
  Her Henry's holy shade;
And ye, that from the stately brow
Of Windsor's heights th' expanse below

Of grove, of lawn, of mead survey,
Whose turf, whose shade, whose flowers among
Wanders the hoary Thames along
His silver-winding way.

Ah, happy hills! ah, pleasing shade!
Ah, fields beloved in vain!
Where once my careless childhood strayed,
A stranger yet to pain!
I feel the gales that from ye blow,
A momentary bliss bestow,
As waving fresh their gladsome wing,
My weary soul they seem to soothe,
And, redolent of joy and youth,
To breathe a second spring.

Say, Father Thames, for thou hast seen
Full many a sprightly race
Disporting on thy margent green
The paths of pleasure trace,
Who foremost now delight to cleave
With pliant arm thy glassy wave?
The captive linnet which enthrall?
What idle progeny succeed
To chase the rolling circle's speed,
Or urge the flying ball?

While some on earnest business bent
Their murmuring labours ply
'Gainst graver hours, that bring constraint
To sweeten liberty:
Some bold adventurers disdain
The limits of their little reign,
And unknown regions dare descry:
Still as they run they look behind,
They hear a voice in every wind,
And snatch a fearful joy.

Gay hope is theirs by fancy fed,
Less pleasing when possessed;
The tear forgot as soon as shed,
The sunshine of the breast:

Theirs buxom health of rosy hue,
Wild wit, invention ever-new,
  And lively cheer of vigour born;
The thoughtless day, the easy night,
The spirits pure, the slumbers light,
  That fly th' approach of morn.

Alas! regardless of their doom,
  The little victims play;
No sense have they of ills to come,
  Nor care beyond to-day:
Yet see how all around 'em wait
The ministers of human fate,
  And black Misfortune's baleful train!
Ah, shew them where in ambush stand
To seize their prey the murderous band!
  Ah, tell them, they are men!

These shall the fury Passions tear,
  The vultures of the mind,
Disdainful Anger, pallid Fear,
  And Shame that skulks behind;
Or pining Love shall waste their youth,
Or Jealousy with rankling tooth,
  That inly gnaws the secret heart,
And Envy wan, and faded Care,
Grim-visaged comfortless Despair,
  And Sorrow's piercing dart.

Ambition this shall tempt to rise,
  Then whirl the wretch from high,
To bitter Scorn a sacrifice,
  And grinning Infamy.
The stings of Falsehood those shall try,
And hard Unkindness' altered eye,
  That mocks the tear it forced to flow;
And keen Remorse with blood defiled,
And moody Madness laughing wild
  Amid severest woe.

Lo, in the vale of years beneath
  A grisly troop are seen,
The painful family of Death,
  More hideous than their Queen:
This racks the joints, this fires the veins,
That every labouring sinew strains,
  Those in the deeper vitals rage:
Lo, Poverty, to fill the band,
That numbs the soul with icy hand,
  And slow-consuming Age.

To each his sufferings; all are men,
  Condemned alike to groan,
The tender for another's pain;
  The unfeeling for his own.
Yet, ah! why should they know their fate,
Since sorrow never comes too late,
  And happiness too swiftly flies?
Thought would destroy their paradise.
No more; where ignorance is bliss,
  'Tis folly to be wise.

HYMN TO ADVERSITY

Daughter of Jove, relentless power,
  Thou tamer of the human breast,
Whose iron scourge and torturing hour
  The bad affright, afflict the best!
Bound in thy adamantine chain,
The proud are taught to taste of pain,
  And purple tyrants vainly groan
With pangs unfelt before, unpitied and alone.

When first thy sire to send on earth
  Virtue, his darling child, designed,
To thee he gave the heavenly birth,
  And bade to form her infant mind.
Stern, rugged nurse! thy rigid lore
With patience many a year she bore;
What sorrow was thou bad'st her know,
And from her own she learned to melt at other's woe.

Scared at thy frown terrific, fly
  Self-pleasing Folly's idle brood,
Wild Laughter, Noise, and thoughtless Joy,
  And leave us leisure to be good:
Light they disperse, and with them go
The summer friend, the flattering foe;
By vain Prosperity received,
To her they vow their truth and are again believed.

Wisdom in sable garb arrayed,
  Immersed in rapturous thought profound,
And Melancholy, silent maid
  With leaden eye, that loves the ground,
Still on thy solemn steps attend;
Warm Charity, the genial friend,
With Justice, to herself severe,
And Pity, dropping soft the sadly-pleasing tear.

Oh, gently on thy suppliant's head,
  Dread goddess, lay thy chastening hand!
Not in thy Gorgon terrors clad,
  Nor circled with the vengeful band
(As by the impious thou art seen),
With thundering voice and threatening mien,
  With screaming Horror's funeral cry,
Despair, and fell Disease, and ghastly Poverty:

Thy form benign, O goddess, wear,
    Thy milder influence impart;
Thy philosophic train be there
    To soften, not to wound, my heart;
The generous spark extinct revive,
Teach me to love and to forgive,
Exact my own defects to scan,
What others are to feel, and know myself a man.

ELEGY

WRITTEN IN A COUNTRY CHURCHYARD

The curfew tolls the knell of parting day,
  The lowing herd winds slowly o'er the lea,
The ploughman homeward plods his weary way,
  And leaves the world to darkness and to me.

Now fades the glimmering landscape on the sight,
  And all the air a solemn stillness holds,
Save where the beetle wheels his droning flight,
  And drowsy tinklings lull the distant folds;

Save that from yonder ivy-mantled tower
  The moping owl does to the moon complain
Of such, as wandering near her secret bower,
  Molest her ancient solitary reign.

Beneath those rugged elms, that yew-tree's shade,
  Where heaves the turf in many a mouldering heap,
Each in his narrow cell forever laid,
  The rude forefathers of the hamlet sleep.

The breezy call of incense-breathing morn,
  The swallow twittering from the straw-built shed,
The cock's shrill clarion, or the echoing horn,
  No more shall rouse them from their lowly bed.

For them no more the blazing hearth shall burn,
  Or busy housewife ply her evening care:
No children run to lisp their sire's return,
  Or climb his knees the envied kiss to share.

Oft did the harvest to their sickle yield,
  Their furrow oft the stubborn glebe has broke;
How jocund did they drive their team afield!
  How bowed the woods beneath their sturdy stroke!

Let not Ambition mock their useful toil,
  Their homely joys, and destiny obscure;
Nor Grandeur hear with a disdainful smile,
  The short and simple annals of the poor.

The boast of heraldry, the pomp of power,
And all that beauty, all that wealth e'er gave,
Await alike th' inevitable hour.
The paths of glory lead but to the grave.

Nor you, ye proud, impute to these the fault,
If Memory o'er their tomb no trophies raise,
Where through the long-drawn aisle and fretted vault
The pealing anthem swells the note of praise.

Can storied urn or animated bust
Back to its mansion call the fleeting breath?
Can Honour's voice provoke the silent dust,
Or Flattery soothe the dull cold ear of Death?

Perhaps in this neglected spot is laid
Some heart once pregnant with celestial fire;
Hands that the rod of empire might have swayed,
Or waked to ecstasy the living lyre.

But Knowledge to their eyes her ample page
Rich with the spoils of time did ne'er unroll;
Chill Penury repressed their noble rage,
And froze the genial current of the soul.

Full many a gem of purest ray serene,
The dark unfathomed caves of ocean bear:
Full many a flower is born to blush unseen,
And waste its sweetness on the desert air.

Some village Hampden, that, with dauntless breast
The little tyrant of his fields withstood;
Some mute inglorious Milton here may rest,
Some Cromwell guiltless of his country's blood.

Th' applause of listening senates to command,
The threats of pain and ruin to despise,
To scatter plenty o'er a smiling land,
And read their history in a nation's eyes,

Their lot forbade: nor circumscribed alone
  Their growing virtues, but their crimes confined;
Forbade to wade through slaughter to a throne,
  And shut the gates of mercy on mankind.

The struggling pangs of conscious truth to hide,
  To quench the blushes of ingenuous shame,
Or heap the shrine of Luxury and Pride
  With incense kindled at the Muse's flame.

Far from the madding crowd's ignoble strife,
  Their sober wishes never learned to stray;
Along the cool sequestered vale of life
  They kept the noiseless tenor of their way.

Yet even these bones from insult to protect,
  Some frail memorial still erected nigh,
With uncouth rhymes and shapeless sculpture decked,
  Implores the passing tribute of a sigh.

Their names, their years, spelt by th' unlettered Muse,
  The place of fame and elegy supply:
And many a holy text around she strews,
  That teach the rustic moralist to die.

For who, to dumb forgetfulness a prey,
  This pleasing anxious being e'er resigned,
Left the warm precincts of the cheerful day,
  Nor cast one longing lingering look behind?

On some fond breast the parting soul relies,
  Some pious drops the closing eye requires;
Even from the tomb the voice of Nature cries,
  Even in our ashes live their wonted fires.

For thee, who mindful of th' unhonoured dead
  Dost in these lines their artless tale relate,
If chance, by lonely contemplation led,
  Some kindred spirit shall inquire thy fate,

Haply some hoary-headed swain may say,
  'Oft have we seen him at the peep of dawn
Brushing with hasty steps the dews away
  To meet the sun upon the upland lawn.

'There at the foot of yonder nodding beech
  That wreathes its old fantastic roots so high,
His listless length at noontide would he stretch,
  And pore upon the brook that babbles by.

'Hard by yon wood, now smiling as in scorn,
  Muttering his wayward fancies he would rove;
Now drooping, woeful-wan, like one forlorn,
  Or crazed with care, or crossed in hopeless love.

'One morn I missed him on the customed hill,
  Along the heath, and near his favourite tree;
Another came; nor yet beside the rill,
  Nor up the lawn, nor at the wood was he;

'The next with dirges due in sad array
  Slow through the church-way path we saw him borne,—
Approach and read (for thou canst read) the lay
  Graved on the stone beneath yon agèd thorn.'

THE EPITAPH

Here rests his head upon the lap of earth
  A youth to fortune and to fame unknown;
Fair Science frowned not on his humble birth,
  And Melancholy marked him for her own.

Large was his bounty, and his soul sincere;
  Heaven did a recompense as largely send:
He gave to Misery (all he had) a tear,
  He gained from Heaven ('twas all he wished) a friend.

No farther seek his merits to disclose,
  Or draw his frailties from their dread abode,
(There they alike in trembling hope repose,)—
  The bosom of his Father and his God.

THE PROGRESS OF POESY

I. 1

Awake, Æolian lyre, awake,
And give to rapture all thy trembling strings!
From Helicon's harmonious springs
A thousand rills their mazy progress take;
The laughing flowers that round them blow
Drink life and fragrance as they flow.
Now the rich stream of music winds along
Deep, majestic, smooth, and strong,
Through verdant vales and Ceres' golden reign:
Now rolling down the steep amain,
Headlong, impetuous, see it pour;
The rocks and nodding groves rebellow to the roar.

I. 2

Oh sovereign of the willing soul,
Parent of sweet and solemn-breathing airs,
Enchanting shell! the sullen Cares
And frantic Passions hear thy soft control.
On Thracia's hills the Lord of War
Has curbed the fury of his car
And dropped his thirsty lance at thy command.
Perching on the sceptred hand
Of Jove, thy magic lulls the feathered king
With ruffled plumes and flagging wing;
Quenched in dark clouds of slumber lie
The terror of his beak and lightnings of his eye.

I. 3

Thee the voice, the dance, obey,
Tempered to thy warbled lay.
O'er Idalia's velvet-green
The rosy-crownèd Loves are seen,
On Cytherea's day,
With antic Sports and blue-eyed Pleasures
Frisking light in frolic measures:
Now pursuing, now retreating,
Now in circling troops they meet;
To brisk notes in cadence beating
Glance their many-twinkling feet.

Slow melting strains their Queen's approach declare:
Where'er she turns the Graces homage pay;
With arms sublime, that float upon the air,
In gliding state she wins her easy way;
O'er her warm cheek and rising bosom move
The bloom of young Desire and purple light of Love.

II. 1

Man's feeble race what ills await:
Labour, and Penury, the racks of Pain,
Disease, and Sorrow's weeping train,
And Death, sad refuge from the storms of Fate!
The fond complaint, my song, disprove,
And justify the laws of Jove.
Say, has he given in vain the heavenly Muse?
Night, and all her sickly dews,
Her spectres wan, and birds of boding cry,
He gives to range the dreary sky;
Till down the eastern cliffs afar
Hyperion's march they spy, and glittering shafts of war.

II. 2

In climes beyond the solar road,
Where shaggy forms o'er ice-built mountains roam,
The Muse has broke the twilight-gloom
To cheer the shivering native's dull abode.
And oft, beneath the odorous shade
Of Chili's boundless forests laid,
She deigns to hear the savage youth repeat,
In loose numbers wildly sweet,
Their feather-cinctured chiefs and dusky loves.
Her track, where'er the goddess roves,
Glory pursue, and generous Shame,
Th' unconquerable Mind, and Freedom's holy flame.

II. 3

Woods that wave o'er Delphi's steep,
Isles that crown th' Ægean deep,
Fields that cool Ilissus laves,
Or where Mæander's amber waves
In lingering labyrinths creep,

How do your tuneful echoes languish,
Mute but to the voice of Anguish?
Where each old poetic mountain
Inspiration breathed around,
Every shade and hallowed fountain
Murmured deep a solemn sound;
Till the sad Nine in Greece's evil hour
Left their Parnassus for the Latian plains:
Alike they scorn the pomp of tyrant Power,
And coward Vice that revels in her chains.
When Latium had her lofty spirit lost,
They sought, O Albion! next, thy sea-encircled coast.

III. 1

Far from the sun and summer-gale,
In thy green lap was Nature's darling laid,
What time, where lucid Avon strayed,
To him the mighty mother did unveil
Her awful face: the dauntless child
Stretched forth his little arms, and smiled.
'This pencil take,' she said, 'whose colours clear
Richly paint the vernal year.
Thine too these golden keys, immortal boy!
This can unlock the gates of Joy;
Of Horror that, and thrilling Fears,
Or ope the sacred source of sympathetic tears.'

III. 2

Nor second he that rode sublime
Upon the seraph-wings of Ecstasy,
The secrets of th' abyss to spy.
He passed the flaming bounds of Place and Time:
The living throne, the sapphire blaze,
Where angels tremble while they gaze,
He saw; but, blasted with excess of light,
Closed his eyes in endless night.
Behold where Dryden's less presumptuous car
Wide o'er the fields of glory bear
Two coursers of ethereal race,
With necks in thunder clothed, and long-resounding pace!

III. 3

Hark! his hands the lyre explore:
Bright-eyed Fancy, hovering o'er,
Scatters from her pictured urn
Thoughts that breathe and words that burn.
But, ah, 'tis heard no more!
O lyre divine, what daring spirit
Wakes thee now? Though he inherit
Nor the pride nor ample pinion
That the Theban Eagle bear,
Sailing with supreme dominion
Through the azure deep of air,
Yet oft before his infant eyes would run
Such forms as glitter in the Muse's ray,
With orient hues unborrowed of the sun:
Yet shall he mount, and keep his distant way
Beyond the limits of a vulgar fate,
Beneath the good how far—but far above the great.

THE BARD

I. 1

'Ruin seize thee, ruthless king!
Confusion on thy banners wait;
Though fanned by conquest's crimson wing,
They mock the air with idle state.
Helm, nor hauberk's twisted mail,
Nor even thy virtues, tyrant, shall avail
To save thy secret soul from nightly fears,
From Cambria's curse, from Cambria's tears!'
Such were the sounds that o'er the crested pride
Of the first Edward scattered wild dismay,
As down the steep of Snowdon's shaggy side
He wound with toilsome march his long array.
Stout Gloucester stood aghast in speechless trance;
'To arms!' cried Mortimer, and couched his quivering lance.

I. 2

On a rock, whose haughty brow
Frowns o'er old Conway's foaming flood,
Robed in the sable garb of woe,
With haggard eyes the poet stood

(Loose his beard and hoary hair
Streamed, like a meteor, to the troubled air),
And with a master's hand and prophet's fire
Struck the deep sorrows of his lyre:
'Hark how each giant oak and desert cave
Sighs to the torrent's awful voice beneath!
O'er thee, oh king! their hundred arms they wave,
Revenge on thee in hoarser murmurs breathe,
Vocal no more, since Cambria's fatal day,
To high-born Hoel's harp or soft Llewellyn's lay.

I. 3

'Cold is Cadwallo's tongue,
That hushed the stormy main;
Brave Urien sleeps upon his craggy bed;
Mountains, ye mourn in vain
Modred, whose magic song
Made huge Plinlimmon bow his cloud-topped head:
On dreary Arvon's shore they lie,
Smeared with gore and ghastly pale;
Far, far aloof th' affrighted ravens sail;
The famished eagle screams, and passes by.
Dear lost companions of my tuneful art,
Dear as the light that visits these sad eyes,
Dear as the ruddy drops that warm my heart,
Ye died amidst your dying country's cries—
No more I weep: they do not sleep!
On yonder cliffs, a grisly band,
I see them sit; they linger yet
Avengers of their native land:
With me in dreadful harmony they join,
And weave with bloody hands the tissue of thy line.

II. 1

'Weave the warp and weave the woof,
The winding-sheet of Edward's race;
Give ample room and verge enough
The characters of hell to trace:
Mark the year, and mark the night,
When Severn shall re-echo with affright
The shrieks of death through Berkley's roofs that ring,
Shrieks of an agonizing king!

She-wolf of France, with unrelenting fangs,
That tear'st the bowels of thy mangled mate,
From thee be born who o'er thy country hangs
The scourge of Heaven: what terrors round him wait!
Amazement in his van, with Flight combined,
And Sorrow's faded form, and Solitude behind.

II. 2

'Mighty victor, mighty lord!
Low on his funeral couch he lies:
No pitying heart, no eye, afford
A tear to grace his obsequies.
Is the Sable Warrior fled?
Thy son is gone; he rests among the dead.
The swarm that in thy noontide beam were born?
Gone to salute the rising morn.
Fair laughs the morn and soft the zephyr blows,
While, proudly riding o'er the azure realm,
In gallant trim the gilded vessel goes,
Youth on the prow, and Pleasure at the helm,
Regardless of the sweeping Whirlwind's sway,
That, hushed in grim repose, expects his evening prey.

II. 3

'Fill high the sparkling bowl,
The rich repast prepare;
Reft of a crown, he yet may share the feast:
Close by the regal chair
Fell Thirst and Famine scowl
A baleful smile upon their baffled guest.
Heard ye the din of battle bray,
Lance to lance, and horse to horse?
Long years of havoc urge their destined course,
And through the kindred squadrons mow their way.
Ye towers of Julius, London's lasting shame,
With many a foul and midnight murther fed,
Revere his consort's faith, his father's fame,
And spare the meek usurper's holy head!
Above, below, the rose of snow,
Twined with her blushing foe, we spread:

The bristled Boar in infant gore
Wallows beneath thy thorny shade.
Now, brothers, bending o'er th' accursed loom,
Stamp we our vengeance deep, and ratify his doom!

III. 1

'Edward, lo! to sudden fate
(Weave we the woof: the thread is spun)
Half of thy heart we consecrate.
(The web is wove. The work is done.)
Stay, oh stay! nor thus forlorn
Leave me unblessed, unpitied, here to mourn!
In yon bright track, that fires the western skies,
They melt, they vanish from my eyes.
But oh! what solemn scenes on Snowdon's height,
Descending slow, their glittering skirts unroll?
Visions of glory, spare my aching sight!
Ye unborn ages, crowd not on my soul!
No more our long-lost Arthur we bewail:
All hail, ye genuine kings, Britannia's issue, hail!

III. 2

'Girt with many a baron bold,
Sublime their starry fronts they rear;
And gorgeous dames, and statesmen old
In bearded majesty, appear.
In the midst a form divine!
Her eye proclaims her of the Briton line;
Her lion-port, her awe-commanding face,
Attempered sweet to virgin-grace.
What strings symphonious tremble in the air,
What strains of vocal transport round her play!
Hear from the grave, great Taliessin, hear:
They breathe a soul to animate thy clay.
Bright Rapture calls, and, soaring as she sings,
Waves in the eye of Heaven her many-coloured wings.

III. 3

'The verse adorn again
Fierce War and faithful Love
And Truth severe, by fairy Fiction dressed.
In buskined measures move

Pale Grief and pleasing Pain,
With Horror, tyrant of the throbbing breast.
A voice, as of the cherub-choir,
Gales from blooming Eden bear;
And distant warblings lessen on my ear,
That, lost in long futurity, expire.
Fond impious man, think'st thou yon sanguine cloud,
Raised by thy breath, has quenched the orb of day?
To-morrow he repairs the golden flood,
And warms the nations with redoubled ray.
Enough for me; with joy I see
The different doom our Fates assign:
Be thine Despair and sceptred Care;
To triumph and to die are mine.'
He spoke, and headlong from the mountain's height
Deep in the roaring tide he plunged to endless night.

THE FATAL SISTERS

AN ODE FROM THE NORSE TONGUE

Now the storm begins to lower,
(Haste, the loom of hell prepare,)
Iron-sleet of arrowy shower
Hurtles in the darkened air.

Glittering lances are the loom,
Where the dusky warp we strain,
Weaving many a soldier's doom,
Orkney's woe, and Randver's bane.

See the grisly texture grow,
('Tis of human entrails made,)
And the weights, that play below,
Each a gasping warrior's head.

Shafts for shuttles, dipped in gore,
Shoot the trembling cords along.
Sword, that once a monarch bore,
Keep the tissue close and strong.

Mista black, terrific maid,
Sangrida, and Hilda see,
Join the wayward work to aid:
'Tis the woof of victory.

Ere the ruddy sun be set,
Pikes must shiver, javelins sing,
Blade with clattering buckler meet,
Hauberk crash, and helmet ring.

(Weave the crimson web of war.)
Let us go, and let us fly,
Where our friends the conflict share,
Where they triumph, where they die.

As the paths of fate we tread,
Wading through th' ensanguined field:
Gondula, and Geira, spread
O'er the youthful king your shield.

We the reins to slaughter give,
Ours to kill, and ours to spare:
Spite of danger he shall live.
(Weave the crimson web of war.)

They, whom once the desert-beach
Pent within its bleak domain,
Soon their ample sway shall stretch
O'er the plenty of the plain.

Low the dauntless earl is laid,
Gored with many a gaping wound:
Fate demands a nobler head;
Soon a king shall bite the ground.

Long his loss shall Erin weep,
Ne'er again his likeness see;
Long her strains in sorrow steep,
Strains of immortality!

Horror covers all the heath,
Clouds of carnage blot the sun.
Sisters, weave the web of death;
Sisters, cease, the work is done.

Hail the task, and hail the hands!
Songs of joy and triumph sing!
Joy to the victorious bands;
Triumph to the younger king.

Mortal, thou that hear'st the tale,
Learn the tenor of our song.
Scotland, through each winding vale
Far and wide the notes prolong.

Sisters, hence with spurs of speed:
Each her thundering falchion wield;
Each bestride her sable steed.
Hurry, hurry to the field.

ODE ON THE PLEASURE ARISING FROM VICISSITUDE

Now the golden Morn aloft
  Waves her dew-bespangled wing;
With vermeil cheek and whisper soft
  She wooes the tardy Spring;
Till April starts, and calls around
The sleeping fragrance from the ground,
And lightly o'er the living scene
Scatters his freshest, tenderest green.

New-born flocks, in rustic dance,
  Frisking ply their feeble feet;
Forgetful of their wintry trance,
  The birds his presence greet;
But chief the sky-lark warbles high
His trembling, thrilling ecstasy,
And, lessening from the dazzled sight,
Melts into air and liquid light.

Rise, my soul! on wings of fire
  Rise the rapturous choir among!
Hark! 'tis Nature strikes the lyre,
  And leads the general song.
[*Four lines lacking in the MS.*]

Yesterday the sullen year
  Saw the snowy whirlwind fly;
Mute was the music of the air,
  The herd stood drooping by:
Their raptures now that wildly flow
No yesterday nor morrow know;
'Tis man alone that joy descries
With forward and reverted eyes.

Smiles on past Misfortune's brow
  Soft Reflection's hand can trace,
And o'er the cheek of Sorrow throw
  A melancholy grace;
While Hope prolongs our happier hour,
Or deepest shades, that dimly lower
And blacken round our weary way,
Gilds with a gleam of distant day.

Still where rosy Pleasure leads
  See a kindred Grief pursue;
Behind the steps that Misery treads,
  Approaching Comfort view:
The hues of bliss more brightly glow
Chastised by sabler tints of woe,
And, blended, form with artful strife
The strength and harmony of life.

See the wretch that long has tossed
  On the thorny bed of pain
At length repair his vigour lost
  And breathe and walk again:
The meanest flowret of the vale,
The simplest note that swells the gale,
The common sun, the air, the skies,
To him are opening Paradise.

Humble Quiet builds her cell
  Near the source whence Pleasure flows;
She eyes the clear crystalline well,
  And tastes it as it goes.

[*The rest is lacking.*]

SAMUEL JOHNSON

From THE VANITY OF HUMAN WISHES

IN IMITATION OF THE TENTH SATIRE OF JUVENAL

In full-blown dignity see Wolsey stand,
Law in his voice, and fortune in his hand:
To him the church, the realm, their powers consign;
Through him the rays of regal bounty shine;
Turned by his nod the stream of honour flows;
His smile alone security bestows.
Still to new heights his restless wishes tower;
Claim leads to claim, and power advances power;
Till conquest unresisted ceased to please,
And rights submitted left him none to seize.
At length his sovereign frowns—the train of state
Mark the keen glance, and watch the sign to hate:
Where'er he turns he meets a stranger's eye;
His suppliants scorn him, and his followers fly;
Now drops at once the pride of awful state—
The golden canopy, the glittering plate,
The regal palace, the luxurious board,
The liveried army, and the menial lord.
With age, with cares, with maladies oppressed,
He seeks the refuge of monastic rest.
Grief aids disease, remembered folly stings,
And his last sighs reproach the faith of kings.

. . . .

When first the college rolls receive his name,
The young enthusiast quits his ease for fame;
Through all his veins the fever of renown
Spreads from the strong contagion of the gown;

O'er Bodley's dome his future labours spread,
And Bacon's mansion trembles o'er his head.
Are these thy views? Proceed, illustrious youth,
And virtue guard thee to the throne of truth!
Yet should thy soul indulge the generous heat,
Till captive science yields her last retreat;
Should reason guide thee with her brightest ray,
And pour on misty doubt resistless day;
Should no false kindness lure to loose delight,
Nor praise relax, nor difficulty fright;
Should tempting novelty thy cell refrain,
And sloth effuse her opiate fumes in vain;
Should beauty blunt on fops her fatal dart,
Nor claim the triumph of a lettered heart;
Should no disease thy torpid veins invade,
Nor melancholy's phantoms haunt thy shade;
Yet hope not life from grief or danger free,
Nor think the doom of man reversed for thee:
Deign on the passing world to turn thine eyes,
And pause awhile from letters, to be wise;
There mark what ills the scholar's life assail,
Toil, envy, want, the patron, and the jail.
See nations slowly wise, and meanly just,
To buried merit raise the tardy bust!

. . . .

On what foundation stands the warrior's pride,
How just his hopes, let Swedish Charles decide.
A frame of adamant, a soul of fire,
No dangers fright him, and no labours tire;
O'er love, o'er fear, extends his wide domain,
Unconquered lord of pleasure and of pain.
No joys to him pacific sceptres yield—
War sounds the trump, he rushes to the field;
Behold surrounding kings their powers combine,
And one capitulate, and one resign:
Peace courts his hand, but spreads her charms in vain;
'Think nothing gained,' he cries, 'till naught remain!
On Moscow's walls till Gothic standards fly,
And all be mine beneath the polar sky!'
The march begins in military state,
And nations on his eye suspended wait.

Stern Famine guards the solitary coast,
And Winter barricades the realms of frost.
He comes; nor want nor cold his course delay —
Hide, blushing Glory, hide Pultowa's day!
The vanquished hero leaves his broken bands,
And shows his miseries in distant lands,
Condemned a needy supplicant to wait
While ladies interpose and slaves debate.
But did not Chance at length her error mend?
Did no subverted empire mark his end?
Did rival monarchs give the fatal wound,
Or hostile millions press him to the ground?
His fall was destined to a barren strand,
A petty fortress, and a dubious hand.
He left the name at which the world grew pale,
To point a moral or adorn a tale.

. . . .

But grant, the virtues of a temperate prime
Bless with an age exempt from scorn or crime;
An age that melts with unperceived decay,
And glides in modest innocence away;
Whose peaceful day Benevolence endears,
Whose night congratulating Conscience cheers;
The general favourite as the general friend:
Such age there is, and who shall wish its end?
  Yet even on this her load Misfortune flings,
To press the weary minutes' flagging wings;
New sorrow rises as the day returns,
A sister sickens, or a daughter mourns.
Now kindred Merit fills the sable bier,
Now lacerated Friendship claims a tear.
Year chases year, decay pursues decay,
Still drops some joy from withering life away;
New forms arise, and different views engage,
Superfluous lags the veteran on the stage,
Till pitying Nature signs the last release,
And bids afflicted worth retire to peace.

. . . .

Where then shall Hope and Fear their objects find?
Must dull Suspense corrupt the stagnant mind?

Must helpless man, in ignorance sedate,
Roll darkling down the torrent of his fate?
Must no dislike alarm, no wishes rise,
No cries invoke the mercies of the skies?—
Enquirer, cease; petitions yet remain,
Which Heaven may hear; nor deem religion vain.
Still raise for good the supplicating voice,
But leave to Heaven the measure and the choice;
Safe in His power, whose eyes discern afar
The secret ambush of a specious prayer.
Implore His aid, in His decisions rest,
Secure, whate'er He gives, He gives the best.
Yet when the sense of sacred presence fires,
And strong devotion to the skies aspires,
Pour forth thy fervours for a healthful mind,
Obedient passions, and a will resigned;
For love, which scarce collective man can fill;
For patience, sovereign o'er transmuted ill;
For faith, that, panting for a happier seat,
Counts death kind Nature's signal of retreat:
These goods for man the laws of Heaven ordain;
These goods He grants, who grants the power to gain;
With these celestial Wisdom calms the mind,
And makes the happiness she does not find.

RICHARD JAGO

From THE GOLDFINCHES

All in a garden, on a currant bush,
  With wondrous art they built their airy seat;
In the next orchard lived a friendly thrush
  Nor distant far a woodlark's soft retreat.

Here blessed with ease, and in each other blessed,
  With early songs they waked the neighbouring groves,
Till time matured their joys, and crowned their nest
  With infant pledges of their faithful loves.

And now what transport glowed in either's eye!
  What equal fondness dealt th' allotted food!
What joy each other's likeness to descry;
  And future sonnets in the chirping brood!

But ah! what earthly happiness can last?
  How does the fairest purpose often fail?
A truant schoolboy's wantonness could blast
  Their flattering hopes, and leave them both to wail.

The most ungentle of his tribe was he,
  No generous precept ever touched his heart;
With concord false, and hideous prosody,
  He scrawled his task, and blundered o'er his part.

On mischief bent, he marked, with ravenous eyes,
  Where wrapped in down the callow songsters lay;
Then rushing, rudely seized the glittering prize,
  And bore it in his impious hands away!

But how shall I describe, in numbers rude,
  The pangs for poor Chrysomitris decreed,
When from her secret stand aghast she viewed
  The cruel spoiler perpetrate the deed?

'O grief of griefs!' with shrieking voice she cried,
  'What sight is this that I have lived to see!
O! that I had in youth's fair season died,
  From love's false joys and bitter sorrows free.'

JOHN DALTON

From A DESCRIPTIVE POEM

. . . . To nature's pride,
Sweet Keswick's vale, the Muse will guide:
The Muse who trod th' enchanted ground,
Who sailed the wondrous lake around,
With you will haste once more to hail
The beauteous brook of Borrodale.
. . . .

Let other streams rejoice to roar
Down the rough rocks of dread Lodore,
Rush raving on with boisterous sweep,
And foaming rend the frighted deep;
Thy gentle genius shrinks away
From such a rude unequal fray;
Through thine own native dale where rise
Tremendous rocks amid the skies,
Thy waves with patience slowly wind,
Till they the smoothest channel find,
Soften the horrors of the scene,
And through confusion flow serene.
Horrors like these at first alarm,
But soon with savage grandeur charm,
And raise to noblest thought the mind:
Thus by the fall, Lodore, reclined,
The craggy cliff, impendent wood,
Whose shadows mix o'er half the flood,
The gloomy clouds which solemn sail,
Scarce lifted by the languid gale.

. . . .

Channels by rocky torrents torn,
Rocks to the lake in thunder borne,
Or such as o'er our heads appear,
Suspended in their mid-career,
To start again at his command
Who rules fire, water, air, and land,
I view with wonder and delight,
A pleasing, though an awful sight.

. . . .

And last, to fix our wandering eyes,
Thy roofs, O Keswick, brighter rise
The lake and lofty hills between,
Where Giant Skiddow shuts the scene.
Supreme of mountains, Skiddow, hail!
To whom all Britain sinks a vale!
Lo, his imperial brow I see
From foul usurping vapours free!
'Twere glorious now his side to climb,
Boldly to scale his top sublime,
And thence—My Muse, these flights forbear,
Nor with wild raptures tire the fair.

JANE ELLIOT

THE FLOWERS OF THE FOREST

I've heard them lilting, at our ewe-milking,
Lasses a-lilting, before the dawn of day;
But now they are moaning, on ilka green loaning;
The Flowers of the Forest are a' wede away.

At bughts in the morning nae blythe lads are scorning;
The lasses are lanely, and dowie, and wae;
Nae daffing, nae gabbing, but sighing and sabbing,
Ilk ane lifts her leglin, and hies her away.

In hairst, at the shearing, nae youths now are jeering,
The bandsters are lyart, and runkled and gray;
At fair or at preaching, nae wooing, nae fleeching—
The Flowers of the Forest are a' wede away.

At e'en, in the gloaming, nae swankies are roaming
'Bout stacks wi' the lasses at bogle to play;
But ilk ane sits eerie, lamenting her dearie—
The Flowers of the Forest are a' wede away.

Dool and wae for the order sent our lads to the Border!
The English, for ance, by guile wan the day;
The Flowers of the Forest, that fought aye the foremost,
The prime of our land, lie cauld in the clay.

We'll hear nae more lilting at our ewe-milking,
Women and bairns are heartless and wae;
Sighing and moaning on ilka green loaning,
The Flowers of the Forest are a' wede away.

CHARLES CHURCHILL

From THE ROSCIAD

[Quin, the Actor]

His eyes, in gloomy socket taught to roll,
Proclaimed the sullen habit of his soul.
Heavy and phlegmatic he trod the stage,
Too proud for tenderness, too dull for rage.
When Hector's lovely widow shines in tears,
Or Rowe's gay rake dependent virtue jeers,
With the same cast of features he is seen
To chide the libertine and court the queen.
From the tame scene which without passion flows,
With just desert his reputation rose.
Nor less he pleased when, on some surly plan,
He was at once the actor and the man.
In Brute he shone unequalled: all agree
Garrick's not half so great a brute as he.
When Cato's laboured scenes are brought to view,
With equal praise the actor laboured too;
For still you'll find, trace passions to their root,
Small difference 'twixt the stoic and the brute.
In fancied scenes, as in life's real plan,
He could not for a moment sink the man.
In whate'er cast his character was laid,
Self still, like oil, upon the surface played.
Nature, in spite of all his skill, crept in:
Horatio, Dorax, Falstaff—still 'twas Quin.

From THE GHOST

[Dr. Johnson]

Pomposo, insolent and loud,
Vain idol of a scribbling crowd,
Whose very name inspires an awe,
Whose every word is sense and law,
For what his greatness hath decreed,
Like laws of Persia and of Mede,

Sacred through all the realm of wit,
Must never of repeal admit;
Who, cursing flattery, is the tool
Of every fawning, flattering fool;
Who wit with jealous eye surveys,
And sickens at another's praise;
Who, proudly seized of learning's throne,
Now damns all learning but his own;
Who scorns those common wares to trade in,
Reasoning, convincing, and persuading,
But makes each sentence current pass
With 'puppy,' 'coxcomb,' 'scoundrel,' 'ass,'
For 'tis with him a certain rule,
The folly's proved when he calls 'fool';
Who, to increase his native strength,
Draws words six syllables in length,
With which, assisted with a frown
By way of club, he knocks us down.

JAMES MACPHERSON

["TRANSLATIONS" FROM "OSSIAN, THE SON OF FINGAL"]

From FINGAL, AN EPIC POEM

[Fingal's Romantic Generosity Toward His Captive Enemy]

'King of Lochlin,' said Fingal, 'thy blood flows in the veins of thy foe. Our fathers met in battle, because they loved the strife of spears. But often did they feast in the hall, and send round the joy of the shell. Let thy face brighten with gladness, and thine ear delight in the harp. Dreadful as the storm of thine ocean, thou hast poured thy valour forth; thy voice has been like the voice of thousands when they engage in war. Raise, to-morrow, raise thy white sails to the wind, thou brother of Agandecca! Bright as the beam of noon, she comes on my mournful soul. I have seen thy tears for the fair one. I spared thee in the halls of Starno, when my sword was red with slaughter, when my eye was full of tears for the maid. Or dost thou choose the fight? The combat which thy fathers gave to Trenmor is thine! that thou mayest depart renowned, like the sun setting in the west!'

'King of the race of Morven!' said the chief of resounding Lochlin, 'never will Swaran fight with thee, first of a thousand heroes! I have seen thee in the halls of Starno: few were thy years beyond my own. When shall I, I said to my soul, lift the spear like the noble Fingal? We have fought heretofore, O warrior, on the side of the shaggy Malmor; after my waves had carried me to thy halls, and the feast of a thousand shells was spread. Let the bards send his name who overcame to future years, for noble was the strife of Malmour! But many of the ships of Lochlin have lost their youths on Lena. Take these, thou king of Morven, and be the friend of Swaran! When thy sons shall come to Gormal, the feast of shells shall be spread, and the combat offered on the vale.'

'Nor ship,' replied the king, 'shall Fingal take, nor land of many hills. The desert is enough to me, with all its deer and woods. Rise on thy waves again, thou noble friend of Agandecca! Spread thy white sails to the beam of the morning; return to the echoing hills of Gormal.' 'Blest be thy soul, thou king of shells,' said Swaran of the dark-brown shield. 'In peace thou art the gale of spring. In war, the mountain-storm. Take now my hand in friendship, king of echoing Selma! Let thy bards mourn those who fell. Let Erin give the sons of Lochlin to earth. Raise high the mossy stones of their fame: that the children of the north hereafter may behold the place where their fathers fought. The hunter may say, when he leans on a mossy tomb, here Fingal and Swaran fought, the heroes of other years. Thus hereafter shall he say, and our fame shall last for ever!'

'Swaran,' said the king of hills, 'to-day our fame is greatest. We shall pass away like a dream. No sound will remain in our fields of war. Our tombs will be lost in the heath. The hunter shall not know the place of our rest. Our names may be heard in song. What avails it when our strength hath ceased? O Ossian, Carril, and

Ullin! you know of heroes that are no more. Give us the song of other years. Let the night pass away on the sound, and morning return with joy.'

We gave the song to the kings. A hundred harps mixed their sound with our voice. The face of Swaran brightened, like the full moon of heaven: when the clouds vanish away, and leave her calm and broad in the midst of the sky.

From THE SONGS OF SELMA

[Colma's Lament]

It is night; I am alone, forlorn on the hill of storms. The wind is heard in the mountain. The torrent pours down the rock. No hut receives me from the rain, forlorn on the hill of winds.

Rise, moon! from behind thy clouds. Stars of the night, arise! Lead me, some light, to the place where my love rests from the chase alone! his bow near him, unstrung; his dogs panting around him. But here I must sit alone, by the rock of the mossy stream. The stream and the wind roar aloud. I hear not the voice of my love! Why delays my Salgar, why the chief of the hill, his promise? Here is the rock, and here the tree! here is the roaring stream! Thou didst promise with night to be here. Ah! whither is my Salgar gone? With thee I would fly, from my father; with thee, from my brother of pride. Our race have long been foes; we are not foes, O Salgar!

Cease a little while, O wind! stream, be thou silent a while! let my voice be heard around. Let my wanderer hear me! Salgar! it is Colma who calls. Here is the tree and the rock. Salgar, my love! I am here. Why delayest thou thy coming? Lo! the calm moon comes forth. The flood is bright in the vale. The rocks are grey on the steep. I see him not on the brow. His dogs come not before him, with tidings of his near approach. Here I must sit alone!

Who lie on the heath beside me? Are they my love and my brother? Speak to me, O my friends! To Colma they give no reply. Speak to me: I am alone! My soul is tormented with fears! Ah, they are dead! Their swords are red from the fight. O my brother! my brother! why hast thou slain my Salgar? Why, O Salgar! hast thou slain my brother? Dear were ye both to me! what shall I say in your praise? Thou wert fair on the hill among thousands! he was terrible in fight. Speak to me; hear my voice; hear me, sons of my love! They are silent; silent for ever! Cold, cold are their breasts of clay. Oh! from the rock on the hill; from the top of the windy steep, speak, ye ghosts of the dead! speak, I will not be afraid! Whither are ye gone to rest? In what cave of the hill shall I find the departed? No feeble voice is on the gale; no answer half-drowned in the storm!

I sit in my grief! I wait for morning in my tears! Rear the tomb, ye friends of the dead. Close it not till Colma come. My life flies away like a dream! why should I stay behind? Here shall I rest with my friends, by the stream of the sounding rock. When night comes on the hill; when the loud winds arise; my ghost shall stand in the blast, and mourn the death of my friends. The hunter shall hear from his booth. He shall fear, but love my voice! For sweet shall my voice be for my friends: pleasant were her friends to Colma!

[The Last Words of Ossian]

Such were the words of the bards in the days of song; when the king heard the music of harps, the tales of other times! The chiefs gathered from all their hills and heard the lovely sound. They praised the voice of Cona [Ossian], the first among a thousand bards! But age is now on my tongue; my soul has failed! I hear at times the ghosts of bards, and learn their pleasant song. But memory fails on my mind. I hear the call of years! They say as they pass along, why does Ossian sing? Soon shall he lie in the narrow house, and no bard shall raise his fame! Roll on, ye dark-brown years; ye bring no joy on your course! Let the tomb open to Ossian, for his strength has failed. The sons of song are gone to rest. My voice remains, like a blast that roars lonely on a sea-surrounded rock, after the winds are laid. The dark moss whistles there; the distant mariner sees the waving trees!

CHRISTOPHER SMART

From A SONG TO DAVID

Strong is the lion—like a coal
His eyeball, like a bastion's mole
  His chest against the foes;
Strong the gier-eagle on his sail;
Strong against tide th' enormous whale
  Emerges as he goes:

But stronger still, in earth and air
And in the sea, the man of prayer,
  And far beneath the tide,
And in the seat to faith assigned,
Where ask is have, where seek is find,
  Where knock is open wide.

Beauteous the fleet before the gale;
Beauteous the multitudes in mail,
  Ranked arms and crested heads;
Beauteous the garden's umbrage mild,
Walk, water, meditated wild,
  And all the bloomy beds;

Beauteous the moon full on the lawn;
And beauteous when the veil's withdrawn
  The virgin to her spouse;
Beauteous the temple, decked and filled,
When to the heaven of heavens they build
  Their heart-directed vows:

Beauteous, yea beauteous more than these,
The shepherd King upon his knees,
  For his momentous trust;
With wish of infinite conceit
For man, beast, mute, the small and great,
  And prostrate dust to dust.

Precious the bounteous widow's mite;
And precious, for extreme delight,
  The largess from the churl;
Precious the ruby's blushing blaze,
And Alba's blest imperial rays,
  And pure cerulean pearl;

Precious the penitential tear;
And precious is the sigh sincere,
  Acceptable to God;
And precious are the winning flowers,
In gladsome Israel's feast of bowers,
  Bound on the hallowed sod:

More precious that diviner part
Of David, even the Lord's own heart,
  Great, beautiful, and new;
In all things where it was intent,
In all extremes, in each event,
  Proof—answering true to true.

Glorious the sun in mid career;
Glorious th' assembled fires appear;
  Glorious the comet's train;
Glorious the trumpet and alarm;
Glorious th' Almighty's stretched-out arm;
  Glorious th' enraptured main;

Glorious the northern lights a-stream;
Glorious the song, when God's the theme;
  Glorious the thunder's roar;
Glorious, Hosannah from the den;
Glorious the catholic amen;
  Glorious the martyr's gore:

Glorious, more glorious, is the crown
Of Him that brought salvation down,
  By meekness called Thy son;
Thou that stupendous truth believed,
And now the matchless deed's achieved,
  Determined, dared, and done.

OLIVER GOLDSMITH

FROM THE TRAVELLER; OR, A PROSPECT OF SOCIETY

As some lone miser, visiting his store,
Bends at his treasure, counts, recounts it o'er,
Hoards after hoards his rising raptures fill,
Yet still he sighs, for hoards are wanting still:
Thus to my breast alternate passions rise,
Pleased with each good that Heaven to man supplies;
Yet oft a sigh prevails, and sorrows fall,
To see the hoard of human bliss so small,
And oft I wish amidst the scene to find
Some spot to real happiness consigned,
Where my worn soul, each wandering hope at rest,
May gather bliss to see my fellows blest.
But where to find that happiest spot below,
Who can direct, when all pretend to know?

. . . .

To kinder skies, where gentler manners reign,
I turn; and France displays her bright domain.
Gay, sprightly land of mirth and social ease,
Pleased with thyself, whom all the world can please,
How often have I led thy sportive choir,
With tuneless pipe, beside the murmuring Loire,
Where shading elms along the margin grew,
And freshened from the wave the zephyr flew!
And haply, though my harsh touch, faltering still,
But mocked all tune and marred the dancer's skill,
Yet would the village praise my wondrous power,
And dance forgetful of the noontide hour.
Alike all ages: dames of ancient days
Have led their children through the mirthful maze;
And the gay grandsire, skilled in gestic lore,
Has frisked beneath the burthen of threescore.
So blessed a life these thoughtless realms display;
Thus idly busy rolls their world away.

Theirs are those arts that mind to mind endear,
For honour forms the social temper here:
Honour, that praise which real merit gains,
Or e'en imaginary worth obtains,
Here passes current; paid from hand to hand,
It shifts in splendid traffic round the land;
From courts to camps, to cottages it strays,
And all are taught an avarice of praise;
They pleased, are pleased; they give, to get, esteem,
Till, seeming blessed, they grow to what they seem.
But while this softer art their bliss supplies,
It gives their follies also room to rise;
For praise, too dearly loved or warmly sought,
Enfeebles all internal strength of thought,
And the weak soul, within itself unblessed,
Leans for all pleasure on another's breast.
Hence Ostentation here, with tawdry art,
Pants for the vulgar praise which fools impart;
Here Vanity assumes her pert grimace,
And trims her robes of frieze with copper-lace;
Here beggar Pride defrauds her daily cheer,
To boast one splendid banquet once a year:
The mind still turns where shifting fashion draws,
Nor weighs the solid worth of self-applause.

. . . .

Vain, very vain, my weary search to find
That bliss which only centres in the mind.
Why have I strayed from pleasure and repose,
To seek a good each government bestows?
In every government, though terrors reign,
Though tyrant kings or tyrant laws restrain,
How small, of all that human hearts endure,
That part which laws or kings can cause or cure!
Still to ourselves in every place consigned,
Our own felicity we make or find:
With secret course, which no loud storms annoy,
Glides the smooth current of domestic joy;
The lifted axe, the agonizing wheel,
Luke's iron crown, and Damiens' bed of steel,
To men remote from power but rarely known,
Leave reason, faith, and conscience all our own.

THE DESERTED VILLAGE

Sweet Auburn! loveliest village of the plain;
Where health and plenty cheered the labouring swain,
Where smiling Spring its earliest visit paid,
And parting summer's lingering blooms delayed:
Dear lovely bowers of innocence and ease,
Seats of my youth, when every sport could please,
How often have I loitered o'er thy green,
Where humble happiness endeared each scene!
How often have I paused on every charm,
The sheltered cot, the cultivated farm,
The never-failing brook, the busy mill,
The decent church that topped the neighbouring hill,
The hawthorn bush, with seats beneath the shade
For talking age and whispering lovers made!
How often have I blest the coming day,
When toil remitting lent its turn to play,
And all the village train, from labour free,
Led up their sports beneath the spreading tree,
While many a pastime circled in the shade,
The young contending as the old surveyed;
And many a gambol frolicked o'er the ground,
And sleights of art and feats of strength went round.
And still, as each repeated pleasure tired,
Succeeding sports the mirthful band inspired;
The dancing pair that simply sought renown
By holding out to tire each other down;
The swain mistrustless of his smutted face,
While secret laughter tittered round the place;
The bashful virgin's side-long looks of love,
The matron's glance that would those looks reprove:
These were thy charms, sweet village! sports like these,
With sweet succession, taught even toil to please:
These round thy bowers their cheerful influence shed:
These were thy charms—but all these charms are fled.
  Sweet smiling village, loveliest of the lawn,
Thy sports are fled, and all thy charms withdrawn
Amidst thy bowers the tyrant's hand is seen,
And desolation saddens all thy green:
One only master grasps the whole domain,
And half a tillage stints thy smiling plain.

No more thy glassy brook reflects the day,
But, choked with sedges, works its weedy way;
Along the glades, a solitary guest,
The hollow sounding bittern guards its nest;
Amidst thy desert walks the lapwing flies,
And tires their echoes with unvaried cries;
Sunk are thy bowers in shapeless ruin all,
And the long grass o'ertops the mouldering wall;
And trembling, shrinking from the spoiler's hand,
Far, far away thy children leave the land.
  Ill fares the land, to hastening ills a prey,
Where wealth accumulates, and men decay:
Princes and lords may flourish, or may fade;
A breath can make them, as a breath has made:
But a bold peasantry, their country's pride,
When once destroyed, can never be supplied.
  A time there was, ere England's griefs began,
When every rood of ground maintained its man;
For him light labour spread her wholesome store,
Just gave what life required, but gave no more:
His best companions, innocence and health;
And his best riches, ignorance of wealth.
  But times are altered; trade's unfeeling train
Usurp the land and dispossess the swain;
Along the lawn, where scattered hamlets rose,
Unwieldy wealth and cumbrous pomp repose,
And every want to opulence allied,
And every pang that folly pays to pride.
These gentle hours that plenty bade to bloom,
Those calm desires that asked but little room,
Those healthful sports that graced the peaceful scene,
Lived in each look, and brightened all the green;
These, far departing, seek a kinder shore,
And rural mirth and manners are no more.
  Sweet Auburn! parent of the blissful hour,
Thy glades forlorn confess the tyrant's power.
Here, as I take my solitary rounds
Amidst thy tangling walks and ruined grounds,
And, many a year elapsed, return to view
Where once the cottage stood, the hawthorn grew,
Remembrance wakes with all her busy train,
Swells at my breast, and turns the past to pain.

In all my wanderings round this world of care,
In all my griefs—and God has given my share—
I still had hopes, my latest hours to crown,
Amidst these humble bowers to lay me down;
To husband out life's taper at the close,
And keep the flame from wasting by repose:
I still had hopes, for pride attends us still,
Amidst the swains to show my book-learned skill,
Around my fire an evening group to draw,
And tell of all I felt, and all I saw;
And, as an hare whom hounds and horns pursue
Pants to the place from whence at first she flew,
I still had hopes, my long vexations past,
Here to return—and die at home at last.

O blest retirement, friend to life's decline,
Retreats from care, that never must be mine,
How happy he who crowns in shades like these
A youth of labour with an age of ease;
Who quits a world where strong temptations try,
And, since 'tis hard to combat, learns to fly!
For him no wretches, born to work and weep,
Explore the mine, or tempt the dangerous deep;
No surly porter stands in guilty state,
To spurn imploring famine from the gate;
But on he moves to meet his latter end,
Angels around befriending Virtue's friend;
Bends to the grave with unperceived decay,
While resignation gently slopes the way;
And, all his prospects brightening to the last,
His Heaven commences ere the world be past!

Sweet was the sound, when oft at evening's close
Up yonder hill the village murmur rose.
There, as I passed with careless steps and slow,
The mingling notes came softened from below;
The swain responsive as the milk-maid sung,
The sober herd that lowed to meet their young,
The noisy geese that gabbled o'er the pool,
The playful children just let loose from school,
The watch-dog's voice that bayed the whispering wind,
And the loud laugh that spoke the vacant mind;—
These all in sweet confusion sought the shade,
And filled each pause the nightingale had made.

But now the sounds of population fail,
No cheerful murmurs fluctuate in the gale,
No busy steps the grass-grown foot-way tread,
For all the bloomy flush of life is fled.
All but yon widowed, solitary thing,
That feebly bends beside the plashy spring:
She, wretched matron, forced in age, for bread,
To strip the brook with mantling cresses spread,
To pick her wintry faggot from the thorn,
To seek her nightly shed, and weep till morn;
She only left of all the harmless train,
The sad historian of the pensive plain.
  Near yonder copse, where once the garden smiled,
And still where many a garden flower grows wild;
There, where a few torn shrubs the place disclose,
The village preacher's modest mansion rose.
A man he was to all the country dear,
And passing rich with forty pounds a year;
Remote from towns he ran his godly race,
Nor e'er had changed, nor wished to change his place;
Unpractised he to fawn, or seek for power,
By doctrines fashioned to the varying hour;
Far other aims his heart had learned to prize,
More skilled to raise the wretched than to rise.
His house was known to all the vagrant train;
He chid their wanderings, but relieved their pain:
The long-remembered beggar was his guest,
Whose beard descending swept his aged breast;
The ruined spendthrift, now no longer proud,
Claimed kindred there, and had his claims allowed;
The broken soldier, kindly bade to stay,
Sate by his fire, and talked the night away,
Wept o'er his wounds, or, tales of sorrow done,
Shouldered his crutch and showed how fields were won.
Pleased with his guests, the good man learned to glow,
And quite forget their vices in their woe;
Careless their merits or their faults to scan,
His pity gave ere charity began.
  Thus to relieve the wretched was his pride,
And e'en his failings leaned to Virtue's side;
But in his duty prompt at every call,
He watched and wept, he prayed and felt, for all;

And, as a bird each fond endearment tries
To tempt its new-fledged offspring to the skies,
He tried each art, reproved each dull delay,
Allured to brighter worlds, and led the way.
  Beside the bed where parting life was laid,
And sorrow, guilt, and pain by turns dismayed,
The reverend champion stood. At his control
Despair and anguish fled the struggling soul;
Comfort came down the trembling wretch to raise,
And his last faltering accents whispered praise.
  At church, with meek and unaffected grace,
His looks adorned the venerable place;
Truth from his lips prevailed with double sway,
And fools, who came to scoff, remained to pray.
The service past, around the pious man,
With steady zeal, each honest rustic ran;
Even children followed with endearing wile,
And plucked his gown to share the good man's smile.
His ready smile a parent's warmth expressed;
Their welfare pleased him, and their cares distressed:
To them his heart, his love, his griefs were given,
But all his serious thoughts had rest in Heaven.
As some tall cliff that lifts its awful form,
Swells from the vale, and midway leaves the storm,
Though round its breast the rolling clouds are spread,
Eternal sunshine settles on its head.
  Beside yon straggling fence that skirts the way,
With blossomed furze unprofitably gay,
There, in his noisy mansion, skilled to rule,
The village master taught his little school.
A man severe he was, and stern to view;
I knew him well, and every truant knew;
Well had the boding tremblers learned to trace
The days' disasters in his morning face;
Full well they laughed with counterfeited glee
At all his jokes, for many a joke had he;
Full well the busy whisper circling round
Conveyed the dismal tidings when he frowned.
Yet he was kind, or, if severe in aught,
The love he bore to learning was in fault:
The village all declared how much he knew;
'Twas certain he could write, and cipher too;

Lands he could measure, terms and tides presage,
And even the story ran that he could gauge;
In arguing, too, the parson owned his skill,
For, even though vanquished, he could argue still;
While words of learned length and thundering sound
Amazed the gazing rustics ranged around;
And still they gazed, and still the wonder grew,
That one small head could carry all he knew.
  But past is all his fame. The very spot
Where many a time he triumphed is forgot.
Near yonder thorn, that lifts its head on high,
Where once the sign-post caught the passing eye,
Low lies that house where nut-brown draughts inspired,
Where graybeard mirth and smiling toil retired,
Where village statesmen talked with looks profound,
And news much older than their ale went round.
Imagination fondly stoops to trace
The parlour splendours of that festive place:
The whitewashed wall, the nicely sanded floor,
The varnished clock that clicked behind the door:
The chest contrived a double debt to pay,
A bed by night, a chest of drawers by day;
The pictures placed for ornament and use,
The twelve good rules, the royal game of goose;
The hearth, except when winter chilled the day,
With aspen boughs and flowers and fennel gay;
While broken tea-cups, wisely kept for show,
Ranged o'er the chimney, glistened in a row.
  Vain transitory splendours could not all
Reprieve the tottering mansion from its fall?
Obscure it sinks, nor shall it more impart
An hour's importance to the poor man's heart.
Thither no more the peasant shall repair
To sweet oblivion of his daily care;
No more the farmer's news, the barber's tale,
No more the woodman's ballad shall prevail;
No more the smith his dusky brow shall clear,
Relax his ponderous strength, and lean to hear;
The host himself no longer shall be found
Careful to see the mantling bliss go round;
Nor the coy maid, half willing to be pressed,
Shall kiss the cup to pass it to the rest.

Yes! let the rich deride, the proud disdain,
These simple blessings of the lowly train;
To me more dear, congenial to my heart,
One native charm, than all the gloss of art.
Spontaneous joys, where Nature has its play,
The soul adopts, and owns their first-born sway;
Lightly they frolic o'er the vacant mind,
Unenvied, unmolested, unconfined.
But the long pomp, the midnight masquerade,
With all the freaks of wanton wealth arrayed—
In these, ere triflers half their wish obtain,
The toiling pleasure sickens into pain;
And, e'en while fashion's brightest arts decoy,
The heart distrusting asks if this be joy.
Ye friends to truth, ye statesmen who survey
The rich man's joys increase, the poor's decay,
'Tis yours to judge, how wide the limits stand
Between a splendid and an happy land.
Proud swells the tide with loads of freighted ore,
And shouting Folly hails them from her shore;
Hoards e'en beyond the miser's wish abound,
And rich men flock from all the world around.
Yet count our gains! This wealth is but a name
That leaves our useful products still the same.
Not so the loss. The man of wealth and pride
Takes up a space that many poor supplied;
Space for his lake, his park's extended bounds,
Space for his horses, equipage, and hounds:
The robe that wraps his limbs in silken sloth
Has robbed the neighbouring fields of half their growth;
His seat, where solitary sports are seen,
Indignant spurns the cottage from the green:
Around the world each needful product flies,
For all the luxuries the world supplies;
While thus the land adorned for pleasure all
In barren splendour feebly waits the fall.
As some fair female unadorned and plain,
Secure to please while youth confirms her reign,
Slights every borrowed charm that dress supplies,
Nor shares with art the triumph of her eyes;
But when those charms are passed, for charms are frail,
When time advances, and when lovers fail,

She then shines forth, solicitous to bless,
In all the glaring impotence of dress.
Thus fares the land by luxury betrayed:
In nature's simplest charms at first arrayed,
But verging to decline, its splendours rise,
Its vistas strike, its palaces surprise;
While, scourged by famine from the smiling land
The mournful peasant leads his humble band,
And while he sinks, without one arm to save,
The country blooms—a garden and a grave.
 Where then, ah! where, shall poverty reside,
To 'scape the pressure of contiguous pride?
If to some common's fenceless limits strayed,
He drives his flock to pick the scanty blade,
Those fenceless fields the sons of wealth divide,
And even the bare-worn common is denied.
 If to the city sped—what waits him there?
To see profusion that he must not share;
To see ten thousand baneful arts combined
To pamper luxury, and thin mankind;
To see those joys the sons of pleasure know
Extorted from his fellow-creature's woe.
Here while the courtier glitters in brocade,
There the pale artist plies the sickly trade;
Here while the proud their long-drawn pomps display,
There the black gibbet glooms beside the way.
The dome where pleasure holds her midnight reign
Here, richly decked, admits the gorgeous train:
Tumultuous grandeur crowds the blazing square,
The rattling chariots clash, the torches glare.
Sure scenes like these no troubles e'er annoy!
Sure these denote one universal joy!
Are these thy serious thoughts?—Ah, turn thine eyes
Where the poor houseless shivering female lies.
She once, perhaps, in village plenty blessed,
Has wept at tales of innocence distressed;
Her modest looks the cottage might adorn,
Sweet as the primrose peeps beneath the thorn:
Now lost to all; her friends, her virtue fled,
Near her betrayer's door she lays her head,
And, pinched with cold, and shrinking from the shower,
With heavy heart deplores that luckless hour,

When idly first, ambitious of the town,
She left her wheel and robes of country brown.
  Do thine, sweet Auburn,—thine, the loveliest train,—
Do thy fair tribes participate her pain?
Even now, perhaps, by cold and hunger led,
At proud men's doors they ask a little bread!
  Ah, no! To distant climes, a dreary scene,
Where half the convex world intrudes between,
Through torrid tracts with fainting steps they go,
Where wild Altama murmurs to their woe.
Far different there from all that charmed before
The various terrors of that horrid shore;
Those blazing suns that dart a downward ray,
And fiercely shed intolerable day;
Those matted woods, where birds forget to sing,
But silent bats in drowsy clusters cling;
Those poisonous fields with rank luxuriance crowned,
Where the dark scorpion gathers death around;
Where at each step the stranger fears to wake
The rattling terrors of the vengeful snake;
Where crouching tigers wait their hapless prey,
And savage men more murderous still than they;
While oft in whirls the mad tornado flies,
Mingling the ravaged landscape with the skies.
Far different these from every former scene,
The cooling brook, the grassy vested green,
The breezy covert of the warbling grove,
That only sheltered thefts of harmless love.
  Good Heaven! what sorrows gloomed that parting day,
That called them from their native walks away;
When the poor exiles, every pleasure passed,
Hung round the bowers, and fondly looked their last,
And took a long farewell, and wished in vain
For seats like these beyond the western main,
And shuddering still to face the distant deep,
Returned and wept, and still returned to weep.
The good old sire the first prepared to go
To new-found worlds, and wept for others' woe;
But for himself, in conscious virtue brave,
He only wished for worlds beyond the grave.
His lovely daughter, lovelier in her tears,
The fond companion of his helpless years,

Silent went next, neglectful of her charms,
And left a lover's for a father's arms.
With louder plaints the mother spoke her woes,
And blest the cot where every pleasure rose,
And kissed her thoughtless babes with many a tear,
And clasped them close, in sorrow doubly dear,
Whilst her fond husband strove to lend relief
In all the silent manliness of grief.
O luxury! thou cursed by Heaven's decree,
How ill exchanged are things like these for thee!
How do thy potions, with insidious joy,
Diffuse their pleasure only to destroy!
Kingdoms by thee, to sickly greatness grown,
Boast of a florid vigour not their own.
At every draught more large and large they grow,
A bloated mass of rank unwieldy woe;
Till sapped their strength, and every part unsound,
Down, down, they sink, and spread a ruin round.
Even now the devastation is begun,
And half the business of destruction done;
Even now, methinks, as pondering here I stand,
I see the rural Virtues leave the land.
Down where yon anchoring vessel spreads the sail,
That idly waiting flaps with every gale,
Downward they move, a melancholy band,
Pass from the shore, and darken all the strand.
Contented Toil, and hospitable Care,
And kind connubial Tenderness, are there;
And Piety with wishes placed above,
And steady Loyalty, and faithful Love.
And thou, sweet Poetry, thou loveliest maid,
Still first to fly where sensual joys invade;
Unfit in these degenerate times of shame
To catch the heart, or strike for honest fame;
Dear charming nymph, neglected and decried,
My shame in crowds, my solitary pride;
Thou source of all my bliss, and all my woe,
That found'st me poor at first, and keep'st me so;
Thou guide by which the nobler arts excel,
Thou nurse of every virtue, fare thee well!
Farewell, and oh! where'er thy voice be tried,
On Torno's cliffs, or Pambamarca's side,

Whether where equinoctial fervours glow,
Or winter wraps the polar world in snow,
Still let thy voice, prevailing over time,
Redress the rigours of th' inclement clime;
Aid slighted truth with thy persuasive strain;
Teach erring man to spurn the rage of gain;
Teach him, that states of native strength possessed,
Though very poor, may still be very blessed;
That trade's proud empire hastes to swift decay,
As ocean sweeps the laboured mole away;
While self-dependent power can time defy,
As rocks resist the billows and the sky.

FROM RETALIATION

Here lies our good Edmund, whose genius was such
We scarcely can praise it or blame it too much;
Who, born for the universe, narrowed his mind,
And to party gave up what was meant for mankind;
Though fraught with all learning, yet straining his throat
To persuade Tommy Townshend to lend him a vote;
Who, too deep for his hearers, still went on refining,
And thought of convincing, while they thought of dining;
Though equal to all things, for all things unfit—
Too nice for a statesman, too proud for a wit,
For a patriot too cool, for a drudge disobedient,
And too fond of the right to pursue the expedient:
In short, 'twas his fate, unemployed or in place, sir,
To eat mutton cold and cut blocks with a razor.

. . . .

Here Cumberland lies, having acted his parts,
The Terence of England, the mender of hearts;
A flattering painter, who made it his care
To draw men as they ought to be, not as they are:
His gallants are all faultless, his women divine,
And Comedy wonders at being so fine—
Like a tragedy-queen he has dizened her out,
Or rather like Tragedy giving a rout;
His fools have their follies so lost in a crowd
Of virtues and feelings that folly grows proud;

And coxcombs, alike in their failings alone,
Adopting his portraits, are pleased with their own.
Say, where has our poet this malady caught,
Or wherefore his characters thus without fault?
Say, was it that, vainly directing his view
To find out men's virtues, and finding them few,
Quite sick of pursuing each troublesome elf,
He grew lazy at last and drew from himself?

. . . .

Here lies David Garrick: describe me, who can,
An abridgment of all that was pleasant in man;
As an actor, confessed without rival to shine;
As a wit, if not first, in the very first line.
Yet with talents like these, and an excellent heart,
The man had his failings, a dupe to his art:
Like an ill-judging beauty his colours he spread,
And beplastered with rouge his own natural red;
On the stage he was natural, simple, affecting—
'Twas only that when he was off he was acting.
With no reason on earth to go out of his way,
He turned and he varied full ten times a day:
Though secure of our hearts, yet confoundedly sick
If they were not his own by finessing and trick;
He cast off his friends as a huntsman his pack,
For he knew when he pleased he could whistle them back.
Of praise a mere glutton, he swallowed what came,
And the puff of a dunce he mistook it for fame;
Till, his relish grown callous, almost to disease,
Who peppered the highest was surest to please.
But let us be candid, and speak out our mind:
If dunces applauded, he paid them in kind;
Ye Kenricks, ye Kellys, and Woodfalls so grave,
What a commerce was yours while you got and you gave!
How did Grub Street re-echo the shouts that you raised,
While he was be-Rosciused and you were bepraised!
But peace to his spirit, wherever it flies
To act as an angel and mix with the skies!
Those poets who owe their best fame to his skill
Shall still be his flatterers, go where he will;

Old Shakespeare receive him with praise and with love,
And Beaumonts and Bens be his Kellys above.

. . . .

Here Reynolds is laid, and, to tell you my mind,
He has not left a better or wiser behind.
His pencil was striking, resistless, and grand;
His manners were gentle, complying, and bland;
Still born to improve us in every part—
His pencil our faces, his manners our heart.
To coxcombs averse, yet most civilly steering,
When they judged without skill he was still hard of hearing;
When they talked of their Raphaels, Correggios, and stuff,
He shifted his trumpet, and only took snuff.

JAMES BEATTIE

From THE MINSTREL; OR, THE PROGRESS OF GENIUS

Fret not thyself, thou glittering child of pride,
That a poor villager inspires my strain;
With thee let pageantry and power abide:
The gentle Muses haunt the sylvan reign;
Where through wild groves at eve the lonely swain
Enraptured roams, to gaze on Nature's charms.
They hate the sensual, and scorn the vain,
The parasite their influence never warms,
Nor him whose sordid soul the love of gold alarms.

Though richest hues the peacock's plumes adorn,
Yet horror screams from his discordant throat.
Rise, sons of harmony, and hail the morn,
While warbling larks on russet pinions float;
Or seek at noon the woodland scene remote,
Where the grey linnets carol from the hill:
O let them ne'er, with artificial note,

To please a tyrant, strain the little bill,
But sing what Heaven inspires, and wander where they will!

. . . .

And yet poor Edwin was no vulgar boy.
Deep thought oft seemed to fix his infant eye.
Dainties he heeded not, nor gaud, nor toy,
Save one short pipe of rudest minstrelsy;
Silent when glad; affectionate, though shy;
And now his look was most demurely sad;
And now he laughed aloud, yet none knew why.
The neighbours stared and sighed, yet blessed the lad;
Some deemed him wondrous wise, and some believed him mad.

. . . .

In truth, he was a strange and wayward wight,
Fond of each gentle and each dreadful scene.
In darkness and in storm he found delight,
Nor less than when on ocean-wave serene
The southern sun diffused his dazzling sheen.
Even sad vicissitude amused his soul;
And if a sigh would sometimes intervene,
And down his cheek a tear of pity roll,
A sigh, a tear, so sweet, he wished not to control.

. . . .

When the long-sounding curfew from afar
Loaded with loud lament the lonely gale,
Young Edwin, lighted by the evening star,
Lingering and listening, wandered down the vale.
There would he dream of graves, and corses pale,
And ghosts that to the charnel-dungeon throng,
And drag a length of clanking chain, and wail,
Till silenced by the owl's terrific song,
Or blast that shrieks by fits the shuddering isles along.

Or when the setting moon, in crimson dyed,
Hung o'er the dark and melancholy deep,
To haunted stream, remote from man, he hied,
Where fays of yore their revels wont to keep;

And there let fancy rove at large, till sleep
A vision brought to his entrancèd sight.
And first, a wildly murmuring wind 'gan creep
Shrill to his ringing ear; then tapers bright,
With instantaneous gleam, illumed the vault of night.

. . . .

Nor was this ancient dame a foe to mirth.
Her ballad, jest, and riddle's quaint device
Oft cheered the shepherds round their social hearth;
Whom levity or spleen could ne'er entice
To purchase chat or laughter at the price
Of decency. Nor let it faith exceed
That Nature forms a rustic taste so nice.
Ah! had they been of court or city breed,
Such delicacy were right marvellous indeed.

Oft when the winter storm had ceased to rave,
He roamed the snowy waste at even, to view
The cloud stupendous, from th' Atlantic wave
High-towering, sail along th' horizon blue;
Where, midst the changeful scenery, ever new,
Fancy a thousand wondrous forms descries,
More wildly great than ever pencil drew—
Rocks, torrents, gulfs, and shapes of giant size,
And glittering cliffs on cliffs, and fiery ramparts rise.

Thence musing onward to the sounding shore,
The lone enthusiast oft would take his way,
Listening, with pleasing dread, to the deep roar
Of the wide-weltering waves. In black array
When sulphurous clouds rolled on th' autumnal day,
Even then he hastened from the haunts of man,
Along the trembling wilderness to stray,
What time the lightning's fierce career began,
And o'er heaven's rending arch the rattling thunder ran.

Responsive to the sprightly pipe when all
In sprightly dance the village youth were joined,
Edwin, of melody aye held in thrall,
From the rude gambol far remote reclined,
Soothed with the soft notes warbling in the wind.

Ah then all jollity seemed noise and folly
To the pure soul by fancy's fire refined!
Ah, what is mirth but turbulence unholy
When with the charm compared of heavenly melancholy!

LADY ANNE LINDSAY

AULD ROBIN GRAY

When the sheep are in the fauld, and the kye at hame,
And a' the warld to rest are gane,
The waes o' my heart fa' in showers frae my e'e,
While my gudeman lies sound by me.

Young Jamie lo'ed me weel, and sought me for his bride;
But saving a croun he had naething else beside;
To make the croun a pund, young Jamie gaid to sea;
And the croun and the pund were baith for me.

He hadna been awa' a week but only twa,
When my father brak his arm, and the cow was stown awa';
My mother she fell sick,—and my Jamie at the sea—
And auld Robin Gray came a-courtin' me.

My father couldna work, and my mother couldna spin;
I toiled day and night, but their bread I couldna win;
Auld Rob maintained them baith, and wi' tears in his e'e
Said, 'Jennie, for their sakes, O, marry me!'

My heart it said nay; I looked for Jamie back;
But the wind it blew high, and the ship it was a wrack;
His ship it was a wrack—Why didna Jamie dee?
Or why do I live to cry, Wae's me!

My father urged me sair: my mother didna speak;
But she looked in my face till my heart was like to break:
They gi'ed him my hand, though my heart was in the sea;
Sae auld Robin Gray he was gudeman to me.

I hadna been a wife a week but only four,
When mournfu' as I sat on the stane at the door,
I saw my Jamie's wraith,—for I couldna think it he,
Till he said, 'I'm come hame to marry thee.'

O sair, sair did we greet, and muckle did we say;
We took but ae kiss, and we tore ourselves away:
I wish that I were dead, but I'm no like to dee;
And why was I born to say, Wae's me!

I gang like a ghaist, and I carena to spin;
I daurna think on Jamie, for that wad be a sin;
But I'll do my best a gude wife aye to be,
For auld Robin Gray he is kind unto me.

JEAN ADAMS

THERE'S NAE LUCK ABOUT THE HOUSE

And are ye sure the news is true,
And are ye sure he's weel?
Is this a time to think of wark?
Ye jauds, fling by your wheel.
Is this the time to think of wark,
When Colin's at the door?
Gi'e me my cloak! I'll to the quay
And see him come ashore.

For there's nae luck about the house,
There's nae luck ava;
There's little pleasure in the house,
When our gudeman's awa'.

Rise up and mak' a clean fireside;
Put on the muckle pot;
Gi'e little Kate her cotton gown,
And Jock his Sunday coat:

And mak' their shoon as black as slaes,
Their hose as white as snaw;
It's a' to please my ain gudeman,
For he's been long awa'.

There's twa fat hens upon the bauk,
Been fed this month and mair;
Mak' haste and thraw their necks about,
That Colin weel may fare;
And mak' the table neat and clean,
Gar ilka thing look braw;
It's a' for love of my gudeman,
For he's been long awa'.

O gi'e me down my bigonet,
My bishop satin gown,
For I maun tell the bailie's wife
That Colin's come to town.
My Sunday's shoon they maun gae on,
My hose o' pearl blue;
'Tis a' to please my ain gudeman,
For he's baith leal and true.

Sae true his words, sae smooth his speech,
His breath's like caller air!
His very foot has music in't,
As he comes up the stair.
And will I see his face again?
And will I hear him speak?
I'm downright dizzy with the thought,—
In troth, I'm like to greet.

The cauld blasts o' the winter wind,
That thrilled through my heart,
They're a' blawn by; I ha'e him safe,
Till death we'll never part:
But what puts parting in my head?
It may be far awa';
The present moment is our ain,
The neist we never saw.

Since Colin's weel, I'm weel content,
    I ha'e nae more to crave;
Could I but live to mak' him blest,
    I'm blest above the lave:
And will I see his face again?
    And will I hear him speak?
I'm downright dizzy wi' the thought,—
    In troth, I'm like to greet.

ROBERT FERGUSSON

THE DAFT DAYS

Now mirk December's dowie face
Glowrs owr the rigs wi' sour grimace,
While, thro' his minimum of space,
    The bleer-eyed sun,
Wi' blinkin' light and stealing pace,
    His race doth run.

From naked groves nae birdie sings;
To shepherd's pipe nae hillock rings;
The breeze nae od'rous flavour brings
    From Borean cave;
And dwyning Nature droops her wings,
    Wi' visage grave.

Mankind but scanty pleasure glean
Frae snawy hill or barren plain,
Whan Winter, 'midst his nipping train,
    Wi' frozen spear,
Sends drift owr a' his bleak domain,
    And guides the weir.

Auld Reikie! thou'rt the canty hole,
A bield for mony a caldrife soul,
What snugly at thine ingle loll,
    Baith warm and couth,
While round they gar the bicker roll
    To weet their mouth.

When merry Yule Day comes, I trow,
You'll scantlins find a hungry mou;
Sma' are our cares, our stamacks fou
    O' gusty gear
And kickshaws, strangers to our view
    Sin' fairn-year.

Ye browster wives, now busk ye bra,
And fling your sorrows far awa';
Then come and gie's the tither blaw
    O' reaming ale,
Mair precious than the Well of Spa,
    Our hearts to heal.

Then, though at odds wi' a' the warl',
Amang oursells we'll never quarrel;
Though Discord gie a cankered snarl
    To spoil our glee,
As lang's there's pith into the barrel
    We'll drink and 'gree.

Fiddlers, your pins in temper fix,
And roset weel your fiddlesticks;
But banish vile Italian tricks
    From out your quorum,
Nor *fortes* wi' *pianos* mix—
    Gie's 'Tullochgorum'!

For naught can cheer the heart sae weel
As can a canty Highland reel;
It even vivifies the heel
    To skip and dance:
Lifeless is he wha canna feel
    Its influence.

Let mirth abound; let social cheer
Invest the dawning of the year;
Let blithesome innocence appear,
    To crown our joy;
Nor envy, wi' sarcastic sneer,
    Our bliss destroy.

And thou, great god of *aqua vitæ!*
Wha sways the empire of this city,—
When fou we're sometimes capernoity,—
    Be thou prepared
To hedge us frae that black banditti,
    The City Guard.

ANONYMOUS

ABSENCE

When I think on the happy days
  I spent wi' you, my dearie;
And now what lands between us lie,
  How can I be but eerie!

How slow ye move, ye heavy hours,
  As ye were wae and weary!
It was na sae ye glinted by
  When I was wi' my dearie.

JOHN LANGHORNE

From THE COUNTRY JUSTICE

General Motives for Lenity

Be this, ye rural Magistrates, your plan:
Firm be your justice, but be friends to man.
He whom the mighty master of this ball
We fondly deem, or farcically call,
To own the patriarch's truth however loth,
Holds but a mansion crushed before the moth.
Frail in his genius, in his heart, too, frail,
Born but to err, and erring to bewail;

Shalt thou his faults with eye severe explore,
And give to life one human weakness more?
Still mark if vice or nature prompts the deed;
Still mark the strong temptation and the need;
On pressing want, on famine's powerful call,
At least more lenient let thy justice fall.

Apology for Vagrants

For him who, lost to every hope of life,
Has long with fortune held unequal strife,
Known to no human love, no human care,
The friendless, homeless object of despair;
For the poor vagrant, feel while he complains,
Nor from sad freedom send to sadder chains.
Alike, if folly or misfortune brought
Those last of woes his evil days have wrought;
Believe with social mercy and with me,
Folly's misfortune in the first degree.
  Perhaps on some inhospitable shore
The houseless wretch a widowed parent bore,
Who, then no more by golden prospects led,
Of the poor Indian begged a leafy bed;
Cold on Canadian hills, or Minden's plain,
Perhaps that parent mourned her soldier slain,
Bent o'er her babe, her eye dissolved in dew,
The big drops mingling with the milk he drew,
Gave the sad presage of his future years,
The child of misery, baptized in tears!

AUGUSTUS MONTAGU TOPLADY

ROCK OF AGES

Rock of Ages, cleft for me,
Let me hide myself in Thee!
Let the water and the blood
From Thy riven side which flowed,
Be of sin the double cure,
Cleanse me from its guilt and power.

Not the labors of my hands
Can fulfil Thy law's demands;
Could my zeal no respite know,
Could my tears forever flow,
All for sin could not atone;
Thou must save, and Thou alone.

Nothing in my hand I bring;
Simply to Thy cross I cling;
Naked, come to Thee for dress;
Helpless, look to Thee for grace;
Foul, I to the fountain fly;
Wash me, Saviour, or I die!

While I draw this fleeting breath,
When my eyestrings break in death,
When I soar through tracts unknown,
See Thee on Thy judgment-throne;
Rock of Ages, cleft for me,
Let me hide myself in Thee!

JOHN SKINNER

TULLOCHGORUM

Come gie's a sang! Montgomery cried,
And lay your disputes all aside;
What signifies 't for folk to chide
    For what's been done before 'em?
Let Whig and Tory all agree,
Whig and Tory, Whig and Tory,
Let Whig and Tory all agree
    To drop their Whig-mig-morum!
Let Whig and Tory all agree
To spend the night in mirth and glee,
And cheerfu' sing, alang wi' me,
    The reel o' Tullochgorum!

O, Tullochgorum's my delight;
It gars us a' in ane unite;
And ony sumph' that keeps up spite,
In conscience I abhor him:
For blythe and cheery we's be a',
Blythe and cheery, blythe and cheery,
Blythe and cheery we's be a',
And mak a happy quorum;

For blythe and cheery we's be a',
As lang as we hae breath to draw,
And dance, till we be like to fa',
The reel o' Tullochgorum!

There needs na be sae great a phrase
Wi' dringing dull Italian lays;
I wadna gi'e our ain strathspeys
For half a hundred score o' 'em:
They're douff and dowie at the best,
Douff and dowie, douff and dowie,
They're douff and dowie at the best,
Wi' a' their variorum;
They're douff and dowie at the best,
Their *allegros* and a' the rest;
They canna please a Scottish taste,
Compared wi' Tullochgorum.

Let warldly minds themselves oppress
Wi' fears of want and double cess,
And sullen sots themselves distress
Wi' keeping up decorum:
Shall we sae sour and sulky sit?
Sour and sulky, sour and sulky,
Shall we sae sour and sulky sit,
Like auld Philosophorum?
Shall we so sour and sulky sit,
Wi' neither sense nor mirth nor wit,
Nor ever rise to shake a fit
To the reel o' Tullochgorum?

May choicest blessings still attend
Each honest, open-hearted friend;
And calm and quiet be his end,

And a' that's good watch o'er him!
May peace and plenty be his lot,
Peace and plenty, peace and plenty,
May peace and plenty be his lot,
And dainties a great store o' em!
May peace and plenty be his lot,
Unstained by any vicious spot,
And may he never want a groat
That's fond o' Tullochgorum!

But for the dirty, yawning fool
Who wants to be Oppression's tool,
May envy gnaw his rotten soul,
And discontent devour him!
May dool and sorrow be his chance,
Dool and sorrow, dool and sorrow,
May dool and sorrow be his chance,
And nane say 'wae's me' for him!
May dool and sorrow be his chance,
Wi' a' the ills that come frae France,
Whae'er he be, that winna dance
The reel o' Tullochgorum!

THOMAS CHATTERTON

[SONGS FROM "ÆLLA, A TRAGYCAL ENTERLUDE, WROTENN BIE THOMAS ROWLEIE"]

[THE BODDYNGE FLOURETTES BLOSHES ATTE THE LYGHTE]

FYRSTE MYNSTRELLE

The boddynge flourettes bloshes atte the lyghte;
The mees be sprenged wyth the yellowe hue;
Ynn daiseyd mantels ys the mountayne dyghte;
The nesh yonge coweslepe blendethe wyth the dewe;
The trees enlefèd, yntoe Heavenne straughte,
Whenn gentle wyndes doe blowe to whestlyng dynne ys brought.

The evenynge commes, and brynges the dewe alonge;
The roddie welkynne sheeneth to the eyne;
Arounde the alestakė Mynstrells synge the songe;
Yonge ivie rounde the doore poste do entwyne;
I laie mee onn the grasse; yette, to mie wylle,
Albeytte alle ys fayre, there lackethe somethynge stylle.

SECONDE MYNSTRELLE

So Adam thoughtenne, whann, ynn Paradyse,
All Heavenn and Erthe dyd hommage to hys mynde;
Ynn Womman alleyne mannès pleasaunce lyes;
As Instrumentes of joie were made the kynde.
Go, take a wyfe untoe thie armes, and see
Wynter and brownie hylles wyll have a charm for thee.

THYRDE MYNSTRELLE

Whanne Autumpne blake and sonne-brente doe appere,
With hys goulde honde guylteynge the falleynge lefe,
Bryngeynge oppe Wynterr to folfylle the yere,
Beerynge uponne hys backe the ripèd shefe;
Whan al the hyls wythe woddie sede ys whyte;
Whanne levynne-fyres and lemes do mete from far the syghte;

Whann the fayre apple, rudde as even skie,
Do bende the tree unto the fructyle grounde;
When joicie peres, and berries of blacke die,
Doe daunce yn ayre, and call the eyne arounde;
Thann, bee the even foule or even fayre,
Meethynckes mie hartys joie ys steyncèd wyth somme care.

SECONDE MYNSTRELLE

Angelles bee wrogte to bee of neidher kynde;
Angelles alleyne fromme chafe desyre bee free:
Dheere ys a somwhatte evere yn the mynde,
Yatte, wythout wommanne, cannot styllèd bee;
Ne seyncte yn celles, botte, havynge blodde and tere,
Do fynde the spryte to joie on syghte of womanne fayre;

Wommen bee made, notte for hemselves, botte manne,
Bone of hys bone, and chyld of hys desire;
Fromme an ynutyle membere fyrste beganne,
Ywroghte with moche of water, lyttele fyre;
Therefore theie seke the fyre of love, to hete
The milkyness of kynde, and make hemselfes complete.

Albeytte wythout wommen menne were pheeres
To salvage kynde, and wulde botte lyve to slea,
Botte wommenne efte the spryghte of peace so cheres,
Tochelod yn Angel joie heie Angeles bee:
Go, take thee swythyn to thie bedde a wyfe;
Bee bante or blessed hie yn proovynge marryage lyfe.

[O, SYNGE UNTOE MIE ROUNDELAIE]

O, synge untoe mie roundelaie!
O, droppe the brynie teare wythe mee!
Daunce ne moe atte hallie daie;
Lycke a reynynge ryver bee:
Mie love ys dedde,
Gon to hys death-bedde,
Al under the wyllowe tree.

Blacke hys cryne as the wyntere nyghte,
Whyte hys rode as the sommer snowe,
Rodde hys face as the mornynge lyghte;
Cale he lyes ynne the grave belowe:
Mie love ys dedde,
Gon to hys deathe-bedde,
Al under the wyllowe tree.

Swote hys tyngue as the throstles note,
Quycke ynn daunce as thoughte canne bee,
Defte hys taboure, codgelle stote;
O! hee lyes bie the wyllowe tree:
Mie love ys dedde,
Gonne to hys deathe-bedde,
Alle underre the wyllowe tree.

Harke! the ravenne flappes hys wynge,
In the briered delle belowe;
Harke! the dethe-owle loude dothe synge,
To the nyghte-mares as heie goe:
Mie love ys dedde,
Gonne to hys deathe-bedde,
Al under the wyllowe tree.

See! the whyte moone sheenes onne hie;
Whyterre ys mie true loves shroude,
Whyterre yanne the mornynge skie,
Whyterre yanne the evenynge cloude:
Mie love ys dedde,
Gon to hys deathe-bedde,
Al under the wyllowe tree.

Heere, uponne mie true loves grave,
Schalle the baren fleurs be layde,
Nee one hallie Seyncte to save
Al the celness of a mayde:
Mie love ys dedde,
Gonne to hys deathe-bedde,
Alle under the wyllowe tree.

Wythe mie hondes I'lle dente the brieres
Rounde his hallie corse to gre;
Ouphante fairie, lyghte youre fyres,
Heere mie boddie stylle schalle bee:
Mie love ys dedde,
Gon to hys death-bedde,
Al under the wyllowe tree.

Comme, wythe acorne-coppe and thorne
Drayne mie hartys blodde awaie;
Lyfe and all yttes goode I scorne,
Daunce bie nete, or feaste by daie:
Mie love ys dedde,
Gon to hys death-bedde,
Al under the wyllowe tree.

Waterre wytches, crownede wythe reytes,
Bere mee to yer leathalle tyde.
I die! I comme! mie true love waytes.—
Thos the damselle spake, and dyed.

AN EXCELENTE BALADE OF CHARITIE

AS WROTEN BIE THE GODE PRIESTE THOMAS ROWLEY, 1464

In Virgynè the sweltrie sun gan sheene,
And hotte upon the mees did caste his raie;
The apple rodded from its palie greene,
And the mole peare did bende the leafy spraie;
The peede chelandri sunge the livelong daie;
'Twas nowe the pride, the manhode, of the yeare,
And eke the grounde was dighte in its most defte au[illegible]re.

The sun was glemeing in the midde of daie,
Deadde still the aire, and eke the welken blue;
When from the sea arist in drear arraie
A hepe of cloudes of sable sullen hue,
The which full fast unto the woodlande drewe,
Hiltring attenes the sunnis fetive face,
And the blacke tempeste swolne and gathered up apace.

Beneathe an holme, faste by a pathwaie side
Which dide unto Seyncte Godwine's covent lede,
A hapless pilgrim moneynge dyd abide,
Pore in his viewe, ungentle in his weede,
Longe bretful of the miseries of neede;
Where from the hailstone coulde the almer flie?
He had no housen theere, ne anie covent nie.

Look in his glommèd face, his spright there scanne:
Howe woe-be-gone, how withered, forwynd, deade!
Haste to thie church-glebe-house, ashrewed manne;
Haste to thie kiste, thie onlie dorture bedde:
Cale as the claie whiche will gre on thie hedde
Is Charitie and Love aminge highe elves;
Knightis and Barons live for pleasure and themselves.

The gathered storme is rype; the bigge drops falle;
The forswat meadowes smethe, and drenche the raine;
The comyng ghastness do the cattle pall,
And the full flockes are drivynge ore the plaine;
Dashde from the cloudes, the waters flott againe;
The welkin opes, the yellow levynne flies,
And the hot fierie smothe in the wide lowings dies.

Liste! now the thunder's rattling clymmynge sound
Cheves slowie on, and then embollen clangs,
Shakes the hie spyre, and, losst, dispended, drowned,
Still on the gallard eare of terroure hanges;
The windes are up, the lofty elmen swanges;
Again the levynne and the thunder poures,
And the full cloudes are braste attenes in stonen showers.

Spurreynge his palfrie oere the watrie plaine,
The Abbote of Seyncte Godwyne's convente came:
His chapournette was drented with the reine,
And his pencte gyrdle met with mickle shame;
He aynewarde tolde his bederoll at the same.
The storme encreasen, and he drew aside
With the mist almes-craver neere to the holme to bide.

His cope was all of Lyncolne clothe so fyne,
With a gold button fastened neere his chynne;
His autremete was edged with golden twynne,
And his shoone pyke a loverds mighte have binne—
Full well it shewn he thoughten coste no sinne;
The trammels of the palfrye pleasde his sighte,
For the horse-millanare his head with roses dighte.

'An almes, sir prieste!' the droppynge pilgrim saide;
'O let me waite within your covente dore,
Till the sunne sheneth hie above our heade,
And the loude tempeste of the aire is oer.
Helpless and ould am I, alas! and poor;
No house, ne friend, ne moneie in my pouche;
All yatte I calle my owne is this my silver crouche.'

'Varlet,' replyd the Abbatte, 'cease your dinne!
This is no season almes and prayers to give.
Mie porter never lets a faitour in;
None touch mie rynge who not in honour live.'
And now the sonne with the blacke cloudes did stryve,
And shettynge on the ground his glairie raie:
The Abbatte spurrde his steede, and eftsoones roadde awaie.

Once moe the skie was blacke, the thounder rolde:
Faste reyneynge oer the plaine a prieste was seen,
Ne dighte full proude, ne buttoned up in golde;
His cope and jape were graie, and eke were clene;
A Limitoure he was of order seene.
And from the pathwaie side then turnèd hee,
Where the pore almer laie binethe the holmen tree.

'An almes, sir priest!' the droppynge pilgrim sayde,
'For sweete Seyncte Marie and your order sake!'
The Limitoure then loosened his pouche threade,
And did thereoute a groate of silver take:
The mister pilgrim dyd for halline shake.
'Here, take this silver; it maie eathe thie care:
We are Goddes stewards all, nete of our owne we bare.

'But ah, unhailie pilgrim, lerne of me
Scathe anie give a rentrolle to their Lorde.
Here, take my semecope—thou arte bare, I see;
'Tis thyne; the Seynctes will give me mie rewarde.'
He left the pilgrim, and his waie aborde.
Virgynne and hallie Seyncte, who sitte yn gloure,
Or give the mittee will, or give the gode man power!

THOMAS DAY

From THE DESOLATION OF AMERICA

I see, I see, swift bursting through the shade,
The cruel soldier, and the reeking blade.
And there the bloody cross of Britain waves,
Pointing to deeds of death an host of slaves.
To them unheard the wretched tell their pain,
And every human sorrow sues in vain:
Their hardened bosoms never knew to melt;
Each woe unpitied, and each pang unfelt.—
See! where they rush, and with a savage joy,
Unsheathe the sword, impatient to destroy.

Fierce as the tiger, bursting from the wood,
With famished jaws, insatiable of blood!
Yet, yet a moment, the fell steel restrain;
Must Nature's sacred ties all plead in vain?
Ah! while your kindred blood remains unspilt,
And Heaven allows an awful pause from guilt,
Suspend the war, and recognize the bands,
Against whose lives you arm your impious hands!—
Not these, the boast of Gallia's proud domains,
Nor the scorched squadrons of Iberian plains;
Unhappy men! no foreign war you wage,
In your own blood you glut your frantic rage;
And while you follow where oppression leads,
At every step, a friend, or brother, bleeds.

. . . .

Devoted realm! what now avails thy claim,
To milder virtue, or sublimer flame?
Or what avails, unhappy land! to trace
The generous labours of thy patriot race?
Who, urged by fate, and fortitude their guide,
On the wild surge their desperate fortune tried;
Undaunted every toil and danger bore,
And fixed their standards on a savage shore;
What time they fled, with an averted eye,
The baneful influence of their native sky,
Where slowly rising through the dusky air,
The northern meteors shot their lurid glare.
In vain their country's genius sought to move,
With tender images of former love,
Sad rising to their view, in all her charms,
And weeping wooed them to her well-known arms.
The favoured clime, the soft domestic air,
And wealth and ease were all below their care,
Since there an hated tyrant met their eyes
And blasted every blessing of the skies.

. . . .

And now, no more by nature's bounds confined
He* spreads his dragon pinions to the wind.
The genius of the West beholds him near,
And freedom trembles at her last barrier.

* The monster, tyranny.

In vain she deemed in this sequestered seat
To fix a refuge for her wandering feet;
To mark one altar sacred to her fame,
And save the ruins of the human name.

. . . .

Lo! Britain bended to the servile yoke,
Her fire extinguished, and her spirit broke,
Beneath the pressure of [a tyrant's] sway,
Herself at once the spoiler and the prey,
Detest[s] the virtues she can boast no more
And envies every right to every shore!
At once to nature and to pity blind,
Wages abhorrèd war with humankind;
And wheresoe'er her ocean rolls his wave,
Provokes an enemy, or meets a slave.
But free-born minds inspired with noble flame,
Attest their origin, and scorn the claim.
Beyond the sweets of pleasure and of rest,
The joys which captivate the vulgar breast;
Beyond the dearer ties of kindred blood;
Or brittle life's too transitory good;
The sacred charge of liberty they prize,
That last, and noblest, present of the skies.

. . . .

Yet, gracious Heaven! though clouds may intervene,
And transitory horrors shade the scene;
Though for an instant virtue sink depressed,
While vice exulting rears her bloody crest;
Thy sacred truth shall still inspire my mind,
To cast the terrors of my fate behind!
Thy power which nature's utmost bound pervades,
Beams through the void, and cheers destruction's shades,
Can blast the laurel on the victor's head,
And smooth the good man's agonizing bed,
To songs of triumph change the captive's groans,
And hurl the powers of darkness from their thrones!

GEORGE CRABBE

From THE LIBRARY

When the sad soul, by care and grief oppressed,
Looks round the world, but looks in vain for rest;
When every object that appears in view,
Partakes her gloom and seems dejected too;
Where shall affliction from itself retire?
Where fade away and placidly expire?
Alas! we fly to silent scenes in vain;
Care blasts the honours of the flowery plain:
Care veils in clouds the sun's meridian beam,
Sighs through the grove, and murmurs in the stream;
For when the soul is labouring in despair,
In vain the body breathes a purer air.

. . . .

Here come the grieved, a change of thought to find;
The curious here, to feed a craving mind;
Here the devout their peaceful temple choose;
And here the poet meets his fav'ring Muse.
With awe, around these silent walks I tread;
These are the lasting mansions of the dead:—
'The dead!' methinks a thousand tongues reply,
'These are the tombs of such as cannot die!
Crowned with eternal fame, they sit sublime,
And laugh at all the little strife of time.'

. . . .

Lo! all in silence, all in order stand,
And mighty folios first, a lordly band;
Then quartos their well-ordered ranks maintain,
And light octavos fill a spacious plain:
See yonder, ranged in more frequented rows,
A humbler band of duodecimos;
While undistinguished trifles swell the scene,
The last new play and frittered magazine.

. . . .

But who are these, a tribe that soar above,
And tell more tender tales of modern love?

A *novel* train! the brood of old Romance,
Conceived by Folly on the coast of France,
That now with lighter thought and gentler fire,
Usurp the honours of their drooping sire;
And still fantastic, vain, and trifling, sing
Of many a soft and inconsistent thing,—
Of rakes repenting, clogged in Hymen's chain,
Of nymph reclined by unpresuming swain,
Of captains, colonels, lords, and amorous knights,
That find in humbler nymphs such chaste delights,
Such heavenly charms, so gentle, yet so gay,
That all their former follies fly away:
Honour springs up, where'er their looks impart
A moment's sunshine to the hardened heart;
A virtue, just before the rover's jest,
Grows like a mushroom in his melting breast.
Much too they tell of cottages and shades,
Of balls, and routs, and midnight masquerades,
Where dangerous men and dangerous mirth reside,
And Virtue goes —— on purpose to be tried.
These are the tales that wake the soul to life,
That charm the sprightly niece and forward wife,
That form the manners of a polished age,
And each pure easy moral of the stage.

From THE VILLAGE

The village life, and every care that reigns
O'er youthful peasants and declining swains;
What labour yields, and what, that labour past,
Age, in its hour of languor, finds at last;
What form the real picture of the poor,
Demand a song—the Muse can give no more.
Fled are those times when, in harmonious strains,
The rustic poet praised his native plains;
No shepherds now, in smooth alternate verse,
Their country's beauty or their nymphs' rehearse:
Yet still for these we frame the tender strain;
Still in our lays fond Corydons complain,
And shepherds' boys their amorous pains reveal—
The only pains, alas! they never feel.

On Mincio's banks, in Cæsar's bounteous reign,
If Tityrus found the Golden Age again,
Must sleepy bards the flattering dream prolong,
Mechanic echoes of the Mantuan song?
From Truth and Nature shall we widely stray,
Where Virgil, not where Fancy, leads the way?
Yes, thus the Muses sing of happy swains,
Because the Muses never knew their pains.
They boast their peasants' pipes; but peasants now
Resign their pipes and plod behind the plough,
And few amid the rural tribe have time
To number syllables and play with rhyme:
Save honest Duck, what son of verse could share
The poet's rapture and the peasant's care,
Or the great labours of the field degrade
With the new peril of a poorer trade?
From this chief cause these idle praises spring—
That themes so easy few forbear to sing,
For no deep thought the trifling subjects ask;
To sing of shepherds is an easy task:
The happy youth assumes the common strain,
A nymph his mistress, and himself a swain;
With no sad scenes he clouds his tuneful prayer,
But all, to look like her, is painted fair.
I grant indeed that fields and flocks have charms
For him that grazes or for him that farms;
But when amid such pleasing scenes I trace
The poor laborious natives of the place,
And see the mid-day sun with fervid ray
On their bare heads and dewy temples play,
While some, with feebler heads and fainter hearts
Deplore their fortune yet sustain their parts,
Then shall I dare these real ills to hide
In tinsel trappings of poetic pride?
No; cast by Fortune on a frowning coast,
Which neither groves nor happy valleys boast;
Where other cares than those the Muse relates,
And other shepherds dwell with other mates;
By such examples taught, I paint the cot
As Truth will paint it and as bards will not.
Nor you, ye poor, of lettered scorn complain:
To you the smoothest song is smooth in vain;

O'ercome by labour and bowed down by time,
Feel you the barren flattery of a rhyme?
Can poets soothe you, when you pine for bread,
By winding myrtles round your ruined shed?
Can their light tales your weighty griefs o'erpower,
Or glad with airy mirth the toilsome hour?
  Lo! where the heath, with withering brake grown o'er,
Lends the light turf that warms the neighbouring poor;
From thence a length of burning sand appears,
Where the thin harvest waves its withered ears;
Rank weeds, that every art and care defy,
Reign o'er the land and rob the blighted rye:
There thistles stretch their prickly arms afar,
And to the ragged infant threaten war;
There poppies nodding, mock the hope of toil;
There the blue bugloss paints the sterile soil;
Hardy and high, above the slender sheaf,
The slimy mallow waves her silky leaf;
O'er the young shoot the charlock throws a shade,
And clasping tares cling round the sickly blade;
With mingled tints the rocky coasts abound,
And a sad splendour vainly shines around.

. . . .

Here, wandering long, amid these frowning fields,
I sought the simple life that Nature yields:
Rapine and Wrong and Fear usurped her place,
And a bold, artful, surly, savage race;
Who, only skilled to take the finny tribe,
The yearly dinner, or septennial bribe,
Wait on the shore, and, as the waves run high,
On the tossed vessel bend their eager eye,
Which to their coast directs its venturous way;
Theirs or the ocean's miserable prey.
  As on their neighbouring beach yon swallows stand,
And wait for favouring winds to leave the land;
While still for flight the ready wing is spread:
So waited I the favouring hour, and fled;
Fled from these shores where guilt and famine reign,
And cried, 'Ah! hapless they who still remain:
Who still remain to hear the ocean roar,
Whose greedy waves devour the lessening shore;

Till some fierce tide, with more imperious sway
Sweeps the low hut and all it holds away;
When the sad tenant weeps from door to door,
And begs a poor protection from the poor!'

But these are scenes where Nature's niggard hand
Gave a spare portion to the famished land;
Hers is the fault, if here mankind complain
Of fruitless toil and labour spent in vain;
But yet in other scenes more fair in view,
Where Plenty smiles—alas! she smiles for few—
And those who taste not, yet behold her store,
Are as the slaves that dig the golden ore—
The wealth around them makes them doubly poor.
Or will you deem them amply paid in health,
Labour's fair child, that languishes with wealth?
Go, then! and see them rising with the sun,
Through a long course of daily toil to run;
See them beneath the Dog-star's raging heat,
When the knees tremble and the temples beat;
Behold them, leaning on their scythes, look o'er
The labour past, and toils to come explore;
See them alternate suns and showers engage,
And hoard up aches and anguish for their age;
Through fens and marshy moors their steps pursue,
When their warm pores imbibe the evening dew;
Then own that labour may as fatal be
To these thy slaves, as thine excess to thee.

Amid this tribe too oft a manly pride
Strives in strong toil the fainting heart to hide;
There may you see the youth of slender frame
Contend with weakness, weariness, and shame;
Yet, urged along, and proudly loth to yield,
He strives to join his fellows of the field;
Till long-contending nature droops at last,
Declining health rejects his poor repast,
His cheerless spouse the coming danger sees,
And mutual murmurs urge the slow disease.

Yet grant them health, 'tis not for us to tell,
Though the head droops not, that the heart is well;
Or will you praise that homely, healthy fare,
Plenteous and plain, that happy peasants share!

Oh! trifle not with wants you cannot feel,
Nor mock the misery of a stinted meal;
Homely, not wholesome, plain, not plenteous, such
As you who praise, would never deign to touch.
  Ye gentle souls, who dream of rural ease,
Whom the smooth stream and smoother sonnet please;
Go! if the peaceful cot your praises share,
Go look within, and ask if peace be there;
If peace be his, that drooping weary sire;
Or theirs, that offspring round their feeble fire;
Or hers, that matron pale, whose trembling hand
Turns on the wretched hearth th' expiring brand.
  Nor yet can Time itself obtain for these
Life's latest comforts, due respect and ease;
For yonder see that hoary swain, whose age
Can with no cares except its own engage;
Who, propped on that rude staff, looks up to see
The bare arms broken from the withering tree,
On which, a boy, he climbed the loftiest bough,
Then his first joy, but his sad emblem now.
  He once was chief in all the rustic trade;
His steady hand the straightest furrow made;
Full many a prize he won, and still is proud
To find the triumphs of his youth allowed;
A transient pleasure sparkles in his eyes,
He hears and smiles, then thinks again and sighs;
For now he journeys to his grave in pain;
The rich disdain him; nay, the poor disdain:
Alternate masters now their slave command,
Urge the weak efforts of his feeble hand,
And, when his age attempts its task in vain,
With ruthless taunts, of lazy poor complain.
  Oft may you see him, when he tends the sheep,
His winter charge, beneath the hillock weep;
Oft hear him murmur to the winds that blow
O'er his white locks and bury them in snow,
When, roused by rage and muttering in the morn,
He mends the broken hedge with icy thorn:—
  'Why do I live, when I desire to be
At once from life and life's long labour free?
Like leaves in spring, the young are blown away,
Without the sorrows of a slow decay;

I, like yon withered leaf, remain behind,
Nipped by the frost, and shivering in the wind;
There it abides till younger buds come on
As I, now all my fellow-swains are gone;
Then from the rising generation thrust,
It falls, like me, unnoticed to the dust.
'These fruitful fields, these numerous flocks I see,
Are others' gain, but killing cares to me;
To me the children of my youth are lords,
Cool in their looks, but hasty in their words:
Wants of their own demand their care; and who
Feels his own want and succours others too?
A lonely, wretched man, in pain I go,
None need my help, and none relieve my woe;
Then let my bones beneath the turf be laid,
And men forget the wretch they would not aid.'
Thus groan the old, till by disease oppressed,
They taste a final woe, and then they rest.
Theirs is yon house that holds the parish poor,
Whose walls of mud scarce bear the broken door;
There, where the putrid vapours, flagging, play,
And the dull wheel hums doleful through the day;
There children dwell who know no parents' care;
Parents, who know no children's love, dwell there!
Heart-broken matrons on their joyless bed,
Forsaken wives, and mothers never wed;
Dejected widows with unheeded tears,
And crippled age with more than childhood fears;
The lame, the blind, and, far the happiest they!
The moping idiot, and the madman gay.
Here too the sick their final doom receive,
Here brought, amid the scenes of grief, to grieve,
Where the loud groans from some sad chamber flow,
Mixed with the clamours of the crowd below;
Here, sorrowing, they each kindred sorrow scan,
And the cold charities of man to man:
Whose laws indeed for ruined age provide,
And strong compulsion plucks the scrap from pride;
But still that scrap is bought with many a sigh,
And pride embitters what it can't deny.
Say, ye, oppressed by some fantastic woes,
Some jarring nerve that baffles your repose;

Who press the downy couch, while slaves advance
With timid eye to read the distant glance;
Who with sad prayers the weary doctor tease
To name the nameless, ever-new, disease;
Who with mock patience dire complaints endure,
Which real pain, and that alone, can cure;
How would ye bear in real pain to lie,
Despised, neglected, left alone to die?
How would ye bear to draw your latest breath
Where all that's wretched paves the way for death?
  Such is that room which one rude beam divides,
And naked rafters form the sloping sides;
Where the vile bands that bind the thatch are seen,
And lath and mud are all that lie between,
Save one dull pane that, coarsely patched, gives way
To the rude tempest, yet excludes the day:
Here on a matted flock, with dust o'erspread,
The drooping wretch reclines his languid head;
For him no hand the cordial cup applies,
Or wipes the tear that stagnates in his eyes;
No friends with soft discourse his pain beguile,
Or promise hope till sickness wears a smile.
  But soon a loud and hasty summons calls,
Shakes the thin roof, and echoes round the walls;
Anon, a figure enters, quaintly neat,
All pride and business, bustle and conceit;
With looks unaltered by these scenes of woe,
With speed that, entering, speaks his haste to go,
He bids the gazing throng around him fly,
And carries fate and physic in his eye:
A potent quack, long versed in human ills,
Who first insults the victim whom he kills;
Whose murderous hand a drowsy Bench protect,
And whose most tender mercy is neglect.
Paid by the parish for attendance here,
He wears contempt upon his sapient sneer;
In haste he seeks the bed where misery lies,
Impatience marked in his averted eyes;
And, some habitual queries hurried o'er,
Without reply he rushes on the door:
His drooping patient, long inured to pain,
And long unheeded, knows remonstrance vain;

He ceases now the feeble help to crave
Of man; and silent sinks into the grave.
  But ere his death some pious doubts arise,
Some simple fears, which 'bold bad' men despise;
Fain would he ask the parish-priest to prove
His title certain to the joys above:
For this he sends the murm'ring nurse, who calls
The holy stranger to these dismal walls:
And doth not he, the pious man, appear,
He, 'passing rich with forty pounds a year?'
Ah! no; a shepherd of a different stock,
And far unlike him, feeds this little flock:
A jovial youth, who thinks his Sunday's task
As much as God or man can fairly ask;
The rest he gives to loves and labours light,
To fields the morning, and to feasts the night;
None better skilled the noisy pack to guide,
To urge their chase, to cheer them or to chide;
A sportsman keen, he shoots through half the day,
And, skilled at whist, devotes the night to play:
Then, while such honours bloom around his head,
Shall he sit sadly by the sick man's bed,
To raise the hope he feels not, or with zeal
To combat fears that e'en the pious feel?

. . . .

And hark! the riots of the green begin,
That sprang at first from yonder noisy inn;
What time the weekly pay was vanished all,
And the slow hostess scored the threatening wall;
What time they asked, their friendly feast to close,
A final cup, and that will make them foes;
When blows ensue that break the arm of toil,
And rustic battle ends the boobies' broil.
  Save when to yonder hall they bend their way,
Where the grave justice ends the grievous fray;
He who recites, to keep the poor in awe,
The law's vast volume—for he knows the law:—
To him with anger or with shame repair
The injured peasant and deluded fair.
Lo! at his throne the silent nymph appears,
Frail by her shape, but modest in her tears;

And while she stands abashed, with conscious eye,
Some favourite female of her judge glides by,
Who views with scornful glance the strumpet's fate,
And thanks the stars that made her keeper great;
Near her the swain, about to bear for life
One certain evil, doubts 'twixt war and wife;
But, while the faltering damsel takes her oath,
Consents to wed, and so secures them both.
 Yet why, you ask, these humble crimes relate,
Why make the poor as guilty as the great?
To show the great, those mightier sons of pride,
How near in vice the lowest are allied;
Such are their natures and their passions such,
But these disguise too little, those too much:
So shall the man of power and pleasure see
In his own slave as vile a wretch as he;
In his luxurious lord the servant find
His own low pleasures and degenerate mind;
And each in all the kindred vices trace
Of a poor, blind, bewildered, erring race;
Who, a short time in varied fortune past,
Die, and are equal in the dust at last.

JOHN NEWTON

A VISION OF LIFE IN DEATH

In evil long I took delight,
 Unawed by shame or fear,
Till a new object struck my sight,
 And stopped my wild career;
I saw One hanging on a Tree
 In agonies and blood,
Who fixed His languid eyes on me,
 As near His cross I stood.

Sure never till my latest breath
 Can I forget that look:
It seemed to charge me with His death,
 Though not a word he spoke:

My conscience felt and owned the guilt,
  And plunged me in despair;
I saw my sins His blood had spilt,
  And helped to nail Him there.

Alas! I know not what I did!
  But now my tears are vain:
Where shall my trembling soul be hid?
  For I the Lord have slain!
A second look He gave, which said,
  'I freely all forgive;
The blood is for thy ransom paid;
  I die, that thou may'st live.'

Thus, while His death my sin displays
  In all its blackest hue,
Such is the mystery of grace,
  It seals my pardon too.
With pleasing grief and mournful joy,
  My spirit now is filled
That I should such a life destroy,—
  Yet live by Him I killed.

WILLIAM COWPER

From TABLE TALK

[The Poet and Religion]

Pity Religion has so seldom found
A skilful guide into poetic ground!
The flowers would spring where'er she deigned to stray,
And every muse attend her in her way.
Virtue indeed meets many a rhyming friend,
And many a compliment politely penned,
But unattired in that becoming vest
Religion weaves for her, and half undressed,
Stands in the desert shivering and forlorn,
A wintry figure, like a withered thorn.

The shelves are full, all other themes are sped,
Hackneyed and worn to the last flimsy thread;
Satire has long since done his best, and curst
And loathsome Ribaldry has done his worst;
Fancy has sported all her powers away
In tales, in trifles, and in children's play;
And 'tis the sad complaint, and almost true,
Whate'er we write, we bring forth nothing new.
'Twere new indeed to see a bard all fire,
Touched with a coal from heaven, assume the lyre,
And tell the world, still kindling as he sung,
With more than mortal music on his tongue,
That He who died below, and reigns above,
Inspires the song, and that his name is Love.

From CONVERSATION

[The Dubious and the Positive]

Dubious is such a scrupulous good man,—
Yes, you may catch him tripping if you can.
He would not with a peremptory tone
Assert the nose upon his face his own;
With hesitation admirably slow,
He humbly hopes—presumes—it may be so.
His evidence, if he were called by law
To swear to some enormity he saw,
For want of prominence and just relief,
Would hang an honest man, and save a thief.
Through constant dread of giving truth offence,
He ties up all his hearers in suspense;
Knows what he knows, as if he knew it not;
What he remembers seems to have forgot;
His sole opinion, whatsoe'er befall,
Centering at last in having none at all.
Yet though he tease and baulk your listening ear,
He makes one useful point exceeding clear;
Howe'er ingenious on his darling theme
A sceptic in philosophy may seem,
Reduced to practice, his beloved rule
Would only prove him a consummate fool;

Useless in him alike both brain and speech,
Fate having placed all truth above his reach;
His ambiguities his total sum,
He might as well be blind and deaf and dumb.
  Where men of judgment creep and feel their way,
The positive pronounce without dismay,
Their want of light and intellect supplied
By sparks absurdity strikes out of pride:
Without the means of knowing right from wrong,
They always are decisive, clear, and strong;
Where others toil with philosophic force,
Their nimble nonsense takes a shorter course,
Flings at your head conviction in the lump,
And gains remote conclusions at a jump;
Their own defect, invisible to them,
Seen in another, they at once condemn,
And, though self-idolized in every case,
Hate their own likeness in a brother's face.
The cause is plain and not to be denied,
The proud are always most provoked by pride;
Few competitions but engender spite,
And those the most where neither has a right.

TO A YOUNG LADY

Sweet stream, that winds through yonder glade,
Apt emblem of a virtuous maid—
Silent and chaste she steals along,
Far from the world's gay busy throng:
With gentle yet prevailing force,
Intent upon her destined course;
Graceful and useful all she does.
Blessing and blest where'er she goes;
Pure-bosomed as that watery glass
And Heaven reflected in her face.

THE SHRUBBERY

O happy shades! to me unblest!
  Friendly to peace, but not to me!
How ill the scene that offers rest,
  And heart that cannot rest, agree!

This glassy stream, that spreading pine,
  Those alders quivering to the breeze,
Might soothe a soul less hurt than mine,
  And please, if anything could please.

But fixed unalterable Care
  Foregoes not what she feels within,
Shows the same sadness everywhere,
  And slights the season and the scene.

For all that pleased in wood or lawn
  While Peace possessed these silent bowers,
Her animating smile withdrawn,
  Has lost its beauties and its powers.

The saint or moralist should tread
  This moss-grown alley, musing, slow,
They seek like me the secret shade,
  But not, like me, to nourish woe!

Me, fruitful scenes and prospects waste
  Alike admonish not to roam;
These tell me of enjoyments past,
  And those of sorrows yet to come.

From THE TASK

[Love of Familiar Scenes]

Scenes that soothed
Or charmed me young, no longer young, I find
Still soothing and of power to charm me still.
And witness, dear companion of my walks,
Whose arm this twentieth winter I perceive
Fast locked in mine, with pleasure such as love,
Confirmed by long experience of thy worth
And well-tried virtues, could alone inspire,
Witness a joy that thou hast doubled long.
Thou knowest my praise of nature most sincere,
And that my raptures are not conjured up
To serve occasions of poetic pomp,
But genuine, and art partner of them all.

How oft upon yon eminence our pace
Has slackened to a pause, and we have borne
The ruffling wind, scarce conscious that it blew,
While admiration feeding at the eye,
And still unsated, dwelt upon the scene.
Thence with what pleasure have we just discerned
The distant plough slow moving, and beside
His labouring team, that swerved not from the track,
The sturdy swain diminished to a boy.
Here Ouse, slow winding through a level plain
Of spacious meads with cattle sprinkled o'er,
Conducts the eye along his sinuous course
Delighted. There, fast rooted in their bank,
Stand, never overlooked, our favourite elms,
That screen the herdsman's solitary hut;
While far beyond, and overthwart the stream,
That, as with molten glass, inlays the vale,
The sloping land recedes into the clouds;
Displaying on its varied side the grace
Of hedge-row beauties numberless, square tower,
Tall spire, from which the sound of cheerful bells
Just undulates upon the listening ear;
Groves, heaths, and smoking villages remote.
Scenes must be beautiful which, daily viewed,
Please daily, and whose novelty survives
Long knowledge and the scrutiny of years:
Praise justly due to those that I describe.

[MAN'S INHUMANITY]

Oh for a lodge in some vast wilderness,
Some boundless contiguity of shade,
Where rumour of oppression and deceit,
Of unsuccessful or successful war,
Might never reach me more! My ear is pained,
My soul is sick, with every day's report
Of wrong and outrage with which earth is filled.
There is no flesh in man's obdurate heart,
It does not feel for man; the natural bond
Of brotherhood is severed as the flax
That falls asunder at the touch of fire.
He finds his fellow guilty of a skin

Not coloured like his own, and, having power
T' enforce the wrong, for such a worthy cause
Dooms and devotes him as his lawful prey.
Lands intersected by a narrow frith
Abhor each other. Mountains interposed
Make enemies of nations who had else
Like kindred drops been mingled into one.
Thus man devotes his brother, and destroys;
And worse than all, and most to be deplored,
As human nature's broadest, foulest blot,
Chains him, and tasks him, and exacts his sweat
With stripes that Mercy, with a bleeding heart,
Weeps when she sees inflicted on a beast.
Then what is man? And what man seeing this,
And having human feelings, does not blush
And hang his head, to think himself a man?
I would not have a slave to till my ground,
To carry me, to fan me while I sleep,
And tremble when I wake, for all the wealth
That sinews bought and sold have ever earned.
No: dear as freedom is, and in my heart's
Just estimation prized above all price,
I had much rather be myself the slave
And wear the bonds than fasten them on him.
We have no slaves at home: then why abroad?
And they themselves, once ferried o'er the wave
That parts us, are emancipate and loosed.
Slaves cannot breathe in England; if their lungs
Receive our air, that moment they are free;
They touch our country, and their shackles fall.
That's noble, and bespeaks a nation proud
And jealous of the blessing. Spread it, then,
And let it circulate through every vein
Of all your empire; that where Britain's power
Is felt, mankind may feel her mercy too.

[Love of England]

England, with all thy faults, I love thee still,
My country! and, while yet a nook is left
Where English minds and manners may be found,
Shall be constrained to love thee. Though thy clime

Be fickle, and thy year, most part, deformed
With dripping rains, or withered by a frost,
I would not yet exchange thy sullen skies
And fields without a flower, for warmer France
With all her vines; nor for Ausonia's groves
Of golden fruitage, and her myrtle bowers.
To shake thy senate, and from heights sublime
Of patriot eloquence to flash down fire
Upon thy foes, was never meant my task;
But I can feel thy fortunes, and partake
Thy joys and sorrows with as true a heart
As any thunderer there. And I can feel
Thy follies too, and with a just disdain
Frown at effeminates, whose very looks
Reflect dishonour on the land I love.
How, in the name of soldiership and sense,
Should England prosper, when such things, as smooth
And tender as a girl, all-essenced o'er
With odours, and as profligate as sweet,
Who sell their laurel for a myrtle wreath,
And love when they should fight,—when such as these
Presume to lay their hand upon the ark
Of her magnificent and awful cause?
Time was when it was praise and boast enough
In every clime, and travel where we might,
That we were born her children; praise enough
To fill the ambition of a private man,
That Chatham's language was his mother tongue,
And Wolfe's great name compatriot with his own.
Farewell those honours, and farewell with them
The hope of such hereafter! They have fallen
Each in his field of glory: one in arms,
And one in council—Wolfe upon the lap
Of smiling Victory that moment won,
And Chatham, heart-sick of his country's shame!
They made us many soldiers. Chatham still
Consulting England's happiness at home,
Secured it by an unforgiving frown
If any wronged her. Wolfe, where'er he fought,
Put so much of his heart into his act,
That his example had a magnet's force,
And all were swift to follow whom all loved.

Those suns are set. Oh, rise some other such!
Or all that we have left is empty talk
Of old achievements, and despair of new.

[COWPER, THE RELIGIOUS RECLUSE]

I was a stricken deer that left the herd
Long since; with many an arrow deep infixed
My panting side was charged, when I withdrew
To seek a tranquil death in distant shades.
There was I found by One who had Himself
Been hurt by th' archers. In His side He bore,
And in His hands and feet, the cruel scars.
With gentle force soliciting the darts,
He drew them forth, and healed, and bade me live.
Since then, with few associates, in remote
And silent woods I wander, far from those
My former partners of the peopled scene,
With few associates, and not wishing more.
Here much I ruminate, as much I may,
With other views of men and manners now
Than once, and others of a life to come.
I see that all are wanderers, gone astray
Each in his own delusions; they are lost
In chase of fancied happiness, still wooed
And never won; dream after dream ensues,
And still they dream that they shall still succeed,
And still are disappointed: rings the world
With the vain stir. I sum up half mankind,
And add two-thirds of the remaining half,
And find the total of their hopes and fears
Dreams, empty dreams.

[THE ARRIVAL OF THE POST]

Hark! 'tis the twanging horn! O'er yonder bridge,
That with its wearisome but needful length
Bestrides the wintry flood, in which the moon
Sees her unwrinkled face reflected bright,
He comes, the herald of a noisy world,
With spattered boots, strapped waist, and frozen locks,
News from all nations lumbering at his back,
True to his charge, the close-packed load behind,

Yet careless what he brings, his one concern
Is to conduct it to the destined inn,
And, having dropped th' expected bag, pass on.
He whistles as he goes, light-hearted wretch,
Cold and yet cheerful; messenger of grief
Perhaps to thousands, and of joy to some,
To him indifferent whether grief or joy.
Houses in ashes, and the fall of stocks,
Births, deaths, and marriages, epistles wet
With tears that trickled down the writer's cheeks
Fast as the periods from his fluent quill,
Or charged with amorous sighs of absent swains
Or nymphs responsive, equally affect
His horse and him, unconscious of them all.
But oh th' important budget, ushered in
With such heart-shaking music, who can say
What are its tidings? Have our troops awaked,
Or do they still, as if with opium drugged,
Snore to the murmurs of th' Atlantic wave?
Is India free, and does she wear her plumed
And jewelled turban with a smile of peace,
Or do we grind her still? The grand debate,
The popular harangue, the tart reply,
The logic, and the wisdom, and the wit,
And the loud laugh—I long to know them all;
I burn to set th' imprisoned wranglers free,
And give them voice and utterance once again.
  Now stir the fire, and close the shutters fast,
Let fall the curtains, wheel the sofa round;
And while the bubbling and loud-hissing urn
Throws up a steamy column, and the cups
That cheer but not inebriate, wait on each,
So let us welcome peaceful evening in.

[The Bastile]

Then shame to manhood, and opprobrious more
To France than all her losses and defeats
Old or of later date, by sea or land,
Her house of bondage worse than that of old
Which God avenged on Pharaoh—the Bastile!

Ye horrid towers, th' abode of broken hearts,
Ye dungeons and ye cages of despair,
That monarchs have supplied from age to age
With music such as suits their sovereign ears—
The sighs and groans of miserable men,
There's not an English heart that would not leap
To hear that ye were fallen at last, to know
That even our enemies, so oft employed
In forging chains for us, themselves were free:
For he that values liberty, confines
His zeal for her predominance within
No narrow bounds; her cause engages him
Wherever pleaded; 'tis the cause of man.
There dwell the most forlorn of human kind,
Immured though unaccused, condemned untried,
Cruelly spared, and hopeless of escape.
There, like the visionary emblem seen
By him of Babylon, life stands a stump,
And filleted about with hoops of brass,
Still lives, though all its pleasant boughs are gone.
To count the hour-bell and expect no change;
And ever as the sullen sound is heard,
Still to reflect that though a joyless note
To him whose moments all have one dull pace,
Ten thousand rovers in the world at large
Account it music—that it summons some
To theatre, or jocund feast, or ball;
The wearied hireling finds it a release
From labour; and the lover, who has chid
Its long delay, feels every welcome stroke
Upon his heart-strings trembling with delight:
To fly for refuge from distracting thought
To such amusements as ingenious woe
Contrives, hard-shifting and without her tools—
To read engraven on the muddy walls,
In staggering types, his predecessor's tale,
A sad memorial, and subjoin his own;
To turn purveyor to an overgorged
And bloated spider, till the pampered pest
Is made familiar, watches his approach,
Comes at his call, and serves him for a friend;
To wear out time in numbering to and fro

The studs that thick emboss his iron door,
Then downward and then upward, then aslant
And then alternate, with a sickly hope
By dint of change to give his tasteless task
Some relish, till, the sum exactly found
In all directions, he begins again:—
Oh comfortless existence! hemmed around
With woes, which who that suffers would not kneel
And beg for exile or the pangs of death?
That man should thus encroach on fellow-man,
Abridge him of his just and native rights,
Eradicate him, tear him from his hold
Upon th' endearments of domestic life
And social, nip his fruitfulness and use,
And doom him for perhaps an heedless word
To barrenness and solitude and tears,
Moves indignation; makes the name of king
(Of king whom such prerogative can please)
As dreadful as the Manichean god,
Adored through fear, strong only to destroy.

[Meditation in Winter]

The night was winter in his roughest mood,
The morning sharp and clear. But now at noon,
Upon the southern side of the slant hills,
And where the woods fence off the northern blast,
The season smiles, resigning all its rage,
And has the warmth of May. The vault is blue
Without a cloud, and white without a speck
The dazzling splendour of the scene below.
Again the harmony comes o'er the vale,
And through the trees I view the embattled tower
Whence all the music. I again perceive
The soothing influence of the wafted strains,
And settle in soft musings as I tread
The walk, still verdant, under oaks and elms,
Whose outspread branches overarch the glade.
The roof, though moveable through all its length
As the wind sways it, has yet well sufficed,
And intercepting in their silent fall
The frequent flakes, has kept a path for me.

No noise is here, or none that hinders thought.
The redbreast warbles still, but is content
With slender notes, and more than half suppressed:
Pleased with his solitude, and flitting light
From spray to spray, where'er he rests he shakes
From many a twig the pendent drops of ice,
That tinkle in the withered leaves below.
Stillness, accompanied with sounds so soft,
Charms more than silence. Meditation here
May think down hours to moments. Here the heart
May give a useful lesson to the head,
And learning wiser grow without his books.
Knowledge and wisdom, far from being one,
Have ofttimes no connection. Knowledge dwells
In heads replete with thoughts of other men,
Wisdom in minds attentive to their own.
Knowledge, a rude unprofitable mass,
The mere materials with which wisdom builds,
Till smoothed and squared and fitted to its place,
Does but encumber whom it seems to enrich.
Knowledge is proud that he has learned so much;
Wisdom is humble that he knows no more.
Books are not seldom talismans and spells,
By which the magic art of shrewder wits
Holds an unthinking multitude enthralled.
Some to the fascination of a name
Surrender judgment hoodwinked. Some the style
Infatuates, and through labyrinths and wilds
Of error leads them, by a tune entranced.
While sloth seduces more, too weak to bear
The insupportable fatigue of thought,
And swallowing therefore, without pause or choice,
The total grist unsifted, husks and all.
But trees, and rivulets whose rapid course
Defies the check of winter, haunts of deer,
And sheepwalks populous with bleating lambs,
And lanes in which the primrose ere her time
Peeps through the moss that clothes the hawthorn root,
Deceive no student. Wisdom there, and Truth,
Not shy as in the world, and to be won
By slow solicitation, seize at once
The roving thought, and fix it on themselves.

[Kindness to Animals]

I would not enter on my list of friends,
Though graced with polished manners and fine sense,
Yet wanting sensibility, the man
Who needlessly sets foot upon a worm.
An inadvertent step may crush the snail
That crawls at evening in the public path;
But he that has humanity, forewarned,
Will tread aside and let the reptile live.
The creeping vermin, loathsome to the sight,
And charged perhaps with venom, that intrudes,
A visitor unwelcome, into scenes
Sacred to neatness and repose—th' alcove,
The chamber, or refectory,—may die:
A necessary act incurs no blame.
Not so when, held within their proper bounds
And guiltless of offence, they range the air,
Or take their pastime in the spacious field:
There they are privileged; and he that hunts
Or harms them there is guilty of a wrong,
Disturbs th' economy of Nature's realm,
Who, when she formed, designed them an abode.

ON THE RECEIPT OF MY MOTHER'S PICTURE

O that those lips had language! Life has passed
With me but roughly since I heard thee last.
Those lips are thine—thy own sweet smile I see,
The same that oft in childhood solaced me;
Voice only fails, else how distinct they say,
'Grieve not, my child, chase all thy fears away!'
The meek intelligence of those dear eyes
(Blest be the art that can immortalize,
The art that baffles Time's tyrannic claim
To quench it) here shines on me still the same.
Faithful remembrancer of one so dear,
O welcome guest, though unexpected here!
Who bidd'st me honour with an artless song,
Affectionate, a mother lost so long,
I will obey, not willingly alone,
But gladly, as the precept were her own:

And, while that face renews my filial grief,
Fancy shall weave a charm for my relief,
Shall steep me in Elysian revery,
A momentary dream that thou art she.
  My mother! when I learned that thou wast dead,
Say, wast thou conscious of the tears I shed?
Hovered thy spirit o'er thy sorrowing son,
Wretch even then, life's journey just begun?
Perhaps thou gav'st me, though unfelt, a kiss;
Perhaps a tear, if souls can weep in bliss—
Ah, that maternal smile! it answers 'Yes.'
I heard the bell tolled on thy burial day,
I saw the hearse that bore thee slow away,
And, turning from my nursery window, drew
A long, long sigh, and wept a last adieu!
But was it such? It was: where thou art gone
Adieus and farewells are a sound unknown.
May I but meet thee on that peaceful shore,
The parting word shall pass my lips no more!
Thy maidens, grieved themselves at my concern,
Oft gave me promise of thy quick return.
What ardently I wished I long believed,
And, disappointed still, was still deceived,
By expectation every day beguiled,
Dupe of to-morrow even from a child.
Thus many a sad to-morrow came and went,
Till, all my stock of infant sorrow spent,
I learnt at last submission to my lot,
But, though I less deplored thee, ne'er forgot.
  Where once we dwelt our name is heard no more:
Children not thine have trod my nursery floor;
And where the gardener Robin, day by day,
Drew me to school along the public way,
Delighted with my bauble coach, and wrapped
In scarlet mantle warm, and velvet-capped,
'Tis now become a history little known
That once we called the pastoral house our own.
Short-lived possession! But the record fair
That memory keeps, of all thy kindness there,
Still outlives many a storm that has effaced
A thousand other themes less deeply traced.
Thy nightly visits to my chamber made,

That thou mightst know me safe and warmly laid;
Thy morning bounties ere I left my home,
The biscuit or confectionary plum;
The fragrant waters on my cheeks bestowed
By thy own hand, till fresh they shone and glowed;
All this, and, more endearing still than all,
Thy constant flow of love, that knew no fall,
Ne'er roughened by those cataracts and breaks
That humour interposed too often makes;
All this, still legible on memory's page,
And still to be so to my latest age,
Adds joy to duty, makes me glad to pay
Such honours to thee as my numbers may,
Perhaps a frail memorial, but sincere,
Not scorned in heaven though little noticed here.
  Could Time, his flight reversed, restore the hours
When, playing with thy vesture's tissued flowers,
The violet, the pink, the jessamine,
I pricked them into paper with a pin
(And thou wast happier than myself the while,
Wouldst softly speak, and stroke my head and smile),
Could those few pleasant days again appear,
Might one wish bring them, would I wish them here?
I would not trust my heart—the dear delight
Seems so to be desired, perhaps I might.
But no—what here we call our life is such,
So little to be loved, and thou so much,
That I should ill requite thee to constrain
Thy unbound spirit into bonds again.
  Thou, as a gallant bark from Albion's coast,
The storms all weathered and the ocean crossed,
Shoots into port at some well-havened isle,
Where spices breathe and brighter seasons smile,
There sits quiescent on the floods, that show
Her beauteous form reflected clear below,
While airs impregnated with incense play
Around her, fanning light her streamers gay,
So thou, with sails how swift, hast reached the shore
'Where tempests never beat nor billows roar,'
And thy loved consort on the dangerous tide
Of life long since has anchored by thy side.

But me, scarce hoping to attain that rest,
Always from port withheld, always distressed,
Me howling blasts drive devious, tempest-tossed,
Sails ripped, seams opening wide, and compass lost,
And day by day some current's thwarting force
Sets me more distant from a prosperous course.
Yet, oh, the thought that thou art safe, and he,
That thought is joy, arrive what may to me.
My boast is not that I deduce my birth
From loins enthroned and rulers of the earth;
But higher far my proud pretensions rise—
The son of parents passed into the skies!
  And now, farewell. Time unrevoked has run
His wonted course, yet what I wished is done:
By contemplation's help, not sought in vain,
I seem t' have lived my childhood o'er again,
To have renewed the joys that once were mine,
Without the sin of violating thine;
And while the wings of Fancy still are free,
And I can view this mimic show of thee,
Time has but half succeeded in his theft—
Thyself removed, thy power to soothe me left.

TO MARY

The twentieth year is well-nigh past,
Since first our sky was overcast;
Ah, would that this might be the last!
My Mary!

Thy spirits have a fainter flow,
I see thee daily weaker grow;
'Twas my distress that brought thee low,
My Mary!

Thy needles, once a shining store,
For my sake restless heretofore,
Now rust disused, and shine no more,
My Mary!

For though thou gladly wouldst fulfil
The same kind office for me still,
Thy sight now seconds not thy will,
My Mary!

But well thou playedst the housewife's part,
And all thy threads with magic art
Have wound themselves about this heart,
My Mary!

Thy indistinct expressions seem
Like language uttered in a dream;
Yet me they charm, whate'er the theme,
My Mary!

Thy silver locks, once auburn bright,
Are still more lovely in my sight
Than golden beams of orient light,
My Mary!

For, could I view nor them nor thee,
What sight worth seeing could I see?
The sun would rise in vain for me,
My Mary!

Partakers of thy sad decline,
Thy hands their little force resign,
Yet, gently pressed, press gently mine,
My Mary!

Such feebleness of limbs thou provest,
That now at every step thou movest
Upheld by two, yet still thou lovest,
My Mary!

And still to love, though pressed with ill,
In wintry age to feel no chill,
With me is to be lovely still,
My Mary!

But ah! by constant heed I know,
How oft the sadness that I show
Transforms thy smiles to looks of woe,
My Mary!

And should my future lot be cast
With much resemblance of the past,
Thy worn-out heart will break at last,
My Mary!

THE CASTAWAY

Obscurest night involved the sky,
The Atlantic billows roared,
When such a destined wretch as I,
Washed headlong from on board,
Of friends, of hope, of all bereft,
His floating home forever left.

No braver chief could Albion boast
Than he with whom he went,
Nor ever ship left Albion's coast
With warmer wishes sent.
He loved them both, but both in vain,
Nor him beheld, nor her again.

Not long beneath the whelming brine,
Expert to swim, he lay;
Nor soon he felt his strength decline,
Or courage die away;
But waged with death a lasting strife,
Supported by despair of life.

He shouted: nor his friends had failed
To check the vessel's course,
But so the furious blast prevailed,
That, pitiless perforce,
They left their outcast mate behind,
And scudded still before the wind.

Some succour yet they could afford;
And such as storms allow,
The cask, the coop, the floated cord,
Delayed not to bestow.
But he (they knew) nor ship nor shore,
Whate'er they gave, should visit more.

Nor, cruel as it seemed, could he
  Their haste himself condemn,
Aware that flight, in such a sea,
  Alone could rescue them;
Yet bitter felt it still to die
Deserted, and his friends so nigh.

He long survives, who lives an hour
  In ocean, self-upheld;
And so long he, with unspent power,
  His destiny repelled;
And ever, as the minutes flew,
Entreated help, or cried 'Adieu!'

At length, his transient respite past,
  His comrades, who before
Had heard his voice in every blast,
  Could catch the sound no more:
For then, by toil subdued, he drank
The stifling wave, and then he sank.

No poet wept him; but the page
  Of narrative sincere,
That tells his name, his worth, his age,
  Is wet with Anson's tear:
And tears by bards or heroes shed
Alike immortalize the dead.

I therefore purpose not, or dream,
  Descanting on his fate,
To give the melancholy theme
  A more enduring date:
But misery still delights to trace
  Its semblance in another's case.

No voice divine the storm allayed,
  No light propitious shone,
When, snatched from all effectual aid,
  We perished, each alone:
But I beneath a rougher sea,
And whelmed in deeper gulfs than he.

WILLIAM LISLE BOWLES

EVENING

Evening! as slow thy placid shades descend,
  Veiling with gentlest hush the landscape still,
  The lonely battlement, the farthest hill
And wood, I think of those who have no friend;
Who now, perhaps, by melancholy led,
  From the broad blaze of day, where pleasure flaunts,
  Retiring, wander to the ringdove's haunts
Unseen; and watch the tints that o'er thy bed
Hang lovely; oft to musing Fancy's eye
  Presenting fairy vales, where the tired mind
  Might rest beyond the murmurs of mankind,
Nor hear the hourly moans of misery!
Alas for man! that Hope's fair views the while
Should smile like you, and perish as they smile!

DOVER CLIFFS

On these white cliffs, that calm above the flood
  Uprear their shadowing heads, and at their feet
  Hear not the surge that has for ages beat,
How many a lonely wanderer has stood!
And, whilst the lifted murmur met his ear,
  And o'er the distant billows the still eve
  Sailed slow, has thought of all his heart must leave
To-morrow; of the friends he loved most dear;
Of social scenes, from which he wept to part!
  Oh! if, like me, he knew how fruitless all
  The thoughts that would full fain the past recall,
Soon would he quell the risings of his heart,
And brave the wild winds and unhearing tide—
The world his country, and his God his guide.

ROBERT BURNS

MARY MORISON

O Mary, at thy window be;
  It is the wished, the trysted hour!
Those smiles and glances let me see
  That make the miser's treasure poor!
How blythely wad I bide the stoure,
  A weary slave frae sun to sun,
Could I the rich reward secure,
  The lovely Mary Morison.

Yestreen, when to the trembling string
  The dance gaed thro' the lighted ha',
To thee my fancy took its wing;
  I sat, but neither heard nor saw:
Tho' this was fair, and that was braw,
  And yon the toast of a' the town,
I sighed, and said amang them a',
  'Ye are na Mary Morison.'

O Mary, canst thou wreck his peace
  Wha for thy sake wad gladly die?
Or canst thou break that heart of his
  Whase only faut is loving thee?
If love for love thou wilt na gie,
  At least be pity to me shown!
A thought ungentle canna be
  The thought o' Mary Morison.

THE HOLY FAIR

Upon a simmer Sunday morn,
  When Nature's face is fair,
I walkèd forth to view the corn,
  An' snuff the caller air.

The rising sun, owre Galston muirs,
  Wi' glorious light was glintin;
The hares were hirplin down the furs,
  The lav'rocks they were chantin
          Fu' sweet that day.

As lightsomely I glowered abroad,
  To see a scene sae gay,
Three hizzies, early at the road,
  Cam skelpin up the way.
Twa had manteeles o' dolefu' black,
  But ane wi' lyart lining;
The third, that gaed a wee a-back,
  Was in the fashion shining
          Fu' gay that day.

The twa appeared like sisters twin,
  In feature, form, an' claes;
Their visage withered, lang an' thin,
  An' sour as onie slaes:
The third cam up, hap-step-an'-lowp,
  As light as onie lambie,
An' wi' a curchie low did stoop,
  As soon as e'er she saw me,
          Fu' kind that day.

Wi' bonnet aff, quoth I, 'Sweet lass,
  I think ye seem to ken me;
I'm sure I've seen that bonie face,
  But yet I canna name ye.'
Quo' she, an' laughin as she spak,
  An' taks me by the han's,
'Ye, for my sake, hae gi'en the feck
  Of a' the Ten Comman's
          A screed some day.

'My name is Fun—your cronie dear,
  The nearest friend ye hae;
An' this is Superstition here,
  An' that's Hypocrisy.

I'm gaun to Mauchline Holy Fair,
  To spend an hour in daffin:
Gin ye'll go there, yon runkled pair,
  We will get famous laughin
                At them this day.'

Quoth I, 'Wi' a' my heart, I'll do 't:
  I'll get my Sunday's sark on,
An' meet you on the holy spot;
  Faith, we'se hae fine remarkin!'
Then I gaed hame at crowdie-time,
  An' soon I made me ready;
For roads were clad frae side to side
  Wi' monie a wearie body,
                In droves that day.

Here farmers gash, in ridin graith,
  Gaed hoddin by their cotters;
There swankies young, in braw braid-claith,
  Are springin owre the gutters.
The lasses, skelpin barefit, thrang,
  In silks an' scarlets glitter;
Wi' sweet-milk cheese in monie a whang,
  An' farls baked wi' butter,
                Fu' crump that day.

When by the plate we set our nose,
  Weel heapèd up wi' ha'pence,
A greedy glowr black-bonnet throws,
  An' we maun draw our tippence.
Then in we go to see the show:
  On every side they're gath'rin,
Some carrying dails, some chairs an' stools,
  An' some are busy bleth'rin
                Right loud that day.

Here stands a shed to fend the showers,
  An' screen our countra gentry,
There Racer Jess, and twa-three whores,
  Are blinkin' at the entry.

Here sits a raw of tittlin' jads,
  Wi' heavin breasts an' bare neck;
An' there a batch o' wabster lads,
  Blackguarding frae Kilmarnock,
            For fun this day.

Here some are thinkin on their sins,
  An' some upo' their claes;
Ane curses feet that fyled his shins,
  Anither sighs and prays;
On this hand sits a chosen swatch,
  Wi' screwed-up grace-proud faces;
On that a set o' chaps, at watch,
  Thrang winkin on the lasses
            To chairs that day.

O happy is that man an' blest
  (Nae wonder that it pride him!)
Whase ain dear lass, that he likes best,
  Comes clinkin down beside him!
Wi' arm reposed on the chair-back,
  He sweetly does compose him;
Which, by degrees, slips round her neck,
  An's loof upon her bosom,
            Unkend that day.

Now a' the congregation o'er
  Is silent expectation;
For Moodie speels the holy door
  Wi' tidings o' damnation.
Should Hornie, as in ancient days,
  'Mang sons o' God present him,
The vera sight o' Moodie's face
  To 's ain het hame had sent him
            Wi' fright that day.

Hear how he clears the points o' faith
  Wi' rattlin an wi' thumpin!
Now meekly calm, now wild in wrath,
  He's stampin an' he's jumpin!

His lengthened chin, his turned-up snout,
  His eldritch squeel an' gestures,
O how they fire the heart devout—
  Like cantharidian plaisters,
          On sic a day!

But hark! the tent has changed its voice;
  There's peace an' rest nae langer;
For a' the real judges rise,
  They canna sit for anger:
Smith opens out his cauld harangues
  On practice and on morals;
An' aff the godly pour in thrangs,
  To gie the jars an' barrels
          A lift that day.

What signifies his barren shine
  Of moral pow'rs an' reason?
His English style an' gesture fine
  Are a' clean out o' season.
Like Socrates or Antonine,
  Or some auld pagan heathen,
The moral man he does define,
  But ne'er a word o' faith in
          That's right that day.

In guid time comes an antidote
  Against sic poisoned nostrum;
For Peebles, frae the water-fit,
  Ascends the holy rostrum:
See, up he's got the word o' God,
  An' meek an' mim has viewed it,
While Common Sense has taen the road,
  An' aff, an' up the Cowgate
          Fast, fast that day.

Wee Miller niest the guard relieves,
  An' orthodoxy raibles,
Tho' in his heart he weel believes
  An' thinks it auld wives' fables;

But faith! the birkie wants a manse,
  So cannilie he hums them,
Altho' his carnal wit an' sense
  Like hafflins-wise o'ercomes him
    At times that day.

Now butt an' ben the change-house fills
  Wi' yill-caup commentators;
Here's crying out for bakes an' gills,
  An' there the pint-stowp clatters;
While thick an' thrang, an' loud an' lang,
  Wi' logic an' wi' Scripture,
They raise a din that in the end
  Is like to breed a rupture
    O' wrath that day.

Leeze me on drink! it gies us mair
  Than either school or college;
It kindles wit, it waukens lear,
  It pangs us fou o' knowledge.
Be 't whisky-gill or penny-wheep,
  Or onie stronger potion,
It never fails, on drinkin deep,
  To kittle up our notion,
    By night or day.

The lads an' lasses, blythely bent
  To mind baith saul an' body,
Sit round the table weel content,
  An' steer about the toddy.
On this ane's dress an' that ane's leuk
  They're makin observations;
While some are cozie i' the neuk,
  An' formin assignations
    To meet some day.

But now the Lord's ain trumpet touts,
  Till a' the hills are rairin,
And echoes back return the shouts;
  Black Russell is na spairin:

His piercin words, like Highlan' swords,
  Divide the joints an' marrow;
His talk o' hell, whare devils dwell,
  Our verra 'sauls does harrow'
                Wi' fright that day!

A vast, unbottomed, boundless pit,
  Filled fou o' lowin brunstane,
Whase ragin flame an' scorchin heat
  Wad melt the hardest whun-stane!
The half-asleep start up wi' fear,
  An' think they hear it roarin,
When presently it does appear
  'Twas but some neebor snorin,
                Asleep that day.

'Twad be owre lang a tale to tell
  How monie stories passed,
An' how they crouded to the yill,
  When they were a' dismissed;
How drink gaed round, in cogs an' caups,
  Amang the furms an' benches,
An' cheese an' bread, frae women's laps,
  Was dealt about in lunches
                An' dawds that day.

In comes a gawsie, gash guidwife,
  An' sits down by the fire,
Syne draws her kebbuck an' her knife;
  The lasses they are shyer;
The auld guidmen about the grace
  Frae side to side they bother,
Till some ane by his bonnet lays
  And gi'es them 't, like a tether,
                Fu' lang that day.

Waesucks for him that gets nae lass,
  Or lasses that hae naething!
Sma' need has he to say a grace,
  Or melvie his braw claithing!

O wives, be mindfu', ance yoursel
  How bonie lads ye wanted,
An' dinna for a kebbuck-heel
  Let lasses be affronted
            On sic a day!

Now Clinkumbell, wi' rattlin tow,
  Begins to jow an' croon;
Some swagger hame the best they dow,
  Some wait the afternoon.
At slaps the billies halt a blink,
  Till lasses strip their shoon;
Wi' faith an' hope, an' love an' drink,
  They're a' in famous tune
            For crack that day.

How monie hearts this day converts
  O' sinners and o' lasses!
Their hearts o' stane, gin night, are gaen
  As saft as onie flesh is.
There's some are fou o' love divine,
  There's some are fou o' brandy;
An' monie jobs that day begin,
  May end in houghmagandie
            Some ither day.

TO A LOUSE

ON SEEING ONE ON A LADY'S BONNET AT CHURCH

Ha! whare ye gaun, ye crowlin ferlie?
Your impudence protects you sairly;
I canna say but ye strunt rarely
      Ower gauze and lace,
Tho', faith, I fear ye dine but sparely
      On sic a place.

Ye ugly, creepin, blastit wonner,
Detested, shunned by saunt an' sinner,
How daur ye set your fit upon her,
      Sae fine a lady!
Gae somewhere else, and seek your dinner
      On some poor body.

Swith! in some beggar's hauffet squattle;
There ye may creep and sprawl and sprattle
Wi' ither kindred jumping cattle,
In shoals and nations,
Whare horn nor bane ne'er daur unsettle
Your thick plantations.

Now haud you there! ye're out o' sight,
Below the fatt'rils, snug an' tight;
Na, faith ye yet! ye'll no be right
Till ye've got on it,
The vera tapmost, tow'ring height
O' Miss's bonnet.

My sooth! right bauld ye set your nose out,
As plump an' grey as onie grozet;
O for some rank, mercurial rozet
Or fell red smeddum!
I'd gie ye sic a hearty dose o't
Wad dress your droddum!

I wad na been surprised to spy
You on an auld wife's flainen toy,
Or aiblins some bit duddie boy,
On's wyliecoat;
But Miss's fine Lunardi—fie!
How daur ye do't!

O Jenny, dinna toss your head,
An' set your beauties a' abread!
Ye little ken what cursèd speed
The blastie's makin!
Thae winks an' finger-ends, I dread,
Are notice takin!

O wad some Power the giftie gie us
To see oursels as ithers see us!
It wad frae monie a blunder free us,
An' foolish notion;
What airs in dress an' gait wad lea'e us,
An' ev'n devotion!

From EPISTLE TO J. LAPRAIK

I am nae poet, in a sense,
But just a rhymer like by chance,
An' hae to learning nae pretence;
    Yet what the matter?
Whene'er my Muse does on me glance,
    I jingle at her.

Your critic-folk may cock their nose,
And say, 'How can you e'er propose,
You wha ken hardly verse frae prose,
    To mak a sang?'
But, by your leaves, my learnèd foes,
    Ye're maybe wrang.

What's a' your jargon o' your schools,
Your Latin names for horns an' stools?
If honest Nature made you fools,
    What sairs your grammers?
Ye'd better taen up spades and shools
    Or knappin-hammers.

A set o' dull, conceited hashes
Confuse their brains in college classes;
They gang in stirks, and come out asses,
    Plain truth to speak;
An' syne they think to climb Parnassus
    By dint o' Greek!

Gie me ae spark o' Nature's fire,
That's a' the learning I desire;
Then, tho' I drudge thro' dub an' mire
    At pleugh or cart,
My Muse, tho' hamely in attire,
    May touch the heart.

THE COTTER'S SATURDAY NIGHT

My loved, my honoured, much respected friend!
  No mercenary bard his homage pays;
With honest pride, I scorn each selfish end,
  My dearest meed a friend's esteem and praise:
  To you I sing, in simple Scottish lays,
The lowly train in life's sequestered scene;
  The native feelings strong, the guileless ways,
What Aiken in a cottage would have been;
Ah, though his worth unknown, far happier there, I ween!

November chill blaws loud wi' angry sugh;
  The shortening winter-day is near a close;
The miry beasts retreating frae the pleugh;
  The blackening trains o' craws to their repose:
  The toil-worn cotter frae his labour goes—
This night his weekly moil is at an end,—
  Collects his spades, his mattocks, and his hoes,
Hoping the morn in ease and rest to spend,
And weary, o'er the moor, his course does hameward bend.

At length his lonely cot appears in view,
  Beneath the shelter of an aged tree;
Th' expectant wee-things, toddlin, stacher through
  To meet their dad, wi' flichterin' noise and glee.
  His wee bit ingle, blinkin bonilie,
His clean hearth-stane, his thrifty wifie's smile,
  The lisping infant, prattling on his knee,
Does a' his weary kiaugh and care beguile,
And makes him quite forget his labour and his toil.

Belyve the elder bairns come drapping in,
  At service out amang the farmers roun';
Some ca' the pleugh, some herd, some tentie rin
  A cannie errand to a neebor town.
  Their eldest hope, their Jenny, woman-grown,
In youthfu' bloom, love sparkling in her e'e,
  Comes hame, perhaps to shew a braw new gown,
Or deposite her sair-won penny-fee,
To help her parents dear if they in hardship be.

With joy unfeigned, brothers and sisters meet,
And each for other's weelfare kindly spiers;
The social hours, swift-winged, unnoticed fleet;
Each tells the uncos that he sees or hears.
The parents, partial, eye their hopeful years;
Anticipation forward points the view.
The mother, wi' her needle and her sheers,
Gars auld claes look amaist as weel's the new;
The father mixes a' wi' admonition due:

Their master's and their mistress's command
The younkers a' are warnèd to obey,
And mind their labours wi' an eydent hand,
And ne'er, tho' out o' sight, to jauk or play:
'And O be sure to fear the Lord alway,
And mind your duty duly, morn and night;
Lest in temptation's path ye gang astray,
Implore His counsel and assisting might:
They never sought in vain that sought the Lord aright!'

But hark! a rap comes gently to the door.
Jenny, wha kens the meaning o' the same,
Tells how a neebor lad came o'er the moor,
To do some errands and convoy her hame.
The wily mother sees the conscious flame
Sparkle in Jenny's e'e, and flush her cheek;
With heart-struck anxious care enquires his name,
While Jenny hafflins is afraid to speak;
Weel-pleased the mother hears it's nae wild, worthless rake.

With kindly welcome Jenny brings him ben:
A strappin' youth, he takes the mother's eye;
Blythe Jenny sees the visit's no ill-taen;
The father cracks of horses, pleughs, and kye.
The youngster's artless heart o'erflows wi' joy,
But blate and laithfu', scarce can weel behave;
The mother, wi' a woman's wiles, can spy
What makes the youth sae bashfu' and sae grave,
Weel-pleased to think her bairn's respected like the lave.

Oh happy love, where love like this is found!
Oh heart-felt raptures! bliss beyond compare!
I've pacèd much this weary, mortal round,
And sage experience bids me this declare:

'If Heaven a draught of heavenly pleasure spare,
One cordial in this melancholy vale,
'Tis when a youthful, loving, modest pair
In other's arms breathe out the tender tale,
Beneath the milk-white thorn that scents the evening gale.'

Is there, in human form, that bears a heart,
A wretch! a villain! lost to love and truth!
That can, with studied, sly, ensnaring art,
Betray sweet Jenny's unsuspecting youth?
Curse on his perjured arts! dissembling smooth!
Are honour, virtue, conscience, all exiled?
Is there no pity, no relenting ruth,
Points to the parents fondling o'er their child?
Then paints the ruined maid, and their distraction wild?

But now the supper crowns their simple board:
The healsome parritch, chief o' Scotia's food:
The soupe their only hawkie does afford,
That 'yont the hallan snugly chows her cood.
The dame brings forth, in complimental mood,
To grace the lad, her weel-hained kebbuck, fell;
And aft he's prest, and aft he ca's it guid;
The frugal wifie, garrulous, will tell
How 't was a towmond auld sin' lint was i' the bell.

The cheerfu' supper done, wi' serious face
They round the ingle form a circle wide;
The sire turns o'er, wi' patriarchal grace,
The big ha'-Bible, ance his father's pride;
His bonnet reverently is laid aside,
His lyart haffets wearing thin and bare;
Those strains that once did sweet in Zion glide,
He wales a portion with judicious care,
And 'Let us worship God!' he says, with solemn air.

They chant their artless notes in simple guise;
They tune their hearts, by far the noblest aim:
Perhaps 'Dundee's' wild-warbling measures rise,
Or plaintive 'Martyrs,' worthy of the name;

Or noble 'Elgin' beets the heavenward flame,
The sweetest far of Scotia's holy lays.
Compared with these, Italian trills are tame;
The tickled ears no heart-felt raptures raise;
Nae unison hae they with our Creator's praise.

The priest-like father reads the sacred page;
How Abram was the friend of God on high;
Or Moses bade eternal warfare wage
With Amalek's ungracious progeny;
Or how the royal bard did groaning lie
Beneath the stroke of Heaven's avenging ire;
Or Job's pathetic plaint and wailing cry;
Or rapt Isaiah's wild, seraphic fire;
Or other holy seers that tune the sacred lyre.

Perhaps the Christian volume is the theme:
How guiltless blood for guilty man was shed;
How He Who bore in Heaven the second name
Had not on earth whereon to lay His head;
How His first followers and servants sped;
The precepts sage they wrote to many a land;
How he, who lone in Patmos banishèd,
Saw in the sun a mighty angel stand,
And heard great Bab'lon's doom pronounced by Heaven's command.

Then kneeling down to Heaven's Eternal King,
The saint, the father, and the husband prays;
Hope 'springs exulting on triumphant wing,'
That thus they all shall meet in future days,
There ever bask in uncreated rays,
No more to sigh or shed the bitter tear,
Together hymning their Creator's praise,
In such society, yet still more dear,
While circling Time moves round in an eternal sphere.

Compared with this, how poor Religion's pride,
In all the pomp of method and of art,
When men display to congregations wide
Devotion's ev'ry grace except the heart!

The Power, incensed, the pageant will desert,
The pompous strain, the sacerdotal stole;
But haply, in some cottage far apart,
May hear, well pleased, the language of the soul,
And in His Book of Life the inmates poor enroll.

Then homeward all take off their several way;
The youngling cottagers retire to rest;
The parent-pair their secret homage pay,
And proffer up to Heaven the warm request
And He who stills the raven's clamorous nest,
And decks the lily fair in flowery pride,
Would, in the way His wisdom sees the best,
For them and for their little ones provide,
But chiefly in their hearts with grace divine preside.

From scenes like these old Scotia's grandeur springs,
That makes her loved at home, revered abroad:
Princes and lords are but the breath of kings,
'An honest man's the noblest work of God.'
And certes in fair virtue's heavenly road,
The cottage leaves the palace far behind:
What is a lordling's pomp? a cumbrous load,
Disguising oft the wretch of human kind,
Studied in arts of hell, in wickedness refined!

O Scotia! my dear, my native soil!
For whom my warmest wish to Heaven is sent!
Long may thy hardy sons of rustic toil
Be blest with health and peace and sweet content!
And O may Heaven their simple lives prevent
From luxury's contagion, weak and vile!
Then, howe'er crowns and coronets be rent,
A virtuous populace may rise the while,
And stand a wall of fire around their much-loved isle.

O Thou, Who poured the patriotic tide
That streamed thro' Wallace's undaunted heart,
Who dared to nobly stem tyrannic pride,
Or nobly die, the second glorious part!

(The patriot's God peculiarly Thou art,
His friend, inspirer, guardian, and reward!)
Oh never, never Scotia's realm desert,
But still the patriot and the patriot-bard
In bright succession raise, her ornament and guard!

TO A MOUSE

ON TURNING HER UP IN HER NEST WITH THE PLOUGH, NOVEMBER, 1785

Wee, sleekit, cowrin, tim'rous beastie,
O what a panic's in thy breastie!
Thou need na start awa sae hasty,
Wi' bickering brattle!
I wad be laith to rin an' chase thee,
Wi' murdering pattle!

I'm truly sorry man's dominion
Has broken Nature's social union,
An' justifies that ill opinion
Which makes thee startle
At me, thy poor, earth-born companion,
An' fellow-mortal!

I doubt na, whyles, but thou may thieve;
What then? poor beastie, thou maun live!
A daimen icker in a thrave
'S a sma' request;
I'll get a blessin' wi' the lave,
An' never miss 't!

Thy wee-bit housie, too, in ruin!
Its silly wa's the win's are strewin!
An' naething now to big a new ane,
O' foggage green!
An' bleak December's win's ensuin,
Baith snell an' keen!

Thou saw the fields laid bare an' waste,
An' weary winter comin fast,
An' cozie here, beneath the blast,
Thou thought to dwell—
Till, crash! the cruel coulter passed
Out thro' thy cell.

That wee bit heap o' leaves an' stibble
Has cost thee monie a weary nibble!
Now thou's turned out, for a' thy trouble,
But house or hald,
To thole the winter's sleety dribble,
An' cranreuch cauld!

But mousie, thou art no thy lane
In proving foresight may be vain:
The best-laid schemes o' mice an' men
Gang aft agley,
An' lea'e us naught but grief an' pain
For promised joy!

Still, thou art blest compared wi' me!
The present only toucheth thee:
But och! I backward cast my e'e,
On prospects drear!
An' forward, tho' I canna see,
I guess an' fear!

TO A MOUNTAIN DAISY

ON TURNING ONE DOWN WITH THE PLOUGH IN APRIL, 1786

Wee, modest, crimson-tippèd flow'r,
Thou's met me in an evil hour,
For I maun crush amang the stoure
Thy slender stem;
To spare thee now is past my pow'r,
Thou bonie gem.

Alas! it's no thy neebor sweet,
The bonie lark, companion meet,

Bending thee 'mang the dewy weet,
    Wi' spreckled breast,
When upward springing, blythe, to greet
    The purpling east.

Cauld blew the bitter-biting north
Upon thy early, humble birth;
Yet cheerfully thou glinted forth
    Amid the storm,
Scarce reared above the parent-earth
    Thy tender form.

The flaunting flow'rs our gardens yield,
High shelt'ring woods and wa's maun shield;
But thou, beneath the random bield
    O' clod or stane,
Adorns the histie stibble-field,
    Unseen, alane.

There, in thy scanty mantle clad,
Thy snawie bosom sunward spread,
Thou lifts thy unassuming head
    In humble guise;
But now the share uptears thy bed,
    And low thou lies!

Such is the fate of artless maid,
Sweet flow'ret of the rural shade!
By love's simplicity betray'd,
    And guileless trust,
Till she, like thee, all soiled is laid,
    Low i' the dust.

Such is the fate of simple bard,
On life's rough ocean luckless starred!
Unskilful he to note the card
    Of prudent lore,
Till billows rage, and gales blow hard,
    And whelm him o'er!

Such fate to suffering worth is giv'n,
Who long with wants and woes has striv'n,

By human pride or cunning driv'n
 To mis'ry's brink;
Till, wrench'd of ev'ry stay but Heav'n,
 He, ruined, sink!

Ev'n thou who mourn'st the daisy's fate,
That fate is thine—no distant date;
Stern Ruin's plough-share drives, elate,
 Full on thy bloom,
Till crush'd beneath the furrow's weight
 Shall be thy doom!

EPISTLE TO A YOUNG FRIEND

I lang hae thought, my youthfu' friend
 A something to have sent you,
Tho' it should serve nae ither end
 Than just a kind memento.
But how the subject-theme may gang,
 Let time and chance determine;
Perhaps it may turn out a sang,
 Perhaps turn out a sermon.

Ye'll try the world soon, my lad;
 And, Andrew dear, believe me,
Ye'll find mankind an unco squad,
 And muckle they may grieve ye:
For care and trouble set your thought,
 Ev'n when your end's attainèd;
And a' your views may come to nought,
 Where ev'ry nerve is strainèd.

I'll no say men are villains a';
 The real, harden'd wicked,
Wha hae nae check but human law,
 Are to a few restricket;
But, och! mankind are unco weak,
 An' little to be trusted;
If self the wavering balance shake,
 It's rarely right adjusted!

Yet they wha fa' in fortune's strife,
  Their fate we shouldna censure,
For still th' important end of life
  They equally may answer;
A man may hae an honest heart,
  Tho' poortith hourly stare him;
A man may tak a neebor's part,
  Yet hae nae cash to spare him.

Aye free, aff-han', your story tell,
  When wi a bosom crony;
But still keep something to yoursel
  Ye scarcely tell to ony.
Conceal yoursel as weel's ye can
  Frae critical dissection;
But keek thro' ev'ry other man,
  Wi' sharpen'd, sly inspection.

The sacred lowe o' weel-placed love,
  Luxuriantly indulge it;
But never tempt th' illicit rove,
  Tho' naething should divulge it;
I wave the quantum o' the sin,
  The hazard of concealing;
But, och! it hardens a' within,
  And petrifies the feeling!

To catch dame Fortune's golden smile,
  Assiduous wait upon her;
And gather gear by ev'ry wile
  That's justified by honour;
Not for to hide it in a hedge,
  Nor for a train attendant;
But for the glorious privilege
  Of being independent.

The fear o' hell's a hangman's whip,
  To haud the wretch in order;
But where ye feel your honour grip,
  Let that aye be your border;

Its slightest touches, instant pause—
  Debar a' side-pretences;
And resolutely keep its laws,
  Uncaring consequences.

The great Creator to revere,
  Must sure become the creature;
But still the preaching cant forbear,
  And ev'n the rigid feature;
Yet ne'er with wits profane to range,
  Be complaisance extended;
An atheist-laugh's a poor exchange
  For Deity offended!

When ranting round in pleasure's ring,
  Religion may be blinded;
Or, if she gie a random sting,
  It may be little minded;
But when on life we're tempest-driv'n—
  A conscience but a canker,
A correspondence fix'd wi' Heav'n
  Is sure a noble anchor!

Adieu, dear amiable Youth!
  Your heart can ne'er be wanting!
May prudence, fortitude, and truth,
  Erect your brow undaunting!
In ploughman phrase, 'God send you speed,'
  Still daily to grow wiser;
And may you better reck the rede,
  Than ever did th' adviser!

A BARD'S EPITAPH

Is there a whim-inspirèd fool,
Owre fast for thought, owre hot for rule,
Owre blate to seek, owre proud to snool?
        Let him draw near;
And owre this grassy heap sing dool,
        And drap a tear.

Is there a bard of rustic song,
Who, noteless, steals the crowds among,
That weekly this area throng?—
Oh, pass not by!
But with a frater-feeling strong
Here heave a sigh.

Is there a man whose judgment clear
Can others teach the course to steer,
Yet runs himself life's mad career
Wild as the wave?—
Here pause—and thro' the starting tear
Survey this grave.

The poor inhabitant below
Was quick to learn and wise to know,
And keenly felt the friendly glow
And softer flame;
But thoughtless follies laid him low,
And stain'd his name!

Reader, attend! whether thy soul
Soars fancy's flights beyond the pole,
Or darkling grubs this earthly hole
In low pursuit;
Know, prudent, cautious self-control
Is wisdom's root.

ADDRESS TO THE UNCO GUID OR THE RIGIDLY RIGHTEOUS

O ye wha are sae guid yoursel,
Sae pious and sae holy,
Ye've nought to do but mark and tell
Your neebour's fauts and folly!
Whase life is like a weel-gaun mill,
Supplied wi' store o' water,
The heapet happer's ebbing still,
And still the clap plays clatter,—

Hear me, ye venerable core,
  As counsel for poor mortals
That frequent pass douce Wisdom's door
  For glaikit Folly's portals;
I for their thoughtless, careless sakes
  Would here propone defences—
Their donsie tricks, their black mistakes,
  Their failings and mischances.

Ye see your state wi' theirs compar'd,
  And shudder at the niffer;
But cast a moment's fair regard,
  What maks the mighty differ?
Discount what scant occasion gave,
  That purity ye pride in,
And (what's aft mair than a' the lave)
  Your better art o' hidin.

Think, when your castigated pulse
  Gies now and then a wallop,
What ragings must his veins convulse
  That still eternal gallop:
Wi' wind and tide fair i' your tail,
  Right on ye scud your sea-way;
But in the teeth o' baith to sail,
  It maks an unco leeway.

See Social Life and Glee sit down,
  All joyous and unthinking,
Till, quite transmugrify'd, they're grown
  Debauchery and Drinking:
O would they stay to calculate
  Th' eternal consequences,
Or—your more dreaded hell to state—
  Damnation of expenses!

Ye high, exalted, virtuous dames,
  Tied up in godly laces,
Before ye gie poor Frailty names,
  Suppose a change o' cases:

A dear-lov'd lad, convenience snug,
  A treach'rous inclination—
But, let me whisper i' your lug,
  Ye're aiblins nae temptation.

Then gently scan your brother man,
  Still gentler sister woman;
Tho' they may gang a kennin wrang,
  To step aside is human:
One point must still be greatly dark,
  The moving *why* they do it;
And just as lamely can ye mark
  How far perhaps they rue it.

Who made the heart, 'tis He alone
  Decidedly can try us;
He knows each chord, its various tone,
  Each spring, its various bias:
Then at the balance, let's be mute,
  We never can adjust it;
What's done we partly may compute,
  But know not what's resisted.

JOHN ANDERSON, MY JO

John Anderson, my jo, John,
  When we were first acquent,
Your locks were like the raven,
  Your bonie brow was brent:
But now your brow is beld, John,
  Your locks are like the snaw;
But blessings on your frosty pow,
  John Anderson, my jo!

John Anderson, my jo, John,
  We clamb the hill thegither;
And monie a cantie day, John,
  We've had wi' ane anither:
Now we maun totter down, John,
  And hand in hand we'll go,
And sleep thegither at the foot,
  John Anderson, my jo!

THE LOVELY LASS OF INVERNESS

The lovely lass of Inverness,
Nae joy nor pleasure can she see;
For e'en to morn she cries, 'Alas!'
And aye the saut tear blin's her e'e:

'Drumossie moor—Drumossie day—
A waefu' day it was to me!
For there I lost my father dear,
My father dear, and brethren three.

'Their winding-sheet the bluidy clay,
Their graves are growing green to see:
And by them lies the dearest lad
That ever blest a woman's e'e!

'Now wae to thee, thou cruel lord,
A bluidy man I trow thou be;
For mony a heart thou hast made sair
That ne'er did wrang to thine or thee!'

A RED, RED ROSE

O, my luv is like a red, red rose,
  That's newly sprung in June:
O, my luv is like the melodie
  That's sweetly played in tune.

As fair art thou, my bonie lass,
  So deep in luve am I;
And I will luve thee still, my dear,
  Till a' the seas gang dry:

Till a' the seas gang dry, my dear,
  And the rocks melt wi' the sun;
And I will luve thee still, my dear,
  While the sands o' life shall run.

And fare thee weel, my only luve!
  And fare thee weel awhile!
And I will come again, my luve,
  Tho' it were ten thousand mile!

AULD LANG SYNE

Should auld acquaintance be forgot,
  And never brought to mind?
Should auld acquaintance be forgot,
  And auld lang syne?

Chorus:

For auld lang syne, my dear,
  For auld lang syne,
We'll tak a cup o' kindness yet,
  For auld lang syne!

And surely ye'll be your pint-stowp,
  And surely I'll be mine;
And we'll take a cup o' kindness yet
  For auld lang syne!

We twa hae run about the braes,
  And pou'd the gowans fine;
But we've wander'd monie a weary fit
  Sin' auld lang syne.

We twa hae paidl'd in the burn,
  Frae morning sun till dine;
But seas between us braid hae roar'd
  Sin' auld lang syne.

And there's a hand, my trusty fiere,
  And gie's a hand o' thine;
And we'll tak a right guid-willie waught,
  For auld lang syne!

SWEET AFTON

Flow gently, sweet Afton, among thy green braes!
Flow gently, I'll sing thee a song in thy praise!
My Mary's asleep by thy murmuring stream,
Flow gently, sweet Afton, disturb not her dream!

Thou stock-dove, whose echo resounds through the glen,
Ye wild whistling blackbirds in yon thorny den,
Thou green-crested lapwing, thy screaming forbear,
I charge you disturb not my slumbering fair!

How lofty, sweet Afton, thy neighbouring hills,
Far marked with the courses of clear winding rills!
There daily I wander as noon rises high,
My flocks and my Mary's sweet cot in my eye.

How pleasant thy banks and green valleys below,
Where wild in the woodlands the primroses blow!
There oft, as mild evening weeps over the lea,
The sweet-scented birk shades my Mary and me.

Thy crystal stream, Afton, how lovely it glides,
And winds by the cot where my Mary resides!
How wanton thy waters her snowy feet lave,
As gathering sweet flowerets she stems thy clear wave!

Flow gently, sweet Afton, among thy green braes!
Flow gently, sweet river, the theme of my lays!
My Mary's asleep by thy murmuring stream,
Flow gently, sweet Afton, disturb not her dream!

THE HAPPY TRIO

O, Willie brew'd a peck o' maut,
  And Rob and Allan cam to see;
Three blyther hearts, that lee-lang night,
  Ye wad na found in Christendie.

Chorus:

We are na fou, we're nae that fou,
But just a drappie in our e'e;
The cock may craw, the day may daw,
And ay we'll taste the barley bree!

Here are we met, three merry boys,
Three merry boys, I trow, are we;
And mony a night we've merry been,
And mony mae we hope to be!

It is the moon, I ken her horn,
That's blinkin in the lift sae hie;
She shines sae bright to wyle us hame,
But, by my sooth, she'll wait a wee!

Wha first shall rise to gang awa,
A cuckold, coward loun is he!
Wha first beside his chair shall fa',
He is the King amang us three!

TO MARY IN HEAVEN

Thou lingering star, with lessening ray,
That lov'st to greet the early morn,
Again thou usher'st in the day
My Mary from my soul was torn.
O Mary! dear departed shade!
Where is thy place of blissful rest?
See'st thou thy lover lowly laid?
Hear'st thou the groans that rend his breast?

That sacred hour can I forget,
Can I forget the hallowed grove,
Where by the winding Ayr we met
To live one day of parting love?
Eternity cannot efface
Those records dear of transports past,
Thy image at our last embrace—
Ah! little thought we 'twas our last!

Ayr, gurgling, kissed his pebbled shore,
  O'erhung with wild woods, thickening green;
The fragrant birch and hawthorn hoar
  Twined amorous round the raptured scene:
The flowers sprang wanton to be pressed,
  The birds sang love on every spray,
Till too, too soon the glowing west
  Proclaimed the speed of wingèd day.

Still o'er these scenes my memory wakes,
  And fondly broods with miser care!
Time but th' impression stronger makes,
  As streams their channels deeper wear.
My Mary, dear departed shade!
  Where is thy place of blissful rest?
See'st thou thy lover lowly laid?
  Hear'st thou the groans that rend his breast?

TAM O' SHANTER: A TALE

Of Brownyis and of Bogillis full is this buke.

—GAWIN DOUGLAS.

When chapman billies leave the street,
And drouthy neebors neebors meet,
As market-days are wearing late,
An' folk begin to tak the gate,
While we sit bousing at the nappy,
An' getting fou and unco happy,
We think na on the lang Scots miles,
The mosses, waters, slaps, and stiles,
That lie between us and our hame,
Whare sits our sulky, sullen dame,
Gathering her brows like gathering storm,
Nursing her wrath to keep it warm.
  This truth fand honest Tam o' Shanter,
As he frae Ayr ae night did canter
(Auld Ayr, wham ne'er a town surpasses
For honest men and bonie lasses).
  O Tam, had'st thou but been sae wise
As taen thy ain wife Kate's advice!

She tauld thee weel thou was a skellum,
A blethering, blustering, drunken blellum,
That frae November till October
Ae market-day thou was nae sober;
That ilka melder wi' the miller
Thou sat as lang as thou had siller;
That ev'ry naig was ca'd a shoe on
The smith and thee gat roaring fou on;
That at the Lord's house, even on Sunday,
Thou drank wi' Kirkton Jean till Monday.
She prophesied that, late or soon,
Thou would be found deep drowned in Doon,
Or catched wi' warlocks in the mirk
By Alloway's auld, haunted kirk.
  Ah, gentle dames, it gars me greet
To think how monie counsels sweet,
How monie lengthened, sage advices,
The husband frae the wife despises!
  But to our tale. Ae market-night
Tam had got planted unco right,
Fast by an ingle, bleezing finely,
Wi' reaming swats, that drank divinely;
And at his elbow, Souter Johnie,
His ancient, trusty, drouthy cronie:
Tam lo'ed him like a very brither;
They had been fou for weeks thegither.
The night drave on wi' sangs and clatter,
And ay the ale was growing better;
The landlady and Tam grew gracious,
Wi' secret favours, sweet and precious;
The souter tauld his queerest stories,
The landlord's laugh was ready chorus;
The storm without might rair and rustle,
Tam did na mind the storm a whistle.
  Care, mad to see a man sae happy,
E'en drowned himself amang the nappy.
As bees flee hame wi' lades o' treasure,
The minutes winged their way wi' pleasure:
Kings may be blest, but Tam was glorious,
O'er a' the ills o' life victorious!
  But pleasures are like poppies spread—
You seize the flow'r, its bloom is shed;

Or like the snow falls in the river,
A moment white—then melts forever;
Or like the borealis race,
That flit ere you can point their place;
Or like the rainbow's lovely form,
Evanishing amid the storm.
Nae man can tether time or tide:
The hour approaches Tam maun ride;
That hour, o' night's black arch the key-stane,
That dreary hour Tam mounts his beast in,
And sic a night he taks the road in
As ne'er poor sinner was abroad in.
  The wind blew as 't wad blawn its last:
The rattling showers rose on the blast;
The speedy gleams the darkness swallowed;
Loud, deep, and lang the thunder bellowed:
That night, a child might understand,
The Deil had business on his hand.
  Weel-mounted on his gray mare Meg,
A better never lifted leg,
Tam skelpit on thro' dub and mire,
Despising wind and rain and fire;
Whiles holding fast his guid blue bonnet,
Whiles crooning o'er some auld Scots sonnet,
While glow'ring round wi' prudent cares,
Lest bogles catch him unawares:
Kirk-Alloway was drawing nigh,
Whare ghaists and houlets nightly cry.
  By this time he was cross the ford,
Whare in the snaw the chapman smoored;
And past the birks and meikle stane,
Whare drunken Charlie brak's neck-bane;
And thro' the whins and by the cairn,
Whare hunters fand the murdered bairn;
And near the thorn, aboon the well,
Whare Mungo's mither hanged hersel.
Before him Doon pours all his floods;
The doubling storm roars thro' the woods;
The lightnings flash from pole to pole;
Near and more near the thunders roll;
When, glimmering thro' the groaning trees,
Kirk-Alloway seemed in a bleeze:

Thro' ilka bore the beams were glancing,
And loud resounded mirth and dancing.
  Inspiring bold John Barleycorn,
What dangers thou canst make us scorn!
Wi' tippenny, we fear nae evil;
Wi' usquebae, we'll face the Devil!
The swats sae reamed in Tammie's noddle,
Fair play, he cared na deils a boddle.
But Maggie stood, right sair astonished,
Till, by the heel and hand admonished,
She ventured forward on the light;
And, vow! Tam saw an unco sight!
  Warlocks and witches in a dance;
Nae cotillion, brent new frae France,
But hornpipes, jigs, strathspeys, and reels,
Put life and mettle in their heels.
A winnock-bunker in the east,
There sat Auld Nick, in shape o' beast;
A towsie tyke, black, grim, and large,
To gie them music was his charge:
He screwed the pipes and gart them skirl,
Till roof and rafters a' did dirl.
Coffins stood round, like open presses,
That shawed the dead in their last dresses,
And, by some devilish cantraip sleight,
Each in its cauld hand held a light:
By which heroic Tam was able
To note, upon the haly table,
A murderer's banes, in gibbet-airns;
Twa span-lang, wee, unchristened bairns;
A thief, new-cutted frae a rape—
Wi' his last gasp his gab did gape;
Five tomahawks, wi' bluid red-rusted;
Five scimitars, wi' murder crusted;
A garter which a babe had strangled;
A knife a father's throat had mangled,
Whom his ain son o' life bereft—
The grey-hairs yet stack to the heft;
Wi' mair of horrible and awfu',
Which even to name wad be unlawfu'.
  As Tammie glowered, amazed and curious,
The mirth and fun grew fast and furious:

The piper loud and louder blew,
The dancers quick and quicker flew;
They reeled, they set, they crossed, they cleekit,
Till ilka carlin swat and reekit,
And coost her duddies to the wark,
And linket at it in her sark!
  Now Tam, O Tam! had thae been queans,
A' plump and strapping in their teens!
Their sarks, instead o' creeshie flannen,
Been snaw-white seventeen-hunder linen!
Thir breeks o' mine, my only pair,
That ance were plush, o' guid blue hair,
I wad hae gi'en them off my hurdies,
For ae blink o' the bonie burdies!
  But withered beldams, auld and droll,
Rigwoodie hags wad spean a foal,
Louping and flinging on a crummock,
I wonder didna turn thy stomach!
  But Tam kend what was what fu' brawlie:
There was ae winsome wench and wawlie,
That night enlisted in the core,
Lang after kend on Carrick shore
(For monie a beast to dead she shot,
An' perished monie a bonie boat,
And shook baith meikle corn and bear,
And kept the country-side in fear).
Her cutty sark, o' Paisley harn,
That while a lassie she had worn,
In longitude tho' sorely scanty,
It was her best, and she was vauntie.—
Ah, little kend thy reverend grannie
That sark she coft for her wee Nannie,
Wi' twa pund Scots ('twas a' her riches),
Wad ever graced a dance o' witches!
  But here my Muse her wing maun cour;
Sic flights are far beyond her power:
To sing how Nannie lap and flang
(A souple jad she was and strang),
And how Tam stood like ane bewitched,
And thought his very een enriched.
Even Satan glowered and fidged fu' fain,
And hotched and blew wi' might and main;

Till first ae caper, syne anither,
Tam tint his reason a' thegither,
And roars out, 'Weel done, Cutty-sark!'
And in an instant all was dark;
And scarcely had he Maggie rallied,
When out the hellish legion sallied.
As bees bizz out wi' angry fyke,
When plundering herds assail their byke;
As open pussie's mortal foes,
When, pop! she starts before their nose;
As eager runs the market-crowd,
When 'Catch the thief' resounds aloud;
So Maggie runs, the witches follow,
Wi' monie an eldritch skriech and hollo.
Ah, Tam! ah, Tam! thou'll get thy fairin!
In hell they'll roast thee like a herrin!
In vain thy Kate awaits thy comin!
Kate soon will be a woefu' woman!
Now do thy speedy utmost, Meg,
And win the key-stane of the brig;
There at them thou thy tail may toss—
A running stream they dare na cross!
But ere the key-stane she could make,
The fient a tail she had to shake!
For Nannie, far before the rest,
Hard upon noble Maggie prest,
And flew at Tam wi' furious ettle;
But little wist she Maggie's mettle!
Ae spring brought off her master hale,
But left behind her ain grey tail:
The carlin claught her by the rump,
And left poor Maggie scarce a stump.
Now, wha this tale o' truth shall read,
Ilk man and mother's son, take heed:
Whene'er to drink you are inclined,
Or cutty sarks run in your mind,
Think ye may buy the joys o'er dear;
Remember Tam o' Shanter's mare.

AE FOND KISS

Ae fond kiss, and then we sever!
Ae farewell, and then forever!
Deep in heart-wrung tears I'll pledge thee;
Warring sighs and groans I'll wage thee.
Who shall say that Fortune grieves him
While the star of hope she leaves him?
Me, nae cheerfu' twinkle lights me,
Dark despair around benights me.

I'll ne'er blame my partial fancy;
Naething could resist my Nancy:
But to see her was to love her,
Love but her and love forever.
Had we never loved sae kindly,
Had we never loved sae blindly,
Never met, or never parted,
We had ne'er been broken-hearted.

Fare-thee-weel, thou first and fairest!
Fare-thee-weel, thou best and dearest!
Thine be ilka joy and treasure,
Peace, enjoyment, love, and pleasure!
Ae fond kiss, and then we sever;
Ae farewell, alas, forever!
Deep in heart-wrung tears I'll pledge thee;
Warring sighs and groans I'll wage thee.

DUNCAN GRAY

Duncan Gray cam here to woo
(Ha, ha, the wooing o't!),
On blythe Yule Night when we were fou
(Ha, ha, the wooing o't!).
Maggie coost her head fu' high,
Looked asklent and unco skeigh,
Gart poor Duncan stand abeigh—
Ha, ha, the wooing o't!

Duncan fleeched, and Duncan prayed
(Ha, ha, the wooing o't!);
Meg was deaf as Ailsa craig
(Ha, ha, the wooing o't!).
Duncan sighed baith out and in,
Grat his een baith bleer't an' blin',
Spak o' lowpin o'er a linn—
Ha, ha, the wooing o't!

Time and chance are but a tide
(Ha, ha, the wooing o't!):
Slighted love is sair to bide
(Ha, ha, the wooing o't!).
'Shall I, like a fool,' quoth he,
'For a haughty hizzie die?
She may gae to—France for me!'—
Ha, ha, the wooing o't!

How it comes let doctors tell
(Ha, ha, the wooing o't!):
Meg grew sick as he grew hale
(Ha, ha, the wooing o't!);
Something in her bosom wrings,
For relief a sigh she brings;
And O her een, they spak sic things!—
Ha, ha, the wooing o't!

Duncan was a lad o' grace
(Ha, ha, the wooing o't!).
Maggie's was a piteous case
(Ha, ha, the wooing o't!):
Duncan could na be her death,
Swelling pity smoored his wrath;
Now they're crouse and canty baith—
Ha, ha, the wooing o't!

HIGHLAND MARY

Ye banks and braes and streams around
The castle o' Montgomery,
Green be your woods and fair your flowers,
Your waters never drumlie!

There Summer first unfald her robes,
  And there the langest tarry!
For there I took the last fareweel
  O' my sweet Highland Mary.

How sweetly bloomed the gay green birk,
  How rich the hawthorn's blossom,
As, underneath their fragrant shade,
  I clasped her to my bosom!
The golden hours, on angel wings,
  Flew o'er me and my dearie;
For dear to me as light and life
  Was my sweet Highland Mary.

Wi' monie a vow and locked embrace,
  Our parting was fu' tender;
And, pledging aft to meet again,
  We tore oursels asunder.
But O fell Death's untimely frost,
  That nipt my flower sae early!
Now green's the sod and cauld's the clay
  That wraps my Highland Mary!

O pale, pale now those rosy lips
  I aft hae kissed sae fondly!
And closed for ay the sparkling glance
  That dwelt on me sae kindly!
And mouldering now in silent dust
  That heart that lo'ed me dearly!
But still within my bosom's core
  Shall live my Highland Mary!

SCOTS, WHA HAE

Scots, wha hae wi' Wallace bled,
Scots, wham Bruce has aften led,
Welcome to your gory bed,
    Or to victorie!

Now's the day, and now's the hour!
See the front o' battle lour!
See approach proud Edward's power—
    Chains and slaverie!

Wha will be a traitor knave?
Wha can fill a coward's grave?
Wha sae base as be a slave?
Let him turn and flee!

Wha for Scotland's king and law
Freedom's sword will strongly draw,
Freeman stand or freeman fa',
Let him follow me!

By Oppression's woes and pains!
By your sons in servile chains!
We will drain our dearest veins,
But they shall be free!

Lay the proud usurpers low!
Tyrants fall in every foe!
Liberty's in every blow!
Let us do or die!

IS THERE FOR HONEST POVERTY

[A MAN'S A MAN FOR A' THAT]

Is there for honest poverty
That hings his head, an' a' that?
The coward slave, we pass him by,—
We dare be poor for a' that!
For a' that, an' a' that,
Our toils obscure, an' a' that:
The rank is but the guinea's stamp;
The man's the gowd for a' that.

What though on hamely fare we dine,
Wear hoddin grey, an' a' that?
Gie fools their silks, and knaves their wine,—
A man's a man for a' that,
For a' that, an' a' that,
Their tinsel show, an' a' that:
The honest man, tho' e'er sae poor,
Is king o' men for a' that.

Ye see yon birkie ca'd 'a lord,'
  Wha struts, an' stares, an' a' that;
Tho' hundreds worship at his word,
  He's but a cuif for a' that,
For a' that, an' a' that,
  His ribband, star, an' a' that:
The man o' independent mind,
  He looks an' laughs at a' that.

A prince can mak a belted knight,
  A marquis, duke, an' a' that!
But an honest man's aboon his might;
  Guid faith, he mauna fa' that!
For a' that, an' a' that,
  Their dignities, an' a' that:
The pith o' sense an' pride o' worth
  Are higher rank than a' that.

Then let us pray that come it may
  (As come it will for a' that),
That sense and worth, o'er a' the earth,
  Shall bear the gree, an' a' that:
For a' that, an' a' that,
  It's comin yet for a' that,
That man to man, the world o'er,
  Shall brithers be for a' that.

LAST MAY A BRAW WOOER

Last May a braw wooer cam down the lang glen,
  And sair wi' his love he did deave me:
I said there was naething I hated like men;
  The deuce gae wi'm to believe me, believe me,
  The deuce gae wi'm to believe me!

He spak o' the darts in my bonie black een,
  And vowed for my love he was dyin:
I said he might die when he liket for Jean;
  The Lord forgie me for lyin, for lyin,
  The Lord forgie me for lyin!

A weel-stocket mailen, himsel for the laird,
  And marriage aff-hand, were his proffers:
I never loot on that I kenned it or cared;
  But thought I might hae waur offers, waur offers,
  But thought I might hae waur offers.

But what wad ye think? in a fortnight or less—
  The Deil tak his taste to gae near her!—
He up the Gate Slack to my black cousin Bess:
  Guess ye how, the jad, I could bear her, could bear her!
  Guess ye how, the jad, I could bear her!

But a' the niest week as I petted wi' care,
  I gaed to the tryste o' Dalgarnock,
And wha but my fine fickle lover was there?
  I glowered as I'd seen a warlock, a warlock,
  I glowered as I'd seen a warlock.

But owre my left shouther I gae him a blink,
  Lest neebours might say I was saucy:
My wooer he capered as he'd been in drink,
  And vowed I was his dear lassie, dear lassie,
  And vowed I was his dear lassie!

I spiered for my cousin fu' couthy and sweet,
  Gin she had recovered her hearin,
And how her new shoon fit her auld shachled feet—
  But, heavens, how he fell a swearin, a swearin!
  But, heavens, how he fell a swearin!

He begged, for Gudesake, I wad be his wife,
  Or else I wad kill him wi' sorrow;
So, e'en to preserve the poor body in life,
  I think I maun wed him to-morrow, to-morrow,
  I think I maun wed him to-morrow!

O, WERT THOU IN THE CAULD BLAST

O, wert thou in the cauld blast,
  On yonder lea, on yonder lea,
My plaidie to the angry airt,
  I'd shelter thee, I'd shelter thee;

Or did misfortune's bitter storms
  Around thee blaw, around thee blaw,
Thy bield should be my bosom,
  To share it a', to share it a'.

Or were I in the wildest waste,
  Sae black and bare, sae black and bare,
The desert were a paradise
  If thou wert there, if thou wert there;
Or were I monarch of the globe,
  Wi' thee to reign, wi' thee to reign,
The brightest jewel in my crown
  Wad be my queen, wad be my queen.

ERASMUS DARWIN

From THE BOTANIC GARDEN

[Procul Este, Profani]

Stay your rude steps! whose throbbing breasts infold
The legion-fiends of glory or of gold!
Stay! whose false lips seductive simpers part,
While cunning nestles in the harlot-heart!—
For you no Dryads dress the roseate bower,
For you no Nymphs their sparkling vases pour;
Unmarked by you, light Graces swim the green,
And hovering Cupids aim their shafts, unseen.

But thou! whose mind the well-attempered ray
Of taste and virtue lights with purer day;
Whose finer sense each soft vibration owns
With sweet responsive sympathy of tones;
(So the fair flower expands its lucid form
To meet the sun, and shuts it to the storm);
For thee my borders nurse the fragrant wreath,
My fountains murmur, and my zephyrs breathe;

Slow slides the painted snail, the gilded fly
Smooths his fine down, to charm thy curious eye;
On twinkling fins my pearly nations play,
Or win with sinuous train their trackless way;
My plumy pairs, in gay embroidery dressed,
Form with ingenious bill the pensile nest,
To love's sweet notes attune the listening dell,
And Echo sounds her soft symphonious shell.

And if with thee some hapless maid should stray,
Disastrous love companion of her way,
Oh, lead her timid steps to yonder glade,
Whose arching cliffs depending alders shade;
There, as meek evening wakes her temperate breeze,
And moonbeams glimmer through the trembling trees,
The rills that gurgle round shall soothe her ear,
The weeping rocks shall number tear for tear;
There as sad Philomel, alike forlorn,
Sings to the night from her accustomed thorn;
While at sweet intervals each falling note
Sighs in the gale, and whispers round the grot;
The sister-woe shall calm her aching breast,
And softer slumbers steal her cares to rest.

[The Sensitive Plant]

Weak with nice sense, the chaste Mimosa stands,
From each rude touch withdraws her timid hands;
Oft as light clouds o'erpass the summer-glade,
Alarmed she trembles at the moving shade;
And feels, alive through all her tender form,
The whispered murmurs of the gathering storm;
Shuts her sweet eyelids to approaching night,
And hails with freshened charms the rising light.
Veiled, with gay decency and modest pride,
Slow to the mosque she moves, an eastern bride,
There her soft vows unceasing love record,
Queen of the bright seraglio of her lord.

WILLIAM BLAKE

TO WINTER

'O Winter! bar thine adamantine doors:
The north is thine; there hast thou built thy dark
Deep-founded habitation. Shake not thy roofs,
Nor bend thy pillars with thine iron car.'

He hears me not, but o'er the yawning deep
Rides heavy; his storms are unchained, sheathèd
In ribbed steel; I dare not lift mine eyes,
For he hath reared his sceptre o'er the world.

Lo! now the direful monster, whose skin clings
To his strong bones, strides o'er the groaning rocks:
He withers all in silence, and in his hand
Unclothes the earth, and freezes up frail life.

He takes his seat upon the cliffs,—the mariner
Cries in vain. Poor little wretch, that deal'st
With storms!—till heaven smiles, and the monster
Is driven yelling to his caves beneath Mount Hecla.

SONG

Fresh from the dewy hill, the merry year
Smiles on my head and mounts his flaming car;
Round my young brows the laurel wreathes a shade,
And rising glories beam around my head.

My feet are winged, while o'er the dewy lawn,
I meet my maiden risen like the morn:
O bless those holy feet, like angels' feet;
O bless those limbs, beaming with heavenly light.

Like as an angel glittering in the sky
In times of innocence and holy joy;
The joyful shepherd stops his grateful song
To hear the music of an angel's tongue.

So when she speaks, the voice of Heaven I hear;
So when we walk, nothing impure comes near;
Each field seems Eden, and each calm retreat;
Each village seems the haunt of holy feet.

But that sweet village where my black-eyed maid
Closes her eyes in sleep beneath night's shade,
Whene'er I enter, more than mortal fire
Burns in my soul, and does my song inspire.

TO THE MUSES

Whether on Ida's shady brow,
Or in the chambers of the East,
The chambers of the sun, that now
From ancient melody have ceased;

Whether in Heaven ye wander fair,
Or the green corners of the earth,
Or the blue regions of the air,
Where the melodious winds have birth;

Whether on crystal rocks ye rove,
Beneath the bosom of the sea
Wandering in many a coral grove
Fair Nine, forsaking Poetry!

How have you left the ancient love
That bards of old enjoyed in you!
The languid strings do scarcely move!
The sound is forced, the notes are few!

INTRODUCTION TO SONGS OF INNOCENCE

Piping down the valleys wild,
Piping songs of pleasant glee,
On a cloud I saw a child,
And he laughing said to me:

'Pipe a song about a Lamb!'
So I piped with merry cheer.
'Piper, pipe that song again;'
So I piped: he wept to hear.

'Drop thy pipe, thy happy pipe;
Sing thy songs of happy cheer:'
So I sang the same again,
While he wept with joy to hear.

'Piper, sit thee down and write
In a book, that all may read.'
So he vanished from my sight,
And I plucked a hollow reed,

And I made a rural pen,
And I stained the water clear,
And I wrote my happy songs
Every child may joy to hear.

THE LAMB

Little Lamb, who made thee?
Dost thou know who made thee?
Gave thee life and bid thee feed
By the stream and o'er the mead;
Gave thee clothing of delight,
Softest clothing, woolly, bright;
Gave thee such a tender voice,
Making all the vales rejoice?
Little Lamb, who made thee?
Dost thou know who made thee?

Little Lamb, I'll tell thee;
Little Lamb, I'll tell thee:
He is callèd by thy name,
For He calls himself a Lamb.
He is meek, and He is mild;
He became a little child.
I a child, and thou a lamb,
We are callèd by His name.
Little Lamb, God bless thee!
Little Lamb, God bless thee!

THE LITTLE BLACK BOY

My mother bore me in the southern wild,
And I am black, but O! my soul is white;
White as an angel is the English child,
But I am black, as if bereaved of light.

My mother taught me underneath a tree,
And, sitting down before the heat of day,
She took me on her lap and kissèd me,
And, pointing to the east, began to say:

'Look on the rising sun,—there God does live,
And gives His light, and gives His heat away;
And flowers and trees and beasts and men receive
Comfort in morning, joy in the noonday.

'And we are put on earth a little space,
That we may learn to bear the beams of love;
And these black bodies and this sunburnt face
Is but a cloud, and like a shady grove.

'For when our souls have learned the heat to bear,
The cloud will vanish; we shall hear His voice,
Saying: "Come out from the grove, my love and care,
And round my golden tent like lambs rejoice."'

Thus did my mother say, and kissèd me;
And thus I say to little English boy.
When I from black and he from white cloud free,
And round the tent of God like lambs we joy,

I'll shade him from the heat, till he can bear
To lean in joy upon our Father's knee;
And then I'll stand and stroke his silver hair,
And be like him, and he will then love me.

A CRADLE SONG

Sweet dreams, form a shade
O'er my lovely infant's head;
Sweet dreams of pleasant streams
By happy, silent, moony beams.

Sweet sleep, with soft down
Weave thy brows an infant crown.
Sweet sleep, Angel mild,
Hover o'er my happy child.

Sweet smiles, in the night
Hover over my delight;
Sweet smiles, mother's smiles,
All the livelong night beguiles.

Sweet moans, dovelike sighs,
Chase not slumber from thy eyes.
Sweet moans, sweeter smiles,
All the dovelike moans beguiles.

Sleep, sleep, happy child,
All creation slept and smiled;
Sleep, sleep, happy sleep,
While o'er thee thy mother weep.

Sweet babe, in thy face
Holy image I can trace.
Sweet babe, once like thee,
Thy Maker lay and wept for me,

Wept for me, for thee, for all,
When He was an infant small.
Thou His image ever see,
Heavenly face that smiles on thee,

Smiles on thee, on me, on all;
Who became an infant small.
Infant smiles are His own smiles;
Heaven and earth to peace beguiles.

HOLY THURSDAY

'Twas on a Holy Thursday, their innocent faces clean,
The children walking two and two, in red and blue and
green,
Grey-headed beadles walked before, with wands as white
as snow,
Till into the high dome of Paul's they like Thames' waters
flow.

O what a multitude they seemed, these flowers of London town!
Seated in companies they sit with radiance all their own.
The hum of multitudes was there, but multitudes of lambs,
Thousands of little boys and girls raising their innocent hands.

Now like a mighty wind they raise to Heaven the voice of song,
Or like harmonious thunderings the seats of Heaven among.
Beneath them sit the agèd men, wise guardians of the poor;
Then cherish pity, lest you drive an angel from your door.

THE DIVINE IMAGE

To Mercy, Pity, Peace, and Love
All pray in their distress;
And to these virtues of delight
Return their thankfulness.

For Mercy, Pity, Peace, and Love
Is God, our Father dear,
And Mercy, Pity, Peace, and Love
Is man, His child and care.

For Mercy has a human heart,
Pity a human face,
And Love, the human form divine,
And Peace, the human dress.

Then every man, of every clime,
That prays in his distress,
Prays to the human form divine,
Love, Mercy, Pity, Peace.

And all must love the human form,
In heathen, Turk, or Jew;
Where Mercy, Love, and Pity dwell
There God is dwelling too.

ON ANOTHER'S SORROW

Can I see another's woe,
And not be in sorrow too?
Can I see another's grief,
And not seek for kind relief?

Can I see a falling tear,
And not feel my sorrow's share?
Can a father see his child
Weep, nor be with sorrow filled?

Can a mother sit and hear
An infant groan, an infant fear?
No, no! never can it be!
Never, never can it be!

And can He who smiles on all
Hear the wren with sorrows small,
Hear the small bird's grief and care,
Hear the woes that infants bear,

And not sit beside the nest,
Pouring pity in their breast;
And not sit the cradle near,
Weeping tear on infant's tear;

And not sit both night and day,
Wiping all our tears away?
O, no! never can it be!
Never, never can it be!

He doth give His joy to all;
He becomes an infant small;
He becomes a man of woe;
He doth feel the sorrow too.

Think not thou canst sigh a sigh,
And thy Maker is not by;
Think not thou canst weep a tear,
And thy Maker is not near.

O! He gives to us His joy
That our grief He may destroy;
Till our grief is fled and gone
He doth sit by us and moan.

THE BOOK OF THEL

Thel's Motto

Does the Eagle know what is in the pit:
Or wilt thou go ask the Mole?
Can Wisdom be put in a silver rod,
Or Love in a golden bowl?

I

The daughters of [the] Seraphim led round their sunny flocks—
All but the youngest: she in paleness sought the secret air,
To fade away like morning beauty from her mortal day:
Down by the river of Adona her soft voice is heard,
And thus her gentle lamentation falls like morning dew:—

'O life of this our spring! why fades the lotus of the water?
Why fade these children of the spring, born but to smile and fall?
Ah! Thel is like a watery bow, and like a parting cloud;
Like a reflection in a glass; like shadows in the water;
Like dreams of infants, like a smile upon an infant's face;
Like the dove's voice; like transient day; like music in the air.
Ah! gentle may I lay me down, and gentle rest my head,
And gentle sleep the sleep of death, and gentle hear the voice
Of Him that walketh in the garden in the evening time.'

The Lily of the Valley, breathing in the humble grass,
Answerèd the lovely maid and said: 'I am a wat'ry weed,
And I am very small, and love to dwell in lowly vales;
So weak, the gilded butterfly scarce perches on my head.
Yet I am visited from heaven, and He that smiles on all
Walks in the valley, and each morn over me spreads His hand,

Saying, "Rejoice, thou humble grass, thou new-born lily flower,
Thou gentle maid of silent valleys and of modest brooks;
For thou shalt be clothèd in light, and fed with morning manna,
Till summer's heat melts thee beside the fountains and the springs,
To flourish in eternal vales." Then why should Thel complain?
Why should the mistress of the vales of Har utter a sigh?'

She ceased, and smiled in tears, then sat down in her silver shrine.

Thel answered: 'O thou little Virgin of the peaceful valley,
Giving to those that cannot crave, the voiceless, the o'ertired;
Thy breath doth nourish the innocent lamb, he smells thy milky garments,
He crops thy flowers while thou sittest smiling in his face,
Wiping his mild and meekin mouth from all contagious taints.
Thy wine doth purify the golden honey; thy perfume,
Which thou dost scatter on every little blade of grass that springs,
Revives the milkèd cow, and tames the fire-breathing steed.
But Thel is like a faint cloud kindled at the rising sun:
I vanish from my pearly throne, and who shall find my place?'

'Queen of the vales,' the Lily answered, 'ask the tender Cloud,
And it shall tell thee why it glitters in the morning sky,
And why it scatters its bright beauty through the humid air.
Descend, O little Cloud, and hover before the eyes of Thel.'

The Cloud descended, and the Lily bowèd her modest head,
And went to mind her numerous charge among the verdant grass.

II

'O little Cloud,' the Virgin said, 'I charge thee tell to me
Why thou complainest not, when in one hour thou fade away;
Then we shall seek thee, but not find. Ah! Thel is like to thee:
I pass away; yet I complain, and no one hears my voice.'

The Cloud then showed his golden head, and his bright form emerged,
Hovering and glittering on the air before the face of Thel.
'O Virgin, know'st thou not our steeds drink of the golden springs
Where Luvah doth renew his horses? Look'st thou on my youth,
And fearest thou, because I vanish and am seen no more,
Nothing remains? O maid, I tell thee, when I pass away,
It is to tenfold life, to love, to peace, and raptures holy:
Unseen descending, weigh my light wings upon balmy flowers,
And court the fair-eyed dew, to take me to her shining tent:
The weeping virgin, trembling, kneels before the risen sun,
Till we arise, linked in a golden band and never part,
But walk united, bearing food to all our tender flowers.'

'Dost thou, O little Cloud? I fear that I am not like thee,
For I walk through the vales of Har, and smell the sweetest flowers,
But I feed not the little flowers; I hear the warbling birds,
But I feed not the warbling birds; they fly and seek their food:
But Thel delights in these no more, because I fade away;
And all shall say, "Without a use this shining woman lived,
Or did she only live to be at death the food of worms?"'

The Cloud reclined upon his airy throne, and answered thus:—

'Then if thou art the food of worms, O Virgin of the skies,
How great thy use, how great thy blessing! Everything
that lives
Lives not alone nor for itself. Fear not, and I will call
The weak Worm from its lowly bed, and thou shalt hear
its voice.
Come forth, Worm of the silent valley, to thy pensive
Queen.'

The helpless Worm arose, and sat upon the Lily's leaf,
And the bright Cloud sailed on, to find his partner in the
vale.

III

Then Thel astonished viewed the Worm upon its dewy bed.

'Art thou a Worm? Image of weakness, art thou but a
Worm?
I see thee like an infant wrappèd in the Lily's leaf.
Ah! weep not, little voice, thou canst not speak, but thou
canst weep.
Is this a Worm? I see thee lay helpless and naked, weep-
ing,
And none to answer, none to cherish thee with mother's
smiles.'
The Clod of Clay heard the Worm's voice, and raised her
pitying head;
She bowed over the weeping infant, and her life exhaled
In milky fondness: then on Thel she fixed her humble
eyes.

'O Beauty of the vales of Har! we live not for ourselves.
Thou seest me, the meanest thing, and so I am indeed.
My bosom of itself is cold, and of itself is dark;
But He that loves the lowly pours His oil upon my head,
And kisses me, and binds His nuptial bands around my
breast,
And says: "Thou mother of my children, I have lovèd thee,
And I have given thee a crown that none can take away."
But how this is, sweet maid, I know not, and I cannot
know;
I ponder, and I cannot ponder; yet I live and love.'

The daughter of beauty wiped her pitying tears with her white veil,
And said: 'Alas! I knew not this, and therefore did I weep.
That God would love a worm I knew, and punish the evil foot
That wilful bruised its helpless form; but that He cherished it
With milk and oil, I never knew, and therefore did I weep;
And I complained in the mild air, because I fade away,
And lay me down in thy cold bed, and leave my shining lot.'

'Queen of the vales,' the matron Clay answered, 'I heard thy sighs,
And all thy moans flew o'er my roof, but I have called them down.
Wilt thou, O queen, enter my house? 'Tis given thee to enter,
And to return: fear nothing; enter with thy virgin feet.'

IV

The eternal gates' terrific porter lifted the northern bar;
Thel entered in, and saw the secrets of the land unknown.
She saw the couches of the dead, and where the fibrous root
Of every heart on earth infixes deep its restless twists:
A land of sorrows and of tears where never smile was seen.

She wandered in the land of clouds through valleys dark, listening
Dolours and lamentations; waiting oft beside a dewy grave
She stood in silence, listening to the voices of the ground,
Till to her own grave-plot she came, and there she sat down,
And heard this voice of sorrow breathèd from the hollow pit.

'Why cannot the ear be closèd to its own destruction?
Or the glistening eye to the poison of a smile?
Why are eyelids stored with arrows ready drawn,
Where a thousand fighting men in ambush lie,
Or an eye of gifts and graces showering fruits and coinèd gold?

Why a tongue impressed with honey from every wind?
Why an ear, a whirlpool fierce to draw creations in?
Why a nostril wide inhaling terror, trembling, and affright?
Why a tender curb upon the youthful, burning boy?
Why a little curtain of flesh on the bed of our desire?'

The Virgin started from her seat, and with a shriek
Fled back unhindered till she came into the vales of Har.

From THE FRENCH REVOLUTION

[Democracy and Peace]

Aumont went out and stood in the hollow porch, his ivory wand in his hand;
A cold orb of disdain revolved round him, and coverèd his soul with snows eternal.
Great Henry's soul shudderèd, a whirlwind and fire tore furious from his angry bosom;
He indignant departed on horses of Heaven. Then the Abbé de Sieyès raised his feet
On the steps of the Louvre; like a voice of God following a storm, the Abbé followed
The pale fires of Aumont into the chamber; as a father that bows to his son,
Whose rich fields inheriting spread their old glory, so the voice of the people bowèd
Before the ancient seat of the kingdom and mountains to be renewèd.

'Hear, O heavens of France! the voice of the people, arising from valley and hill,
O'erclouded with power. Hear the voice of valleys, the voice of meek cities,
Mourning oppressèd on village and field, till the village and field is a waste.
For the husbandman weeps at blights of the fife, and blasting of trumpets consume
The souls of mild France; the pale mother nourishes her child to the deadly slaughter.

When the heavens were sealed with a stone, and the terrible sun closed in an orb, and the moon
Rent from the nations, and each star appointed for watchers of night,
The millions of spirits immortal were bound in the ruins of sulphur heaven
To wander enslaved; black, depressed in dark ignorance, kept in awe with the whip
To worship terrors, bred from the blood of revenge and breath of desire
In bestial forms, or more terrible men; till the dawn of our peaceful morning,
Till dawn, till morning, till the breaking of clouds, and swelling of winds, and the universal voice;
Till man raise his darkened limbs out of the caves of night. His eyes and his heart
Expand—Where is Space? where, O sun, is thy dwelling? where thy tent, O faint slumbrous Moon?
Then the valleys of France shall cry to the soldier: "Throw down thy sword and musket,
And run and embrace the meek peasant." Her nobles shall hear and shall weep, and put off
The red robe of terror, the crown of oppression, the shoes of contempt, and unbuckle
The girdle of war from the desolate earth. Then the Priest in his thunderous cloud
Shall weep, bending to earth, embracing the valleys, and putting his hand to the plough,
Shall say, "No more I curse thee; but now I will bless thee: no more in deadly black
Devour thy labour; nor lift up a cloud in thy heavens, O laborious plough;
That the wild raging millions, that wander in forests, and howl in law-blasted wastes,
Strength maddened with slavery, honesty bound in the dens of superstition,
May sing in the village, and shout in the harvest, and woo in pleasant gardens
Their once savage loves, now beaming with knowledge, with gentle awe adornèd;
And the saw, and the hammer, the chisel, the pencil, the pen, and the instruments

Of heavenly song sound in the wilds once forbidden, to
teach the laborious ploughman
And shepherd, delivered from clouds of war, from pestilence, from night-fear, from murder,
From falling, from stifling, from hunger, from cold, from
slander, discontent, and sloth,
That walk in beasts and birds of night, driven back by
the sandy desert,
Like pestilent fogs round cities of men; and the happy
earth sing in its course,
The mild peaceable nations be openèd to heaven, and men
walk with their fathers in bliss."
Then hear the first voice of the morning: "Depart, O
clouds of night, and no more
Return; be withdrawn cloudy war, troops of warriors depart, nor around our peaceable city
Breathe fires; but ten miles from Paris let all be peace,
nor a soldier be seen!"'

From A SONG OF LIBERTY

The Eternal Female groaned! It was heard over all the earth.

Albion's coast is sick, silent. The American meadows faint!

Shadows of Prophecy shiver along by the lakes and the rivers, and mutter across the ocean. France, rend down thy dungeon!

. . . .

Look up! look up! O citizen of London, enlarge thy countenance! O Jew, leave counting gold! return to thy oil and wine. O African! black African! Go, wingèd thought, widen his forehead!

. . . .

With thunder and fire, leading his starry hosts through the waste wilderness, he promulgates his ten commands, glancing his beamy eyelids over the deep in dark dismay.

Where the son of fire in his eastern cloud, while the morning plumes her golden breast,

Spurning the clouds written with curses, stamps the stony law to dust, loosing the eternal horses from the dens of night, crying: *Empire is no more! and now the lion and wolf shall cease.*

CHORUS

Let the Priests of the Raven of dawn no longer, in deadly black, with hoarse note curse the sons of joy! Nor his accepted brethren—whom, tyrant, he calls free—lay the bound or build the roof! Nor pale Religion's lechery call that virginity that wishes but acts not!

For everything that lives is holy!

THE FLY

Little Fly,
Thy summer's play
My thoughtless hand
Has brushed away.

Am not I
A fly like thee?
Or art not thou
A man like me?

For I dance,
And drink, and sing,
Till some blind hand
Shall brush my wing.

If thought is life
And strength and breath,
And the want
Of thought is death;

Then am I
A happy fly,
If I live
Or if I die.

THE TIGER

Tiger! Tiger! burning bright
In the forests of the night,
What immortal hand or eye
Could frame thy fearful symmetry?

In what distant deeps or skies
Burnt the fire of thine eyes?
On what wings dare he aspire?
What the hand dare seize the fire?

And what shoulder, and what art,
Could twist the sinews of thy heart?
And when thy heart began to beat,
What dread hand? and what dread feet?

What the hammer? what the chain?
In what furnace was thy brain?
What the anvil? what dread grasp
Dare its deadly terrors clasp?

When the stars threw down their spears,
And watered heaven with their tears,
Did he smile his work to see?
Did he who made the Lamb make thee?

Tiger! Tiger! burning bright
In the forests of the night,
What immortal hand or eye,
Dare frame thy fearful symmetry?

HOLY THURSDAY

Is this a holy thing to see
In a rich and fruitful land,
Babes reduced to misery,
Fed with cold and usurous hand?

Is that trembling cry a song?
Can it be a song of joy?
And so many children poor?
It is a land of poverty!

And their sun does never shine,
And their fields are bleak and bare,
And their ways are filled with thorns:
It is eternal winter there.

For where'er the sun does shine,
And where'er the rain does fall,
Babe can never hunger there,
Nor poverty the mind appal.

THE GARDEN OF LOVE

I went to the Garden of Love,
And saw what I never had seen:
A chapel was built in the midst,
Where I used to play on the green.

And the gates of this chapel were shut,
And 'Thou shalt not' writ over the door;
So I turned to the Garden of Love,
That so many sweet flowers bore;

And I saw it was fillèd with graves,
And tombstones where flowers should be;
And priests in black gowns were walking their
rounds,
And binding with briars my joys and desires.

A LITTLE BOY LOST

'Nought loves another as itself,
Nor venerates another so,
Nor is it possible to Thought
A greater than itself to know:

'And, Father, how can I love you
Or any of my brothers more?
I love you like the little bird
That picks up crumbs around the door.'

The Priest sat by and heard the child,
In trembling zeal he seized his hair:
He led him by his little coat,
And all admired the priestly care.

And standing on the altar high,
'Lo! what a fiend is here!' said he,
'One who sets reason up for judge
Of our most holy Mystery.'

The weeping child could not be heard,
The weeping parents wept in vain;
They stripped him to his little shirt,
And bound him in an iron chain;

And burned him in a holy place,
Where many had been burned before:
The weeping parents wept in vain.
Are such things done on Albion's shore?

THE SCHOOLBOY

I love to rise in a summer morn
When the birds sing on every tree;
The distant huntsman winds his horn,
And the skylark sings with me.
O! what sweet company.

But to go to school in a summer morn,
O! it drives all joy away;
Under a cruel eye outworn,
The little ones spend the day
In sighing and dismay.

Ah! then at times I drooping sit,
And spend many an anxious hour,
Nor in my book can I take delight,
Nor sit in learning's bower,
Worn through with the dreary shower.

How can the bird that is born for joy
Sit in a cage and sing?
How can a child, when fears annoy,
But droop his tender wing,
And forget his youthful spring?

O! father and mother, if buds are nipped
And blossoms blown away,
And if the tender plants are stripped
Of their joy in the springing day,
By sorrow and care's dismay,

How shall the summer arise in joy,
Or the summer fruits appear?
Or how shall we gather what griefs destroy,
Or bless the mellowing year,
When the blasts of winter appear?

LONDON

I wander through each chartered street,
Near where the chartered Thames does flow,
And mark in every face I meet
Marks of weakness, marks of woe.

In every cry of every man,
In every infant's cry of fear,
In every voice, in every ban,
The mind-forged manacles I hear.

How the chimney-sweeper's cry
Every blackening church appals;
And the hapless soldier's sigh
Runs in blood down palace walls

But most through midnight streets I hear
How the youthful harlot's curse
Blasts the new-born infant's tear,
And blights with plagues the marriage hearse.

From AUGURIES OF INNOCENCE

To see a World in a grain of sand,
And a Heaven in a wild flower,
Hold Infinity in the palm of your hand,
And Eternity in an hour.

A robin redbreast in a cage
Puts all Heaven in a rage.
A dove-house filled with doves and pigeons
Shudders hell through all its regions.
A dog starved at his master's gate
Predicts the ruin of the state.
A horse misused upon the road
Calls to Heaven for human blood.
Each outcry of the hunted hare
A fibre from the brain does tear.
A skylark wounded in the wing,
A cherubim does cease to sing.
The game-cock clipped and armed for fight
Does the rising sun affright.
Every wolf's and lion's howl
Raises from hell a human soul.
The wild deer, wandering here and there,
Keeps the human soul from care.
The lamb misused breeds public strife,
And yet forgives the butcher's knife.
The bat that flits at close of eve
Has left the brain that won't believe.
The owl that calls upon the night
Speaks the unbeliever's fright.
He who shall hurt the little wren
Shall never be beloved by men.
He who the ox to wrath has moved
Shall never be by woman loved.
The wanton boy that kills the fly
Shall feel the spider's enmity.
He who torments the chafer's sprite
Weaves a bower in endless night.
The caterpillar on the leaf
Repeats to thee thy mother's grief.

Kill not the moth nor butterfly,
For the Last Judgment draweth nigh.
He who shall train the horse to war
Shall never pass the polar bar.
The beggar's dog and widow's cat,
Feed them, and thou wilt grow fat.

. . . .

The babe that weeps the rod beneath
Writes revenge in realms of death.
The beggar's rags fluttering in air,
Does to rags the heavens tear.
The soldier, armed with sword and gun,
Palsied strikes the summer's sun.
The poor man's farthing is worth more
Than all the gold on Afric's shore.
One mite wrung from the labourer's hands
Shall buy and sell the miser's lands;
Or, if protected from on high,
Does that whole nation sell and buy.
He who mocks the infant's faith
Shall be mocked in age and death.
He who shall teach the child to doubt
The rotting grave shall ne'er get out.
He who respects the infant's faith
Triumphs over hell and death.

From MILTON

And did those feet in ancient time
  Walk upon England's mountains green?
And was the holy Lamb of God
  On England's pleasant pastures seen?

And did the countenance divine
  Shine forth upon our clouded hills?
And was Jerusalem builded here
  Among these dark Satanic mills?

Bring me my bow of burning gold!
  Bring me my arrows of desire!
Bring me my spear! O clouds, unfold!
  Bring me my chariot of fire!

I will not cease from mental fight,
Nor shall my sword sleep in my hand,
Till we have built Jerusalem
In England's green and pleasant land.

[Reason and Imagination]

The negation is the Spectre, the reasoning power in man:
This is a false body, an incrustation over my immortal
Spirit, a selfhood which must be put off and annihilated alway.
To cleanse the face of my spirit by self-examination,
To bathe in the waters of life, to wash off the not human,
I come in self-annihilation and the grandeur of inspiration;
To cast off rational demonstration by faith in the Saviour,
To cast off the rotten rags of memory by inspiration,
To cast off Bacon, Locke, and Newton from Albion's covering,
To take off his filthy garments and clothe him with imagination;
To cast aside from poetry all that is not inspiration,
That it no longer shall dare to mock with the aspersion of madness
Cast on the inspirèd by the tame high finisher of paltry blots.
Indefinite or paltry rhymes, or paltry harmonies,
Who creeps into state government like a caterpillar to destroy;
To cast off the idiot questioner, who is always questioning,
But never capable of answering; who sits with a sly grin
Silent plotting when to question, like a thief in a cave;
Who publishes doubt and calls it knowledge; whose science is despair,
Whose pretence to knowledge is envy, whose whole science is
To destroy the wisdom of ages, to gratify ravenous envy
That rages round him like a wolf, day and night, without rest.
He smiles with condescension; he talks of benevolence and virtue,

And those who act with benevolence and virtue they murder time on time.
These are the destroyers of Jerusalem! these are the murderers
Of Jesus! who deny the faith and mock at eternal life,
Who pretend to poetry that they may destroy imagination
By imitation of nature's images drawn from remembrance.
These are the sexual garments, the abomination of desolation,
Hiding the human lineaments, as with an ark and curtains
Which Jesus rent, and now shall wholly purge away with fire,
Till generation is swallowed up in regeneration.

From JERUSALEM

[To the Deists]

I saw a Monk of Charlemaine
Arise before my sight:
I talked with the Grey Monk as we stood
In beams of infernal light.

Gibbon arose with a lash of steel,
And Voltaire with a racking wheel;
The schools, in clouds of learning rolled,
Arose with war in iron and gold.

'Thou lazy Monk!' they sound afar,
'In vain condemning glorious war;
And in your cell you shall ever dwell:
Rise, War, and bind him in his cell!'

The blood red ran from the Grey Monk's side,
His hands and feet were wounded wide,
His body bent, his arms and knees
Like to the roots of ancient trees.

When Satan first the black bow bent
And the moral law from the Gospel rent,
He forged the law into a sword,
And spilled the blood of mercy's Lord.

Titus! Constantine! Charlemaine!
O Voltaire! Rousseau! Gibbon! Vain
Your Grecian mocks and Roman sword
Against this image of his Lord;

For a tear is an intellectual thing;
And a sigh is the sword of an angel king;
And the bitter groan of a martyr's woe
Is an arrow from the Almighty's bow.

GEORGE CANNING

From THE PROGRESS OF MAN

[Matrimony in Otaheite]

There laughs the sky, there zephyrs frolic train,
And light-winged loves, and blameless pleasures reign:
There, when two souls congenial ties unite,
No hireling bonzes chant the mystic rite;
Free every thought, each action unconfined,
And light those fetters which no rivets bind.
There in each grove, each sloping bank along,
And flowers and shrubs, and odorous herbs among,
Each shepherd clasped, with undisguised delight,
His yielding fair one—in the captain's sight;
Each yielding fair, as chance or fancy led,
Preferred new lovers to her sylvan bed.
Learn hence each nymph, whose free aspiring mind
Europe's cold laws, and colder customs bind;
O! learn what Nature's genial laws decree!
What Otaheite is, let Britain be!

. . . .

Of whist or cribbage mark th' amusing game;
The partners changing, but the sport the same:
Else would the gamester's anxious ardour cool,
Dull every deal, and stagnant every pool.
—Yet must one man, with one unceasing wife,
Play the long rubber of connubial life.

Yes! human laws, and laws esteemed divine,
The generous passion straighten and confine;
And, as a stream, when art constrains its course,
Pours its fierce torrent with augmented force,
So passion, narrowed to one channel small,
Unlike the former,—does not flow at all.
For Love then only flaps his purple wings
When uncontrolled by priestcraft or by kings.

From THE NEW MORALITY

[Anti-Patriotism and Sentimentality]

With unsparing hand,
Oh, lash these vile impostures from the land!
First, stern Philanthropy,—not she who dries
The orphan's tears, and wipes the widow's eyes;
Not she who, sainted Charity her guide,
Of British bounty pours the annual tide,—
But French Philanthropy, whose boundless mind
Glows with the general love of all mankind;
Philanthropy, beneath whose baneful sway
Each patriot passion sinks, and dies away.
Taught in her school t' imbibe thy mawkish strain,
Condorcet! filtered through the dregs of Paine,
Each pert adept disowns a Briton's part,
And plucks the name of England from his heart.
What! shall a name, a word, a sound, control
Th' aspiring thought, and cramp th' expansive soul?
Shall one half-peopled island's rocky round
A love that glows for all creation bound?
And social charities contract the plan
Framed for thy freedom, universal man?
No—through th' extended globe his feelings run
As broad and general as th' unbounded sun!
No narrow bigot he: his reasoned view
Thy interests, England, ranks with thine, Peru!
France at our doors, he seeks no danger nigh,
But heaves for Turkey's woes th' impartial sigh;
A steady patriot of the world alone,
The friend of every country but his own.

Next comes a gentler virtue.—Ah, beware
Lest the harsh verse her shrinking softness scare.
Visit her not too roughly; the warm sigh
Breathes on her lips; the tear-drop gems her eye.
Sweet Sensibility, who dwells inshrined
In the fine foldings of the feeling mind;
With delicate Mimosa's sense endued,
Who shrinks, instinctive, from a hand too rude;
Or, like the anagillis, prescient flower,
Shuts her soft petals at th' approaching shower.
  Sweet child of sickly fancy! her of yore
From her loved France Rousseau to exile bore;
And while 'midst lakes and mountains wild he ran,
Full of himself, and shunned the haunts of man,
Taught her o'er each lone vale and Alpine steep
To lisp the story of his wrongs, and weep;
Taught her to cherish still in either eye,
Of tender tears a plentiful supply,
And pour them in the brooks that babbled by:
Taught by nice scale to mete her feelings strong,
False by degrees, and exquisitely wrong;
For the crushed beetle first, the widowed dove,
And all the warbled sorrows of the grove,
Next for poor suffering guilt,—and last of all,
For parents, friends, a king and country's fall.
  Mark her fair votaries, prodigal of grief,
With cureless pangs, and woes that mock relief,
Droop in soft sorrow o'er a faded flower,
O'er a dead jackass pour the pearly shower:
But hear, unmoved, of Loire's ensanguined flood
Choked up with slain; of Lyons drenched in blood;
Of crimes that blot the age, the world, with shame,
Foul crimes, but sicklied o'er with freedom's name,—
Altars and thrones subverted, social life
Trampled to earth, the husband from the wife,
Parent from child, with ruthless fury torn;
Of talents, honour, virtue, wit, forlorn
In friendless exile; of the wise and good
Staining the daily scaffold with their blood.
Of savage cruelties that scare the mind,
The rage of madness with hell's lusts combined,
Of hearts torn reeking from the mangled breast,
They hear—and hope, that all is for the best!

CAROLINA, LADY NAIRNE

THE LAND O' THE LEAL

I'm wearin' awa', John,
Like snaw-wreaths in thaw, John,
I'm wearin' awa'
To the land o' the leal.
There's nae sorrow there, John,
There's neither cauld nor care, John,
The day is aye fair
In the land o' the leal.

Our bonnie bairn's there, John,
She was baith gude and fair, John;
And oh! we grudged her sair
To the land o' the leal.
But sorrow's sel' wears past, John,
And joy's a-comin' fast, John,
The joy that's aye to last
In the land o' the leal.

Sae dear that joy was bought, John,
Sae free the battle fought, John,
That sinfu' man e'er brought
To the land o' the leal.
Oh! dry your glistening e'e, John,
My soul langs to be free, John,
And angels beckon me
To the land o' the leal.

Oh! haud ye leal and true, John,
Your day it's wearin' through, John,
And I'll welcome you
To the land o' the leal.
Now fare-ye-weel, my ain John,
This warld's cares are vain, John,
We'll meet, and we'll be fain
In the land o' the leal.

INDEX

INDEX OF AUTHORS

INDEX OF TITLES

INDEX OF FIRST LINES

GLOSSARY

A',	all.	*Bane*,	bone.
Abeigh,	off.	*Bante*,	cursed.
Aboon,	above.	*Barefit*,	barefoot.
Aborde,	went on.	*Bauk*,	cross-beam.
Abread,	abroad.	*Bauldly*,	boldly.
Acquent,	acquainted.	*Bear*,	barley.
Ae,	one.	*Bederoll*,	string of beads.
Aff,	off.	*Beet*,	fan, kindle.
Aften,	often.	*Beld*,	bald.
Agley,	askew.	*Bell*,	flower.
Aiblins,	maybe.	*Belyve*,	by and by.
Ain,	own.	*Ben*,	inner room, parlor, inside.
Airt,	direction, quarter.	*Bicker*,	bowl.
Aith,	oath.	*Bickering*,	hurrying.
Alane,	alone.	*Bield*,	shelter.
Alang,	along.	*Big*,	build.
Albeytte,	albeit.	*Bigonet*,	linen cap.
Alestake,	alehouse sign.	*Billie*,	fellow.
Alleyne,	alone.	*Birk*,	birch.
Almer,	beggar.	*Birkie*,	conceited fellow.
Amaist,	almost.	*Bizz*,	buzz.
Amang, aming,	among.	*Black-bonnet*,	elder.
An,	if.	*Blake*,	bleak.
Ance,	once.	*Blastie*,	damned creature.
Ane,	one.	*Blastit*,	damned.
Arist,	arose.	*Blate*,	shy.
Ashrewed,	accursed.	*Blaw*,	blow, draught.
Asklent,	askance.	*Bleer't*,	bleared.
Asteer,	astir.	*Bleeze*,	blaze.
Astonied,	stunned.	*Blellum*,	babbler.
Atte,	at.	*Blethering*,	gabbling.
Attene,	at one.	*Blin*,	blind.
Auld,	old.	*Blink*,	glance, moment.
Aumere,	mantle.	*Bloshes*,	blushes.
Autremete,	robe.	*Bluid*,	blood.
Ava,	at all.	*Boddle*,	farthing.
Awa,	away.	*Boddynge*,	budding.
Aynewarde,	backward.	*Bogillis*,	hobgoblins.
		Bogle,	bogie.
Bairn,	child.	*Bonie*,	pretty.
Baith,	both.	*Bonilie*,	prettily.
Bake,	biscuit.	*Bonnet*,	cap.
Bandsters,	binders of sheaves.	*Bore*,	chink.
		Botte,	but.

Bra, fine.
Brae, hillside.
Braid, broad.
Braid-claith, broadcloth.
Brak, broke.
Braste, burst.
Brattle, scamper, clatter.
Braw, *brawlie*, fine.
Bree, liquor.
Breeks, breeches.
Bretful, brimful.
Brent, straight.
Brig, bridge.
Brither, brother.
Brogues, breeches.
Brownyis, brownies.
Browster, brewer.
Brunstane, brimstone.
Bught, pen, inclosure.
Buke, book.
Burdies, girls.
Burn, brook.
Busk, dress, make ready.
Bustine, fustian.
But, *butt*, outer room, kitchen, without.
Byke, hive.

Ca', call, drive.
Cadgy, cheerful, gay.
Cairn, heap of stones.
Caldrife, cool, spiritless.
Cale, cold.
Caller, cool.
Canna, cannot.
Cannie, careful, crafty.
Cannilie, craftily.
Cantie, *canty*, cheerful, jolly.
Cantraip, magic, witchcraft
Capernoity, ill-natured.
Carlin, old woman.
Cates, dainties.
Cauld, cold.
Caup, cup.
Celness, coldness.
Cess, excise, tax.
Chafe, chafing.
Change-house, tavern.
Chapman, peddler.
Chapournette, hat.
Chelandri, goldfinch.
Cheres, cheers.
Cheves, moves.
Chirm, chirp.
Chows, chews.
Church-glebe-house, grave.
Claes, clothes.
Claithing, clothing.
Clamb, climbed.
Claught, seized.
Cleek, catch up.
Clinkin, smartly.
Clinkumbell, the bell-ringer.
Clymmynge, noisy.
Cockernony, woman's hair gathered up with a band.
Cofte, bought.
Cog, basin.
Cood, cud.
Coost, cast.
Corbie, raven.
Core, company.
Cotter, tenant of a cottage.
Coulter, ploughshare.
Countra, country.
Cour, stoop.
Couth, *couthy*, sociable, affable.
Crack, chat, instant.
Craig, rock.
Cranreuch, hoar-frost.
Craw, crow.
Creeshie, greasy.
Croon, loll, murmur.
Crouche, crucifix.
Croun, crown.
Crouse, proud, lively.
Crowdie, porridge, breakfast.
Crowlin, crawling.
Crummock, crooked staff.
Crump, crisp.
Cryne, hair.
Cuif, dolt.
Curchie, curtsy.
Cutty, short.

Daffing, frolicking.
Daft, foolish.
Dail, board, plank.
Daimen, rare, occasional.
Daur, dare.
Daw, dawn.
Dawd, lump.
Deave, deafen.
Dee, die.

Defeat, defeated.
Defte, neat.
Deil, devil.
Dente, fasten.
Dheere, there.
Die, dye.
Differ, difference.
Dine, noon.
Dirl, vibrate, ring.
Dit, shut.
Domes, volumes.
Donsie, reckless.
Dool, pain, grief.
Dorture, slumber.
Douce, grave, prudent.
Douff, dull, sad.
Dow, can.
Dowie, drooping, gloomy.
Drappie, small drop.
Drenche, drink.
Drented, drenched.
Dringing, droning.
Droddum, breech.
Drouthy, thirsty.
Drowsyhed, drowsiness.
Drumlie, muddy.
Dub, puddle.
Duddie, ragged.
Duddies, rags.
Dwyning, failing, pining.
Dyke, wall.
Dynne, noise.

Eathe, ease.
E'e, eye.
Een, eyes.
Eerie, uncanny, timorous.
Efte, often.
Eftsoons, forthwith.
Eldritch, unearthly.
Embollen, swollen.
Enlefed, leafed out.
Ermelin, ermine.
Ettle, aim.
Eydent, diligent.

Fa', befall, fall.
Fairin', a gift from a fair.
Fairn-year, last year.
Faitour, vagabond.
Fand, found.
Farl, meal cake.
Fash, bother.
Fatt'rils, falderals, finery.
Faut, fault.
Feck, bulk.
Fell, deadly, pungent.
Fend, keep off.
Ferlie, ferly, wonder.
Fetive, festive.
Fidge, fidget.
Fient, fiend, devil.
Fiere, chum.
Fit, foot.
Flainen, flannen, flannel.
Flang, kicked.
Fleech, wheedle.
Flet, remonstrated.
Flichterin', fluttering.
Fling, waving.
Flott, fly.
Flourettes, flowers.
Foggage, coarse grass.
Forswat, sunburned.
Forwind, dried up.
Fou, very, drunk, full.
Fourth, fouth, abundance, plenty.
Frae, from.
Fructyle, fruitful.
Fu', full, very.
Furm, long seat.
Fyke, fuss.
Fyle, soil.

Gab, mouth.
Gabbing, talking.
Gae, go.
Gaed, gaid, went.
Gallard, frightened.
Gane, gone.
Gang, go.
Gar, make.
Gart, made.
Gash, shrewd, self-complacent.
Gat, got.
Gate, way.
Gaun, gawn, going.
Gawsie, buxom, jolly.
Gear, things, goods.
Geck, mock.
Ghaist, ghost.
Ghastness, ghastliness.
Gibbet-airn, gibbet-iron.
Gie, gi'e, give.
Gie's, give us, give me.
Giftie, little gift.

Gill, glass of whiskey.
Gin, if, by.
Glaikit, foolish.
Glint, flash.
Glommed, gloomy.
Gloure, glory.
Gowan, wild daisy.
Gowd, gold.
Gowk, fool.
Grane, groan.
Grat, wept.
Gre, grow.
Gree, prize.
'Gree, agree.
Greet, weep.
Grein, long for.
Grozet, gooseberry.
Gude, *guid*, good.
Gudeman, *guidman*, husband.
Guidwife, married woman, mistress of the house.
Guidwillie, full of good will.
Gusty, savory.
Guylteynge, gilding.

Ha', hall.
Hae, have.
Haffets, temples, side-locks.
Hafflins, half.
Hafflins-wise, about half.
Hairst, harvest-time.
Hald, holding, possession.
Halesome, wholesome.
Hallan, partition-wall.
Hallie, holy.
Halline, gladness.
Haly, holy.
Hamely, homely.
Hap-step-an'-loup, hop, step, and jump.
Harn, coarse linen.
Hartsome, hearty, merry.
Hash, stupid fellow, dolt.
Haud, hold, keep.
Hawkie, cow.
Hawslock, throat-lock, choicest wool.
Heapet, heaped.
Heie, they.
Het, hot.
Hie, high. highly.
Hight, was called.
Hiltring, hiding.
Hing, hang.
Hinny, honey, sweet.
Hirple, hop.
Histie, bare, dry.
Hizzie, girl, jade.
Hoddin, jogging.
Hoddin grey, undyed woolen.
Holme, evergreen oak.
Hornie, the Devil.
Hotch, jerk.
Houghmagandie, fornication, disgrace.
Houlet, owl.
Hound, incite to pursuit.
Hum, humbug.
Hurdies, buttocks.

Icker, ear of grain.
Ilka, each. every.
Ingle, fireside.

Jad, jade.
Jape, surplice.
Jauds, jades.
Jauk, trifle.
Jaw, strike, dash.
Jo, sweetheart.
Joicie, juicy.
Jow, swing.

Kebbuck, cheese.
Kebbuck-heel, last bit of cheese.
Keek, peep.
Kelpie, water-spirit.
Ken, know.
Kend, known.
Kennin, trifle.
Kest, cast.
Kiaugh, fret.
Kickshaws, delicacies.
Kiltit, tucked up.
Kirk, church.
Kiste, coffin.
Kittle, tickle.
Knappin-hammer, hammer for breaking stone.
Kye, kine, cattle.
Kynde, nature, species, womankind.

Lade, load.
Laird, lord, land-owner.
Laith, loath.
Laithfu', sheepish, bashful.
Landscip, landscape.
Lane, lone.
Lang, long.
Lap, leaped.
Lave, rest.
Lav'rock, lark.
Lear, learning.
Leel, loyal.
Lee-lang, live-long.
Leeze me on, commend me to.
Leglen, leglin, milk-pail.
Lemes, gleams.
Leugh, laughed.
Leuk, look.
Levynne, lightning.
Lift, sky.
Lilt, sing merrily.
Limitour, begging friar.
Linkan, tripping.
Linket, tripped.
Linn, waterfall.
Lint, flax.
Loan, loaning, lane, path.
Loo'ed, loved.
Loof, palm.
Loot, let.
Loun, clown, rascal.
Loup, leap.
Loverds, lords.
Lowe, flame.
Lowin, flaming.
Lowings, flashes.
Lowp, leap.
Lug, ear.
Lunardi, balloon, bonnet.
Luv, love.
Lyart, gray, gray-haired.

Mailen, farm.
Mair, more.
Mantels, mantles.
Mar, more.
Maun, must.
Maut, malt.
Mees, meadows.
Meikle, big.
Meldcr, grinding of grain.
Melvie, soil with meal.
Mim, prim.
Mirk, dark.
Misca'd, miscalled.
Mist, poor.
Mittie, mighty.
Moe, more.
Mole, soft.
Moneynge, moaning.
Monie, mony, many.
Mou, mouth.
Muckle, much, great.
Muir, heath.

Na, nae, no, not.
Naething, nothing.
Naig, nag.
Nappy, ale.
Ne, no.
Neebor, neighbor.
Neidher, neither.
Neist, next.
Nesh, tender.
Nete, night, naught.
Neuk, nook, corner.
Niffer, exchange.
No, not.

Onie, ony, any.
Ouphant, elfin.
Owr, owre, ower, over.

Paidle, paddle, wade.
Pall, appal.
Pang, cram.
Parritch, porridge.
Pattle, plough-staff.
Peed, pied.
Pencte, painted.
Penny-wheep, small beer.
Peres, pears.
Perishe, destroy.
Pet, be in a pet.
Pheeres, mates.
Pint-stowp, two-quart measure, flagon.
Plaidie, shawl used as cloak.
Plaister, plaster.
Pleugh, plough.
Poortith, poverty.
Pou, pull, pluck.
Pow, pate.
Prankt, gayly adorned.
Press, cupboard.
Propine, propone, present.
Pund, pound.

Pussie,	hare.
Pyke,	peaked.
Quean,	lass.
Quorum,	company.
Raible,	rattle off.
Rair,	roar.
Rant,	song, lay.
Rape,	rope.
Raw,	row.
Reaming,	foaming.
Reck,	observe.
Rede,	counsel.
Red up,	cleared up.
Reek,	smoke.
Reikie,	(smoky), Edinburgh.
Restricket,	restricted.
Reveled,	ravelled, troublesome.
Reynynge,	running
Reytes,	water-flags, iris.
Rig,	ridge.
Rigwoodie,	lean, tough.
Rin,	run.
Rodde, roddie,	ruddy.
Rodded,	grew red.
Rode,	skin.
Roset, rozet,	rosin.
Rowan,	rolling.
Rudde,	ruddy.
Runkled,	wrinkled.
Sabbing,	sobbing.
Sae,	so.
Saftly,	softly.
Sair,	serve, sore, sorely.
Sang,	song.
Sark,	shirt, chemise.
Saul,	soul.
Saunt,	saint.
Saut,	salt.
Scantlins,	scarcely.
Scoured,	ran.
Screed,	rip, rent.
Sede,	seed.
Semecope,	jacket.
Sets,	patterns.
Seventeen-hunder,	very fine (linen).
Shachled,	feeble, shapeless.
Shaw,	show.
Shiel,	shelter.
Shool,	shovel.
Shoon,	shoes.
Shouther,	shoulder.
Sic,	such.
Siller,	silver, money.
Simmer,	summer.
Sin',	since.
Skeigh,	skittish.
Skellum,	good-for-nothing.
Skelp,	run quickly.
Skiffing,	moving along lightly.
Skirl,	squeal, scream.
Skriech,	screech.
Slaes,	sloes.
Slap,	gap in a fence.
Slea,	slay.
Sleekit,	sleek.
Slid,	smooth.
Smeddum,	powder.
Smethe,	smoke.
Smoor,	smother.
Smothe,	vapor.
Snaw,	snow.
Snell,	bitter.
Snooded,	bound up with a fillet.
Snool,	cringe.
Solan,	gannet.
Soote,	sweet.
Souter,	cobbler.
Spak,	spoke.
Spean,	wean.
Speel,	climb.
Spier,	ask, inquire.
Spraing,	stripe.
Sprattle,	scramble.
Spreckled,	speckled.
Sprenged,	sprinkled.
Spryte,	spirit.
Squattle,	squat.
Stacher,	stagger, totter.
Stane,	stone.
Steer,	stir.
Steyned,	stained.
Stibble,	stubble.
Still,	ever.
Stirk,	young steer.
Stole,	robe.
Stonen,	stony.
Stote,	stout.
Stoure,	dust, struggle.
Stown,	stolen.
Strang,	strong.
Strath,	river-valley.
Strathspeys,	dances for two persons.

Straughte, stretched.
Strunt, strut.
Sugh, sough, moan.
Sumph', blockhead.
Swanges, swings.
Swankie, strapping youth.
Swat, sweated.
Swatch, sample.
Swats, foaming new ale.
Swith, shoo! begone!
Swote, sweet.
Swythyn, quickly.
Syne, since, then.

Taen, taken.
Tapmost, topmost.
Tauld, told.
Tent, watch.
Tentie, heedful.
Tere, muscle.
Thae, those.
Thieveless, useless.
Thilk, that same.
Thir, these.
Thole, endure.
Thrang, throng, throng-ing, busy.
Thrave, twenty-four sheaves.
Thraw, twist.
Thrawart, perverse.
Tint, lost.
Tippeny, twopenny (ale).
Tither, the other.
Tittlin', whispering.
Tochelod, dowered? dipped?
Tod, fox.
Tout, toot, blast.
Tow, rope.
Towmond, twelvemonth.
Towsie, shaggy.
Toy, cap.
Transmugrify'd, changed, metamorphosed.
Tryste, appointment, fair.
Twa, *tway*, two.
Tyke, cur, dog.

Unco, uncommon, very.
Uncos, news, wonders.
Unfald, unfold.
Ungentle, mean.
Unhailie. unhappy.
Unkend, unknown, disregarded.
Usquabae, whiskey.

Vauntie, proud.
Vera, *verra*, very.
Vest, robe.
View, appearance.
Virginè, the Virgin (in the zodiac).

Wabster, weaver.
Wad, would.
Wae, woe, sad.
Waesucks, alas.
Waff, stray, wandering.
Wale, choice.
Wark, work.
Warld, world.
Warlock, wizard.
Wa's, walls.
Water-fit, river's mouth.
Waught, draught.
Wauking, waking.
Wawlie, goodly.
Wear up, gather in.
Wede, passed, faded.
Weede, attire.
Weel, well.
Weel-hained, carefully saved.
Ween, believe.
Weet, wet.
Weir, war.
Wha, who.
Wham, whom.
Whang, large piece, slice.
Whare, where.
Whase, whose.
Whestling, whistling.
Whig-mig-morum, talking politics.
Whinging, whining.
Whins, furze.
Whunstane, hard rock, mill-stone.
Whyles, sometimes.
Winna, will not.
Winnock-bunker, window-seat.
Woddie, woody.
Wonner, wonder.
Woo, wool.
Wood, mad.
Wordy, worthy.

Wrack,	wreck.
Wraith,	spectre.
Wrang,	wrong.
Wyle,	lure, entice.
Wyliecoat,	undervest.
Yanne,	than.
Yatte	that.
Yblent,	blended.
Yer,	your.
Yestreen,	last night.
Yill,	ale.
Ymolten,	melted.
Ynutyle,	useless.
Younkers,	youngsters.
Yttes,	its.

The Modern Student's Library

NOVELS

AUSTEN: Pride and Prejudice
With an introduction by WILLIAM DEAN HOWELLS

BUNYAN: The Pilgrim's Progress
With an introduction by SAMUEL MCCHORD CROTHERS

ELIOT: Adam Bede
With an introduction by LAURA JOHNSON WYLIE, formerly Professor of English, Vassar College

GALSWORTHY: The Patrician
With an introduction by BLISS PERRY, Professor of English Literature, Harvard University

HARDY: The Return of the Native
With an introduction by J. W. CUNLIFFE, Professor of English, Columbia University

HAWTHORNE: The Scarlet Letter
With an introduction by STUART P. SHERMAN, late Literary Editor of the New York *Herald Tribune*

MEREDITH: Evan Harrington
With an introduction by GEORGE F. REYNOLDS, Professor of English Literature, University of Colorado

MEREDITH: The Ordeal of Richard Feverel
With an introduction by FRANK W. CHANDLER, Professor of English and Comparative Literature, and Dean of the College of Liberal Arts, University of Cincinnati

SCOTT: The Heart of Midlothian
With an introduction by WILLIAM P. TRENT, Professor of English Literature, Columbia University

STEVENSON: The Master of Ballantrae
With an introduction by H. S. CANBY, Assistant Editor of the *Yale Review* and Editor of the *Saturday Review*

THACKERAY: The History of Pendennis
With an introduction by ROBERT MORSS LOVETT, Professor of English, University of Chicago
2 vols.; $1.50 *per set*

TROLLOPE: Barchester Towers
With an introduction by CLARENCE D. STEVENS, Professor of English, University of Cincinnati

WHARTON: Ethan Frome
With a special introduction by EDITH WHARTON

POETRY

BROWNING: Poems and Plays
Edited by HEWETTE E. JOYCE, Assistant Professor of English, Dartmouth College

BROWNING: The Ring and the Book
Edited by FREDERICK MORGAN PADELFORD, Professor of English, University of Washington

TENNYSON: Poems
Edited by J. F. A. PYRE, Professor of English, University of Wisconsin

WHITMAN: Leaves of Grass
Edited by STUART P. SHERMAN, late Literary Editor of the New York *Herald Tribune*

WORDSWORTH: Poems
Edited by GEORGE M. HARPER, Professor of English, Princeton University

AMERICAN SONGS AND BALLADS
Edited by LOUISE POUND, Professor of English, University of Nebraska

ENGLISH POETS OF THE EIGHTEENTH CENTURY
Edited by ERNEST BERNBAUM, Professor of English, University of Illinois

MINOR VICTORIAN POETS
Edited by JOHN D. COOKE, Professor of English, University of Southern California

ROMANTIC POETRY OF THE EARLY NINETEENTH CENTURY
Edited by ARTHUR BEATTY, Professor of English, University of Wisconsin

ESSAYS AND MISCELLANEOUS PROSE

ADDISON AND STEELE: Selections
Edited by WILL D. HOWE, formerly head of the Department of English, Indiana University

ARNOLD: Prose and Poetry
Edited by ARCHIBALD L. BOUTON, Professor of English and Dean of the Graduate School, New York University

BACON: Essays
Edited by MARY AUGUSTA SCOTT, late Professor of the English Language and Literature, Smith College

BROWNELL: American Prose Masters
Edited by STUART P. SHERMAN, late Literary Editor of the New York *Herald Tribune*

BURKE: Selections
Edited by LESLIE NATHAN BROUGHTON, Assistant Professor of English, Cornell University

CARLYLE: Past and Present
Edited by EDWIN MIMS, Professor of English, Vanderbilt University

CARLYLE: Sartor Resartus
Edited by ASHLEY H. THORNDIKE, Professor of English, Columbia University

EMERSON: Essays and Poems
Edited by ARTHUR HOBSON QUINN, Professor of English, University of Pennsylvania

FRANKLIN AND EDWARDS: Selections
Edited by CARL VAN DOREN, Associate Professor of English, Columbia University

HAZLITT: Essays
Edited by PERCY V. D. SHELLY, Professor of English, University of Pennsylvania

LINCOLN: Selections
Edited by NATHANIEL WRIGHT STEPHENSON, author of "Lincoln: His Personal Life"

MACAULAY: Historical Essays
Edited by CHARLES DOWNER HAZEN, Professor of History, Columbia University

MEREDITH: An Essay on Comedy
Edited by LANE COOPER, Professor of the English Language and Literature, Cornell University

PARKMAN: The Oregon Trail
Edited by JAMES CLOYD BOWMAN, Professor of English, Northern State Normal College, Marquette, Mich.

POE: Tales
Edited by JAMES SOUTHALL WILSON, Edgar Allan Poe Professor of English, University of Virginia

RUSKIN: Selections and Essays
Edited by FREDERICK WILLIAM ROE, Professor of English, University of Wisconsin

STEVENSON: Essays
Edited by WILLIAM LYON PHELPS, Lampson Professor of English Literature, Yale University

SWIFT: Selections
Edited by HARDIN CRAIG, Professor of English, University of Iowa

THOREAU: A Week on the Concord and Merrimack Rivers
Edited by ODELL SHEPARD, James J. Goodwin Professor of English, Trinity College

CONTEMPORARY ESSAYS
Edited by ODELL SHEPARD, James J. Goodwin Professor of English, Trinity College

CRITICAL ESSAYS OF THE EARLY NINETEENTH CENTURY
Edited by RAYMOND M. ALDEN, late Professor of English, Leland Stanford University

SELECTIONS FROM THE FEDERALIST
Edited by JOHN S. BASSETT, late Professor of History, Smith College

NINETEENTH CENTURY LETTERS
Edited by BYRON JOHNSON REES, late Professor of English, Williams College.

ROMANTIC PROSE OF THE EARLY NINETEENTH CENTURY
Edited by CARL H. GRABO, Professor of English, University of Chicago

SEVENTEENTH CENTURY ESSAYS
Edited by JACOB ZEITLIN, Associate Professor of English, University of Illinois

BIOGRAPHY

BOSWELL: Life of Johnson
Abridged and Edited by CHARLES GROSVENOR OSGOOD, Professor of English, Princeton University

CROCKETT: Autobiography of David Crockett
Edited by HAMLIN GARLAND

PHILOSOPHY SERIES

Editor, Ralph Barton Perry

Professor of Philosophy, Harvard University

ARISTOTLE: Selections
Edited by W. D. ROSS, Professor of Philosophy, Oriel College, University of Oxford

BACON: Selections
Edited by MATTHEW THOMPSON MCCLURE, Professor of Philosophy, University of Illinois

BERKELEY: Selections
Edited by MARY W. CALKINS, Professor of Philosophy and Psychology, Wellesley College

DESCARTES: Selections
Edited by RALPH M. EATON, Assistant Professor of Philosophy, Harvard University

HEGEL: Selections
Edited by JACOB LOEWENBERG, Professor of Philosophy, University of California

HUME: Selections
Edited by CHARLES W. HENDEL, JR., Associate Professor of Philosophy, Princeton University

KANT: Selections
Edited by THEODORE M. GREENE, Associate Professor of Philosophy, Princeton University

LOCKE: Selections
Edited by STERLING P. LAMPRECHT, Professor of Philosophy, Amherst College

PLATO: The Republic
With an introduction by C. M. BAKEWELL, Professor of Philosophy, Yale University

PLATO: Selections
Edited by RAPHAEL DEMOS, Assistant Professor of Philosophy, Harvard University

SCHOPENHAUER: Selections
Edited by DEWITT H. PARKER, Professor of Philosophy, University of Michigan

MEDIEVAL PHILOSOPHY
Edited by RICHARD MCKEON, Assistant Professor of Philosophy, Columbia University

FRENCH SERIES

Editor, Horatio Smith

Professor of French Language and Literature, Brown University

BALZAC: Le Père Goriot
With an introduction by HORATIO SMITH, Professor of French Language and Literature, Brown University

FLAUBERT: Madame Bovary
With an introduction by CHRISTIAN GAUSS, Dean of the College, Princeton University

FRENCH ROMANTIC PROSE
Edited by W. W. COMFORT, President, Haverford College

MOLIÈRE: Three Plays
Edited by WILLIAM A. NITZE and HILDA L. NORMAN, University of Chicago

VOLTAIRE: Candide and Other Philosophical Tales
Edited by MORRIS BISHOP, Assistant Professor of the Romance Languages and Literature, Cornell University